the
GASLIGHT
effect

the
GASLIGHT
effect

how to SPOT and SURVIVE the HIDDEN MANIPULATION others use to CONTROL YOUR LIFE

Dr Robin Stern
Foreword by Naomi Wolf

ff

First published in Great Britain in 2008
by Fusion Press, a division of Satin Publications Ltd
101 Southwark Street
London SE1 0JF
UK
info@visionpaperbacks.co.uk
www.visionpaperbacks.co.uk
Publisher: Sheena Dewan

First published in the United States in 2007 by Morgan Road Books,
an imprint of The Doubleday Broadway Publishing Group,
a division of Random House, Inc., New York.

ISBN: 978-1-905745-31-9

2 4 6 8 10 9 7 5 3 1

Cover design by ok?design
Book design by Chris Welch

Printed and bound in the UK by
J. H. Haynes & Co Ltd, Sparkford

TO MY FAMILY THEN
My loving parents, Rosalind and David Stern,
who taught me to believe in people
My wonderful brother, Eric Stern, whose clarity and conviction
continues to give me strength

TO MY FAMILY NOW
My sweetheart, Frank Moretti, whose love and support,
in every way, made this writing possible
My beloved and amazing children, Scott and Melissa,
who fill my heart with joy, every day!

TO MY MANY PATIENTS, AND STUDENTS, AND THE
YOUNG PEOPLE I HAVE MENTORED . . . with whom
I walked the road and from whom I learned so much.

contents

acknowledgments

I am deeply grateful to so many people from various times of my life whose teaching, friendship, support, and collaboration created the foundation for my work and who have continued to inspire me through the writing of this book.

I feel so blessed to have met Amy Hertz. From our first resonant conversation, I hoped that she would be my editor! Amy's broad vision, love of stories, and attention to detail have made it possible to reach a wide audience. Her authenticity and striving for excellence pushed my thinking. Heartfelt thanks also to her assistant Julie Miesionczek.

I also am beyond grateful to have met my amazing agent, Richard Pine, who brilliantly thought of the title for the book. His wisdom and guidance, patience with many drafts, and belief in the important subject matter inspired me to craft the strongest proposal and best book possible. My heartfelt thanks to co-agent Janis Vallely for her enthusiasm from the beginning, and for her deep listening, sharing, insight, and input on both the proposal and manuscript of this book.

My greatest thanks go to Rachel Kranz, whose genius, work ethic, and originality are remarkable. I am grateful for the hours and hours of deep conversation, of pushing back and forth, and of synchronicity. Rachel's incisive thinking, in addition to her gift as a writer, made this the best book it could be. And none of these people would have been in my life were it not for Mike Frankfurt. For some wonderful, reason, Mike, in his generosity and kindness, was the man behind the scenes in friendship, in support, from the beginning of this project.

Very special thanks to Les Lenoff, my friend and colleague, who has painstakingly reviewed and reviewed my manuscript and offered brilliant insight and guidance in translating very difficult psychological concepts for a wider audience. Deep gratitude to my dear friend Naomi Wolf, cofounder of the Woodhull Institute for Ethical Leadership, who was literally by my side when I realized, years ago, that I really needed to bring public attention to the huge problem of emotional abuse. Thank you so much for all of your support and your contributions to this book. I am so grateful to Wende Jager-Hyman, executive director of the Woodhull Institute, and hugs to Helen Churko and Susan Devenyi for meaningful conversations, reviewing chapters of this manuscript and giving me important feedback. I thank all the women and men of Woodhull—board members, fellows, faculty, guests, and friends—for holding the vision of educating and empowering women to speak their truth; at Woodhull, young women are empowered, through skill-building and self-understanding, to make their dreams come true. Among my many extraordinary Woodhull colleagues, a special thank-you to Gina Amaro, Cheri Anisman, Marlene Arnold, Kenny Becker, Steve Becker, Tara Bracco, Melissa Bradley, Karla Jackson Brewer, Ken Burrows, Phyllis Chesler, Beth Fenton, Joan Finsilver, Jennifer Gandin, Beth Greenberg, Erica Jong, Jennifer Jones, Karen Kisslinger, Chris Le, Jan Leonard, Joanna Lipper, Margot Magowan, Nicola Miner, Gretchen Mullin, Monica Rosen, Rashmi Sharma, Rosa and Joey Shipley, Agapi Stassinopoulos, and Jacquette Timmons.

I am deeply grateful to my research assistant, Andrés Richner, whose research skills, intelligence, generosity, and heart-centered view of the world have been invaluable in this writing.

To my teachers and mentors: I have journeyed a long road to writing this book and learned so much from so many along the way. Thanks to Marty Livingston, Anne Brooks, the late Sig Bernd, and all of whom taught me so much about their relationships. Deep gratitude to my colleagues and mentors Manny Shapiro and Frank Lachmann. To my many other teachers at Postgraduate Center for Mental Health, especially Marvin Aronson, Alex Broden, Al Brok, Arthur Gray, Jeffrey Kleinberg, Jerry Leff, the late Michael Lindenman, and Bill Meaders—thank you for the opportunity to learn from all of you. Thanks also to my academic mentor, the late Phillip Merrifield, as well as to Elazar Pedhazur and Teresa Jordan. Special thanks to Bernie Weitzman of the graduate faculty, New School for Social Research. Thanks to my colleagues and friends at Teachers College—Shawna Bushell, Chuck Kinzer, Xiadong Lin, Susan Lowes, and Robbie McClintock—and thanks for our wonderful conversations to Carole Saltz of TC Press, and to New York University Graduate School of Education. Special thanks to Andy Cohen for years of compassion and support for my family. Thanks to my colleagues from Educators for Social Responsibility.

I feel a profound sense of gratitude to Daniel Goleman, whose work in emotional intelligence, leadership, and social intelligence has helped to shape my professional interests for more than ten years. My gratitude for deep learning in this field of study also goes to my colleagues and mentors Richard Boyatzis, Cary Cherniss, and J. Theodore Repa. Special thanks to Ted and Betty Repa for important conversations and Maine hospitality.

I am also grateful for those special moments when important knowing emerged from informal, engaged conversations, so thanks to Kathy Anderson, Loryn Ashlee, Kimberlee Auerbach, Jonathan Baliet, Arlene Basset, Sheila Brown, Linda Bruene Butler, Joanne Cassullo, Rachel Chou, Gardner Dunnan, Diana Feldman, Paula Jaye, Amishi Jha, Susan Kahn, Caroline Keating, Theo Koffler, Lisa Lahey, Jere Martin, Max McKlintock, Florence Meyer, Margaret Miele, Deb Oneil, John Pellitteri, Judy Rabinor, Alice Ray, Rose Rodriguez, Charles Rosenberg, Stephen Rudin, Sharon Salzberg, Michele Savitz, Deborah Schoeberlein, Michelle Seligson, Claudia Shelton, Beryl Snyder, Francee Sugar, and Deborah and Leonard Wolf. Very special thanks to Helen Churko for many insightful "present" conversations. Thanks for those important times of talking and sharing to the "moms of Trevor," including Debbie Ashe, Anna Condo, Joan Finkelstein, Lise Gollogly, Shelley

Kaplan, Ona Lyndquist, Adrienne Packer, Elana Roberts, Cathy Steck, Traci Werbel, and Kate White. Thanks to friends from other places and from years ago: Claire and Larry Aidem, Sheila Katt Beck, Linda Berko, Denise Bleckner, Kate Cannon, Wendy Dubit, Sheila Erlich, Judi Fishman, the late Karen Harte, Joan Hoberman, John Hughes, Ruth and Alan Jacobs, Linda Jacobson, Pat Launer, Jacquie Norris, Suzanne Roff, Lynn Schachter, Susan Schachtman, Wendy Schuman, Mark Seides, Cathy Weitz, and Genie Wing.

Thank you to the faculty, staff, and leadership of The School at Columbia University, and especially to Diane Dillon, whose support for this project has been so important to me. Thank you to the Summer Principals Academy at Teachers College, and to Tom Haferd, Terry Maltbia, and Craig Richards for times of teaching and learning. Thanks to Project Renewal for your important work in the world: Carmella B'Hahn, Marthy Eddy, Linda Lantieri, Madhavi Nambiar, and Lynne Hurdle Price. Special thanks to my dear friend Linda for joining me in the inner circle; to Allison Leopold, who gave generously of her home and her time in conversation; and to my buddy and collaborator Janet Patti, for hours and days of honest conversation.

Thanks to Hunter Leadership Center, including Marcia Knoll and Jade Young, and to all of the participants in the Star Factor Training—I have learned from you all. I have been blessed with so many wonderful students and young people to mentor and work with: the many young women of Woodhull—you know who you are!—as well as Rachel Brod, Ellie Ciofli, Shira Garber, Julie Henderson, Debbie Hoberman, Joie Jager Hyman, Lauren Hyman, Anna Ingram, Deborah Keisch, Colleen McLean, Katherine O'Neal, Lori Ramsey, Alex Ritt, Deborah Rosenzweig, Glynnis Scanlon, Shetal Shah, Erin Shakespeare, Nava Silton, Rachel Simmons, Bonnie Schneider, Michele Taubeblat, Melissa Ulto, and Claudia Veritas. I've been particularly inspired by my friend, colleague, and almost family member, Courtney Martin, one of the most extraordinary young women I've ever known.

For important work in guiding people on their life journeys, and for talking with me about emotional abuse and this project, thanks to Angeles Arrien, Marti Tamm Loring, Margaret Miele, Andrew Morrison, and Anne

Patterson. Thanks especially to my patients and to the many people who have shared their stories of gaslighting relationships and other types of emotional abuse. This work has benefited enormously from your sharing and I am grateful. Thanks to Rachel Simmons and Phyllis Chesler, who gave generously of their time and intellect in reading the manuscript.

Finally, I thank my dear friends, whose wisdom and insight inform every page of this book. Thank you for years of conversation to Robin Bernstein, Suzi Epstein, Tripp Evans, Donna Klein, Dana Launer, Ken Perlin, Jerry Salzberg, and Claudia Shelton. Thanks to Marilyn and Norm Goldstein for always being a reality check. Special thanks to Madaleine Berley for her clear vision. And thanks for those wonderful cousins' times and talks with Cheryl Filler, Leslie Sporn, Mona Van Cleef, and Terry Yagoda.

I want to express my profound gratitude to Avalina Gordon, who has worked with my family for twenty years. Without Lina, I could not have finished school, completed postgraduate work, or held my household together. Many thanks also to others who have made it possible for me to balance my work life and home life for many years: Izzy Baldi, Leonard Finkel, Enrique Santiago Michel, Josie Oliveira, Anna Woloczyn, and especially Teresa Gonzales at Columbia University.

None of my work or my home life would have been possible without the extraordinary gifts I received from my parents, Roz and Dave Stern (who is watching from above), who believed in me and encouraged me to find my dreams. I love them and am forever grateful. A big hug and thanks to my second parents, Elaine and Artie Kreisberg, and to my lifelong friend Billy Kreisberg. Special thanks to my lifelong best friend, Jan K. Rosenberg, whose friendship means the world to me. Much love and profound appreciation to my brother, Eric Stern, who has always been there—no matter what. Thanks to my sister-in-law, Jacquie Savitz Stern, for her inner beauty and for her commitment to our family. Bozzin Deedin and bundles of thanks to my nephews and niece: Justin, Daniel, and Julie. Special thanks to Kiki, Tonio, and Nicco for hanging in there. And words cannot express my deep gratitude to my sweetheart, Frank Moretti, whose commitment in every way to me and to my children has been greater than any of us could have asked for. From our inspiring dinner-table conversations, to the trips to the Po, to building bookcases, to beasty on the road, I thank you with all my heart. And finally, all my love up to the sky, the moon, and all the stars for my brilliant, compassionate, and creative children, Scott and Melissa, whose shining faces make my day, every day. I am truly blessed.

foreword

Sometimes life presents us with interesting coincidences.

When Robin Stern first told me she was thinking of writing about the subject of emotional abuse, we were sitting in a playground watching my children play. Outside the playground a path meandered. A four- or five-year-old boy who had been walking next to his father ran exuberantly down the path ahead for a moment, then tripped on some gravel and fell hard. He was clearly hurt and struggling not to cry. His father's face tightened: "What have you done to yourself now?" he snapped, pulling the boy roughly to his feet by one arm. "You are so clumsy I can't even believe it. I tell you to be more careful all the time."

It was an awful moment. We, the adults, were flinching at the failure of empathy shown by the father. We wondered if we should say something. But what was even more painful was watching the child try to recompose himself and try to make sense of what his father had said. He seemed visibly trying to interpret his father's words to make them somehow not be cruel. You could almost hear him thinking, "I am clumsy. I am hurt not because my father has just wounded my feelings but because I did not listen to my father better. It is my fault."

I urged Dr. Stern at that moment to take her inclinations seriously and write such a book. I am very glad that she has done so. Emotional abuse is a subject that is finally receiving the serious attention it deserves, and a great deal has recently been written about it. People are more likely these days to see emotional abuse for what it is, whereas a generation ago the same interactions were often more socially acceptable, especially when it came to child-rearing—seen as "tough love" or "character building." However, the particular kind of emotional abuse that Dr. Stern identifies and explores in *The Gaslight Effect*—abuse that is more covert and controlling—has not been examined with the empathy and insight that she brings to it from her years of clinical practice, and especially from her unique interest in the emotional well-being of young women. It is good news that she has written about this issue from the breadth of her experience.

Dr. Stern works with scores of bright, talented, idealistic young women, many of them from loving families, who find themselves caught up in relationships that demonstrate variations of this kind of abuse. She does a miraculous job of helping them remember and then work from their own lost sources of strength and self-respect, and they reclaim their lives in the process. Now readers across the country will have the benefit of her wisdom that these young women have had Dr. Stern's explanation of how to identify this kind of covert emotional control and abuse, and how to resist it, is a very important tool for young women in particular to use, if they wish to safeguard their emotional well-being, resist others' efforts to control and manipulate them, and choose relationships that support and nurture their development.

But while I know first-hand, from watching Dr. Stern mentor young women, how healing her insights into the Gaslight Effect can be, I do not believe that the value of this exploration is restricted to women. Men and women alike suffer emotional abuse and control when they are boys and girls at the hands of adults; while the majority of the examples here, drawn from Dr. Stern's practice, are about the abuse of women, I have also seen countless men open up and describe their own struggles to be free of such toxic interactions when Dr. Stern has described what she is working on—and gain a measure of release and freedom from hearing her analysis. Parents in particular should read this book: so often the ways in which we wound children's sense of self—or manipulate them emotionally—are entirely unconscious. The more aware we become about the fact that any of us, no matter how well-intentioned, can inadvertently emotionally wound or manipulate a child in our care, the better it will be for the next generation.

Readers are fortunate to have a psychotherapist such as Dr. Stern so sincerely committed to their emotional growth and personal development; every page is written from her heart. Even more important, every page moves us closer toward truly recognizing what happened to that little guy in the park—and understanding the adults who might identify with him.

This book will help so many find new self-respect and strength.

—Naomi Wolf

chapter 1

What Is Gaslighting?

K atie is a friendly, upbeat person who walks down the street with a smile for everyone. Her job as a sales rep means that she's often talking to new people, which she loves. An attractive woman in her late twenties, she went through a long period of dating before she finally settled on her current boyfriend, Brian.

Brian can be sweet, protective, and considerate, but he's also an anxious, fearful guy who treats every new person with suspicion. When the two of them go on a walk together, Katie is outgoing and talkative, easily falling into conversation with the man who stops to ask directions or the woman whose dog cuts across their path. Brian, though, is full of criticism. Can't she see how people are laughing at her? She thinks they like these casual conversations, but they're actually rolling their eyes and wondering why she's so chatty. And that man who asked them for directions? He was only trying to seduce her—she should have seen how he leered at her the moment her back was turned. Besides, behaving in such a manner is highly disrespectful to him, her boyfriend. How does she think it makes him feel to see her making eyes at every guy she passes?

At first, Katie laughs off her boyfriend's complaints. She's been like this all her life, she tells him, and she enjoys being friendly. But after weeks of relentless criticism, she starts to doubt herself. Maybe people *are* laughing and leering at her. Maybe she *is* being flirtatious and rubbing her boyfriend's nose in it—what a terrible way to treat the man who loves her!

Eventually, when Katie walks down the street, she can't decide how to behave. She doesn't want to give up her warm and friendly approach to the world—but now, whenever she smiles at a stranger, she can't help imagining what Brian would think.

LIZ IS A top-level executive in a major advertising firm. A stylish woman in her late forties with a solid, twenty-year marriage and no children, she's worked hard to get where she is, pouring all her extra energy into her career. Now she seems to be on the verge of reaching her goal, in line to take over the company's New York office.

Then, at the last minute, someone else is brought in to take the job. Liz swallows her pride and offers to give him all the help she can. At first, the new boss seems charming and appreciative. But soon Liz starts to notice that she's being left out of important decisions and not invited to major meetings. She hears rumors that clients are being told she doesn't want to work with them anymore and has recommended that they speak to her new boss instead. When she complains to her colleagues, they look at her in bewilderment. "But he always praises you to the skies," they insist. "Why would he say such nice things if he was out to get you?"

Finally, Liz confronts her boss, who has a plausible explanation for every incident. "Look," he says kindly at the end of the meeting. "I think you're being way too sensitive about all this—maybe even a little paranoid. Would you like a few days off to destress?"

Liz feels completely disabled. She *knows* she's being sabotaged—but why is she the only one who thinks so?

MITCHELL IS A grad student in his mid-twenties who's studying to become an electrical engineer. Tall, gangly, and somewhat shy, he's taken a long time to find the right woman, but he's just begun dating someone he really likes. One day, his girlfriend mildly points out that Mitchell still dresses like a little boy. Mitchell is mortified, but he sees what she means. Off he goes to a local department store, where he asks the personal shopper to help him choose an entire wardrobe. The clothes make him feel like a new man—sophisticated, attractive—and he enjoys the appreciative glances women give him on the bus ride home.

But when he wears the new clothes to Sunday dinner at his parents' home, his mother bursts out laughing. "Oh, Mitchell, that outfit is all wrong for you—you look ridiculous," she says. "Please, dear, the next time you go shopping, let me help you." When Mitchell feels hurt and asks his mother to apologize, she shakes her head sadly. "I was only trying to help," she says. "And I'd like an apology from *you* for that tone of voice."

Mitchell is confused. He liked his new clothes—but maybe he *does* look ridiculous. And has he really been rude to his mother?

Understanding the Gaslight Effect

Katie, Liz, and Mitchell have one thing in common: they're all suffering from the Gaslight Effect. The Gaslight Effect results from a relationship between two people: a gaslighter, who needs to be right in order to preserve his own sense of self and his sense of having power in the world; and a gaslightee, who allows the gaslighter to define her sense of reality because she idealizes him and seeks his approval. Gaslighters and gaslightees can be of either gender, and gaslighting can happen in any type of relationship. But I'm going to call gaslighters "he" and gaslightees "she," since that's the pairing I most often see in my practice. I'll explore a variety of relationships—with friends, family, bosses, and colleagues—but the male-female romantic pairing will be my major focus.

For example, Katie's gaslighting boyfriend insists that the world is a dangerous place and that Katie's behavior is inappropriate and insensitive. When he feels stressed or threatened, he *has* to be right about these issues, and he has to get Katie to agree that he is. Katie values the relationship and doesn't want to lose Brian, so she starts to see things from his point of view. Maybe the people they meet *are* laughing at her. Maybe she *is* being flirtatious. Gaslighting has begun.

Likewise, Liz's boss insists that he really cares about her and that any concerns she has are because she's paranoid. Liz wants her boss to think well of her—after all, her career is at stake—so she starts to doubt her own perceptions and tries to adopt his. But her boss's view of things really doesn't make sense to Liz. If he's *not* trying to sabotage her, why is she missing all those meetings? Why are her clients failing to return her calls? Why is she feeling so worried and confused? Liz is so trusting that she just can't believe anyone could be as blatantly manipulative as her boss seems to be; she *has* to be doing something that warrants his terrible treatment. Wishing desperately for her boss to be right, but knowing deep down that he isn't, makes Liz feels completely disoriented, no longer sure of what she sees or what she knows. Her gaslighting is in full swing.

Mitchell's mother insists that she's entitled to say anything she wants to her son and that he is being rude if he objects. Mitchell would like to see his mother as a good, loving person, not as someone who says mean things to him. So when she hurts his feelings, he blames himself, not her. Both Mitchell and his mother agree: the mother is right, and Mitchell is wrong. Together, they are creating the Gaslight Effect.

Of course, Katie, Liz, and Mitchell all have other choices. Katie might ignore her boyfriend's negative remarks, ask him to stop making them, or as a last resort, break up with him. Liz could say to herself, "Wow, this new boss is a piece of work. Well; maybe that smarmy charm has fooled everyone else in this company—but not me!" Mitchell might reply calmly, "Sorry, Mom, but you're the one who owes *me* an apology." All of them could decide that, on some basic level, they are willing to live with their gaslighters' disapproval. *They* know they are good, capable, lovable people, and that's all that matters.

If our three gaslightees were able to take this attitude, there would be no gaslighting. Maybe their gaslighters would still behave badly, but their behavior would no longer have such a pernicious effect. Gaslighting works only when you believe what the gaslighter says and need him to think well of you.

The problem is, gaslighting is insidious. It plays on our worst fears, our most anxious thoughts, our deepest wishes to be understood, appreciated, and loved. When someone we trust, respect, or love speaks with great certainty—especially if there's a grain of truth in his words, or if he's hit on one of our pet anxieties—it can be very difficult not to believe him. And when we idealize the gaslighter—when we want to see him as the love of our life, an admirable boss, or a wonderful parent—then we have even more difficulty sticking to our own sense of reality. Our gaslighter needs to be right, we need to win his approval, and so the gaslighting goes on.

Of course, neither of you may be aware of what's really happening. The gaslighter may genuinely believe every word he tells you or sincerely feel that he's only saving you from yourself. Remember: He's being driven by his own needs. Your gaslighter might seem like a strong, powerful man, or he may appear to be an insecure, tantrum-throwing little boy; either way, he *feels* weak and powerless. To feel powerful and safe, he *has* to prove that he is right, and he *has* to get you to agree with him.

Meanwhile, you have idealized your gaslighter and are desperate for his approval, although you may not consciously realize this. But if there's even a little piece of you that thinks you're not good enough by yourself—if even a small part of you feels you need your gaslighter's love or approval to be whole—then you are susceptible to gaslighting. And a gaslighter will take advantage of that vulnerability to make you doubt yourself, over and over again.

Are You Being Gaslighted?

TURN UP YOUR GASLIGHT RADAR.
CHECK FOR THESE TWENTY TELLTALE SIGNS

Gaslighting may not involve all of these experiences or feelings, but if you recognize yourself in any of them, give it extra attention.

1. You are constantly second-guessing yourself.
2. You ask yourself, "Am I too sensitive?" a dozen times a day.

(continued)

3. You often feel confused and even crazy at work.

4. You're always apologizing to your mother, father, boyfriend, boss.

5. You wonder frequently if you are a "good enough" girlfriend/wife/employee/friend/daughter.

6. You can't understand why, with so many apparently good things in your life, you aren't happier.

7. You buy clothes for yourself, furnishings for your apartment, or other personal purchases with your partner in mind, thinking about what he would like instead of what would make you feel great.

8. You frequently make excuses for your partner's behavior to friends and family.

9. You find yourself withholding information from friends and family so you don't have to explain or make excuses.

10. You know something is terribly wrong, but you can never quite express what it is, even to yourself.

11. You start lying to avoid the put-downs and reality twists.

12. You have trouble making simple decisions.

13. You think twice before bringing up certain seemingly innocent topics of conversation.

14. Before your partner comes home, you run through a checklist in your head to anticipate anything you might have done wrong that day.

15. You have the sense that you used to be a very different person—more confident, more fun-loving, more relaxed.

16. You start speaking to your husband through his secretary so you don't have to tell him things you're afraid might upset him.

17. You feel as though you can't do anything right.

18. Your kids begin trying to protect you from your partner.

19. You find yourself furious with people you've always gotten along with before.

20. You feel hopeless and joyless.

How I Discovered the Gaslight Effect

I've been a therapist in private practice for the past twenty years, as well as a teacher, leadership coach, consultant, and fellow at the Woodhull Institute for Ethical Leadership, where I help develop and facilitate trainings for women of all ages. In all these domains, I constantly encounter women who are strong, smart, successful. Yet I kept hearing the same story: Somehow, many of these confident, high-achieving women were being caught in demoralizing, destructive, and bewildering relationships. Although the woman's friends and colleagues might have seen her as empowered and capable, she had come to view herself as incompetent—a person who could trust neither her own abilities nor her own perception of the world.

There was something sickeningly familiar about these stories, and gradually I realized that not only was I hearing them professionally but they also mirrored experiences my friends and I had had. In every case, a seemingly powerful woman was involved in a relationship with a lover, spouse, friend, colleague, boss, or family member who caused her to question her own sense of reality and left her feeling anxious, confused, and deeply depressed. These relationships were all the more striking because in other domains the women seemed so strong and together. But there was always that one special person— loved one, boss, or relative—whose approval she kept trying to win, even as his treatment of her went from bad to worse. Finally, I was able to give this painful condition a name: the Gaslight Effect, after the old movie *Gaslight*.

This classic 1944 film is the story of Paula, a young, vulnerable singer (played by Ingrid Bergman) who marries Gregory, a charismatic, mysterious older man (played by Charles Boyer). Unbeknownst to Paula, her beloved husband is trying to drive her insane in order to take over her inheritance. He continually tells her she is ill and fragile, rearranges household items and then accuses her of doing so, and most deviously of all, manipulates the gas so that she sees the lights dim for no apparent reason. Under the spell of her husband's diabolical scheme, Paula starts to believe that she is going mad. Confused and scared, she begins to act hysterical, actually becoming the fragile, disoriented person that he keeps telling her she is. In a vicious downward spiral, the more she doubts herself, the more confused and hysterical she becomes. She is desperate for her husband to approve of her and to tell her he loves her, but he keeps refusing to do so, insisting that she is insane. Her return to sanity and self-assertion comes only when a police inspector reassures her that he, too, sees the dimming of the light.

As *Gaslight* makes clear, a gaslighting relationship always involves two people. Gregory needs to seduce Paula to make himself feel powerful and in control. But Paula is also eager to be seduced. She has idealized this strong, handsome man, and she desperately wants to believe that he'll cherish and protect her. When he starts behaving badly, she's reluctant to blame him for it or to see him differently; she'd rather preserve her romantic image of the perfect husband. Her insecurity about herself and her idealization of him offer the perfect opening for his manipulation.

In *Gaslight,* the gaslighter is after something tangible. He consciously wants to drive his wife mad so that he can take possession of her property. Few real-life gaslighters are so diabolical—though the effects of their behavior may be wicked indeed. From the gaslighter's point of view, however, he's just protecting himself. A gaslighter has such a flawed sense of self that he can't tolerate the slightest challenge to the way he sees things. However he decides to explain the world to himself, that's how you must see it, too—or leave him prey to unbearable anxiety.

Suppose you smile at a guy at a party and your gaslighter feels uncomfortable. The guy not involved in gaslighting might say, "Yeah, I'm the jealous type" or "I know you weren't doing anything wrong, honey, but it makes me crazy to see you having fun with other men." He's willing to at least consider that his discomfort may be caused by the situation or by his own insecurities. Even if you actually *were* flirting—even if you were flirting outrageously—the nongaslighter could potentially recognize that your behavior, objectionable as he finds it, wasn't intended to make him feel lousy, even though he may also ask you to stop.

The gaslighter, though, never considers that his own jealousy, insecurity, or paranoia might be involved. He clings to his own explanation: He feels bad because you're a flirt. He's not satisfied simply knowing this, either; he has to get you to agree. If you don't, you'll be treated to hours of anger, coldness, hurt feelings, or seemingly reasonable criticism. ("I don't know why you can't see how deeply you're hurting me. Don't my feelings matter to you at *all?*")

But it takes two to tango, and gaslighting can take place only when there's a willing gaslightee, someone who idealizes the gaslighter and desperately wants his approval. If you're not open to gaslighting, you might simply laugh and brush off the criticism when your jealous boyfriend wrongly accuses you of flirting. But what if you can't bear the thought that he sees you in such a bad light? Then you might start to argue, trying to get him to change *his* mind. ("Honey, I *wasn't* flirting. That was a perfectly innocent smile.") Just as the gaslighter is desperate to get his girlfriend to apologize, so is the gaslightee desperate to win her boyfriend's approval. She may become willing to do *anything* to make things right with her boyfriend—even accepting his negative, critical view of her.

Gaslighting: From Bad to Worse

Gaslighting tends to work in stages. At first, it may be relatively minor—indeed, you may not even notice it. When your boyfriend accuses you of deliberately trying to undermine him by showing up late to his office party, you attribute it to his nerves or assume he didn't really mean it or perhaps even begin to wonder whether you were trying to undermine him—but then you let it go.

Eventually, though, gaslighting becomes a bigger part of your life, preoccupying your thoughts and overwhelming your feelings. Finally, you're mired in full-scale depression, hopeless and joyless, unable even to remember the person you once were, with your own point of view and your own sense of self.

Of course, you may not proceed through all three stages. But for many women, gaslighting goes from bad to worse.

Stage 1: Disbelief

Stage 1 is characterized by disbelief. Your gaslighter says something outrageous—"That guy who asked us for directions was really just trying to get you into bed!"—and you can't quite believe your ears. You think you've misunderstood, or maybe he has, or maybe he was just joking. The comment seems so off the wall, you might let it go. Or perhaps you try to correct the error but without a whole lot of energy. Maybe you even get into long, involved arguments, but you're still pretty certain of your own point of view. Although you'd *like* your gaslighter's approval, you don't yet feel desperate for it.

Katie remains in this stage for several weeks. She keeps trying to convince her boyfriend that he's simply wrong about her and the people she meets, that she's not flirting with anyone and no one is flirting with her. Sometimes Katie feels she's just on the verge of getting Brian to understand—but he never quite does. Then she worries: Was it him? Was it her? He can be so sweet when things are good; why does he get so weird sometimes? As you can see, the relatively mild gaslighting of Stage 1 can leave you feeling confused, frustrated, and anxious.

Stage 2: Defense

Stage 2 is marked by the need to defend yourself. You search for evidence to prove your gaslighter wrong and argue with him obsessively, often in your head, desperately trying to win his approval.

Liz is a Stage 2 gaslightee. All she can think about is how much she wants her boss to see things her way. After their meeting, she replays every conversation with her boss over and over—on the way to work, at lunch with her friends, as she's trying to fall asleep. She just *has* to find a way to show him she's right. Maybe then he'll approve of her and everything will be fine again.

Mitchell is also in Stage 2. He has idealized his mother so much that part of him actually wants her to be right. Okay, Mitchell thinks after he and his mother disagree. I guess I *was* a little rude. Then he feels terrible about being such a bad son. But at least he doesn't have to feel terrible about having such a bad mother. He can keep trying to win her approval without acknowledging her bad behavior.

You know you're in Stage 2 if you frequently feel obsessive, sometimes desperate. You're no longer sure you can win your gaslighter's approval—but you haven't given up hope.

Stage 3: Depression

Stage 3 gaslighting is the most difficult of all: depression. At this point, you are actively trying to prove that your gaslighter is right, because then maybe you could do things his way and *finally* win his approval. Stage 3 is exhausting, though, and you are often too worn out to argue.

My patient Melanie was fully ensconced in Stage 3. Melanie was a lovely woman of about thirty-five who worked as a marketing analyst for a major New York corporation. When she first came to see me, though, I would scarcely have taken her for a top executive. Huddled in a shapeless sweater and trembling with exhaustion, she sat on the edge of my couch, weeping uncontrollably.

The incident that had provoked her visit was a trip to the supermarket. She had been rushing up and down the aisles, trying to gather the groceries she needed for the dinner party she was giving that night for her husband and his colleagues. Jordan had asked her to prepare her special grilled salmon steaks, pointing out that his friends were health-conscious and would expect wild salmon. But when Melanie got to the fish counter, she discovered that only farm-raised salmon was available. She had two choices: buy the inferior fish or plan another main course.

"I just started shaking," she told me as her sobs subsided. "All I could think was how disappointed Jordan would be. The look on his face as I told him that I couldn't find the salmon, that it just wasn't there. The questions I would face—'Did you not think to go early enough, Melanie? You've made this dish before, you know what's involved. Didn't you care enough about this evening? I've told you how important it was to me. What mattered more to *you*, Melanie, than making sure this dinner came off properly? No, please, tell me, I'd really like to know.' "

Melanie took a deep breath and reached for a Kleenex. "The thing about those questions is, they just don't stop. I've tried to laugh it off, to explain, even to apologize. I've tried to *tell* him why something doesn't work—but he never believes me." She slumped a little farther down on the couch and pulled her sweater around her more tightly. "He's probably right. I used to be so organized, so on top of things. But even I can see what a mess I've become. I don't know *why* I can't do anything right anymore. I just can't."

Melanie was an extreme example of the Gaslight Effect—someone who had so completely bought into her gaslighter's negative view of her that she could no longer access her true self. To some extent, Melanie was right: She had actually become the helpless, incompetent person that her gaslighter kept telling her she was. She had so idealized her husband and wanted so desperately to win his approval that she took his side even when he accused her of something she knew she hadn't done—in this case, being careless about his party. It was easier to give in and agree that Jordan was right than face the fact that he was behaving badly and she would probably never win his wholehearted, permanent approval, which she needed—or thought she did—to complete her sense of self.

The Three Stages of Gaslighting: A Twisting Path

The descent through gaslighting's three stages is by no means inevitable. Some people live their lives in Stage 1, either in the same relationship or in a series of frustrating friendships, love affairs, or work situations. They find themselves having the same kinds of arguments again and again, and when the relationship gets too painful, they simply break it off. Then they run right out and find another gaslighter to restart the cycle.

Some people are constantly battling the demons of Stage 2. They can still function, but their thoughts and emotions are consumed by the gaslighting relationship. We've probably all had at least one girlfriend who can't talk about anything but her crazy boss or her nagging mother or her insensitive boyfriend. Stuck in Stage 2, she can only keep having that one conversation, over and over again. Even if all her other relationships are terrific, the gaslighting poisons everything.

Sometimes a relationship—especially one in Stage 2—alternates, so that the partners take turns being the gaslighter or switch roles entirely. You may have "permission" to gaslight your partner about emotional issues, for example, telling him what he "really means" when he says or does something you don't like. He, meanwhile, may be allowed to lay down the law about your behavior in social situations, accusing you of talking too much at a party or making the guests uncomfortable with your political opinions. Each of you keeps trying to be right or to get the other's approval—but about different kinds of topics.

Sometimes, too, a relationship works well for several months or even years before the gaslighting begins. Perhaps it presents occasional gaslighting moments, maybe even some rough patches along the way, but basically, the relationship is a healthy one. Then the husband loses his job, or the friend gets divorced, or the mother becomes frustrated with the difficulties of aging, and the gaslighting begins in earnest, because that's when the gaslighter feels threatened and turns to gaslighting in order to feel powerful. Or perhaps *you* feel threatened, so you suddenly become much more desperate to win your gaslighter's approval. Your desperation makes him feel powerless, he reasserts his power by getting you to agree that he's right and you're wrong—about something, anything—and so the gaslighting begins.

Sometimes you'll have a girlfriend who for years gaslighted her spouse, her child, or another friend—but not you. Not realizing what was going on in that other relationship, you may even have taken her side, bonding with her over how badly that other person was behaving. Then the husband leaves, the child grows up, or the other friend gets tired of the abuse, and suddenly she has no one left to gaslight but *you*. Used to sympathizing with her complaints, you may go for weeks or even months before realizing that you don't like the way she's now treating you.

Being gaslighted by someone whom you've trusted for years can be even more debilitating than entering into a gaslighting relationship from the start. Because your trust has a solid foundation, it's all the more bewildering when you find yourself being badly treated—and you may be even more likely to blame yourself. How could the problem be him? It must be you.

In any of these cases, gaslighting may remain at the Stage 1 or Stage 2 level, or go back and forth between them—and that's painful enough. When gaslighting proceeds to Stage 3, however, the results can be truly devastating. By this point, gaslighting has rendered you hopeless, helpless, and joyless, incapable of making even the smallest decision, wandering in a vast, uncharted desert without maps or landmarks. You can barely remember who you were before the gaslighting relationship began. All you know is that there's something terribly wrong—probably with you. After all, if you were a really *good* person, a really *competent* person, you'd be able to win your gaslighter's approval. Wouldn't you?

After treating dozens of women who struggle with this pattern, and after experiencing it myself, I can attest to the fact that the Gaslight Effect is truly soul-destroying. Perhaps the worst moment is when you realize how far you've gotten from what you used to consider your best self—your *true* self. You've lost your self-confidence, your self-esteem, your perspective, your courage. Worst of all, you've lost your joy. All that matters to you is getting your gaslighter to approve of you. And by Stage 3, you're beginning to understand that you never will.

Three Types of Gaslighters

Gaslighting comes in many forms. Some of it looks like abuse, but some of it can look as though your partner is being a good guy or even a romantic lover. So let me give you a few ideas of the shapes gaslighting might take.

The Glamour Gaslighter: When He Creates a Special World for You

Suppose your boyfriend hasn't called you for two weeks, even though you've left him several messages. Then, when he shows up, he's carrying a huge bouquet of your favorite flowers, a bottle of expensive champagne, and tickets to a weekend in the country. You're angry and frustrated. Where was he? Why didn't he return your calls? But he refuses to accept that there was anything wrong with his unexplained absence and insists you join him in enjoying this romantic occasion he's just created. Like all gaslighters, he's distorting reality and demanding that you agree with his distorted view; he's behaving as though he's done nothing out of the ordinary, acting as though *you're* the unreasonable one for being upset. But the glamour and romance may cover up how badly he's behaving and how distressing you first found it.

That's what I call a Glamour Gaslighter. Some guys engage continuously in this type of gaslighting; others, like Katie's possessive boyfriend, Brian, may try this type of glamour move only occasionally, after a particularly upsetting fight, perhaps. Either way, Glamour Gaslighting can be very confusing—you *know* something is wrong, but you love the romance. So if you can't get him to agree with you that there's a problem, then you start to agree with him that everything must be fine.

As I look back on my own relationship with a Glamour Gaslighter, I have the sense of having fallen under his magic spell, entering an enchanted world where my beloved and I were the luckiest lovers the world had ever known. The gaslighter is often at his charming best at the beginning of a relationship, and the very qualities that cause trouble later on can help him make a good impression in these early stages. He lets you know you're the most wonderful woman in the world, the only one who's ever understood him, the fairy-tale princess who has magically transformed his life. He'll transform your life, too, he implies or even promises, he'll shower you with affection, take you to wonderful places, sweep you off your feet with gifts or intimate confessions or sexual attention of a kind you've never known before. You feel close to him, wonderful, special. He glows, and you glow with him. For women who believe that falling in love can be magical—and who among us doesn't believe that sometimes?—the Glamour Gaslighter can be the most attractive man in the world, because creating that magic is his specialty.

Okay, so what's wrong with this picture?

Certainly, falling in love *can* be a magical experience, and I'd be the last to discourage you from enjoying a new romance. Sometimes, though, the men most skilled at creating "magic" are the ones who love mainly the *idea* of a relationship. They've had lots of practice setting the stage for their romantic dramas—all they need is their leading lady, and when you come along, you're practically handed a script and swept up into the grand production. This can be thrilling for a while—the fancy restaurants, the romantic gestures, the intimate moments, the sex. This is a guy who likes being the leading man.

Even in the early glamorous phase, you might spot signs of trouble that you choose to disregard because everything else is so magical. When Katie and Brian were first dating, for example, Katie loved Brian's romantic gestures—the time he brought her flowers or gave her a foot rub—but she was disturbed as well by the way he periodically accused her of being too flirtatious or too naïve. Because she loved the romantic attention, though, she convinced herself that the accusations weren't important, that they'd disappear after Brian got to know her better, or perhaps even that she'd misunderstood them.

In other Glamour Gaslighting relationships, everything may be truly perfect until the first glitch occurs—the first time he accuses you of something you didn't do and expects you to agree. You might continue in that romantic glow for several weeks or even months before he makes an accusation or blames *you* for being upset at his disappearing for two weeks and failing to return your calls. By then, however, you're invested in the romance, so even though you may not like the bad behavior or the gaslighting, you cling to the relationship, hoping desperately to regain that former glow.

As I listened to one of my clients describe her growing discomfort with one of these Glamour Gaslighters, I found myself seeing the image of a snow globe, a crystal ball that encloses a lovely, fragile world. The globe is so beautiful—until it shatters. Then an entire world is destroyed, and there's no way to put it back again.

Often, especially during Stage 1, Glamour Gaslighting may be interspersed with periods of romantic tenderness, so you can't quite identify what the problem is. You might even hate the gaslighting but think it's a small price to pay for the closeness and warmth. If, like Katie, you've been single for a while, or if you and your gaslighter have children together, you may dread the thought of leaving the relationship—even if it's a bad relationship—and of course, that dynamic makes the good times all the more precious. "See," Katie would tell herself when her increasingly bad-tempered boyfriend brought her roses, gave her a foot rub, or surprised her with a bottle of her favorite perfume. "He really does love me. I'm sure this other stuff will clear up."

Meanwhile, though, Katie's sense of self was being progressively undermined. She was beginning to see herself as her boyfriend saw her— overeager, inappropriately flirtatious, ridiculous—and she started to draw back from her usual friendly responses.

Sometimes, too, the good times come in direct response to the bad ones. A gaslighter might harangue you for hours about your bad behavior. Then, when you're almost in tears, he'll apologize profusely. "Please forgive me— you know how I get sometimes," he might say. "I just can't stand the thought of losing you." He might use gifts, sex, or other intimacies to restore your former closeness—a response that you greet with almost unbearable relief. See, you weren't wrong—he *is* a terrific guy! The more upsetting the bad behavior becomes, the more welcome is the good behavior that seems to erase it and return you to those early magical days. Some women spend months, years, a lifetime hoping for that trip back into the past.

There are many ways glamour and romance can play into a relationship, and of course, not all of them are negative. But if your guy is using romance to distract you from your own feelings—if he brings you flowers to stop you criticizing his lateness, or insults you in front of his friends and immediately follows it with an extravagant compliment that takes your breath away, so that you begin to doubt your own perception that anything is wrong—then you are involved in glamour gaslighting.

Is your guy a Glamour Gaslighter? See if the items on this checklist ring any bells.

Are You Involved with a Glamour Gaslighter?

Although some of the items on this checklist are negative, many are neutral or positive. But if you are concerned that your partner is using glamour to distract you from your feelings, even the positive items may indicate gaslighting.

- Do you often feel as though the two of you have your own special world?
- Would you describe your guy as "the most romantic man I've ever known"?
- Are your fights and disagreements typically followed by intense times of closeness or romance, marked by special presents, greater intimacy, better sex?
- Are your friends impressed by how romantic your guy is?
- Are your friends nervous about how romantic your guy is?
- Does your impression of your guy not match your friends' impression of him?
- Does he behave markedly differently in public than in private?
- Is he the kind of guy who needs to charm everyone in the room?
- Do you sometimes feel that he has a whole repertoire of romantic ideas that don't necessarily fit your moods, tastes, or history together?
- Does he insist on being romantic—sexually or otherwise—when you've said you aren't in the mood?
- Do you feel a marked discrepancy between your experience early in the relationship and your sense of it now?

P.S. It's not only romantic partners who can be Glamour Gaslighters. Many bosses, colleagues, even friends and relatives can sweep us up into a wonderful fantasy world, whose price is the gaslighting we'd prefer to ignore.

If your Glamour Gaslighter is a man and you're a woman, he may infuse every situation with his sexual charm, even if there's no chance that an actual sexual relationship will ever develop. In other words, he gaslights you by insisting that you act as though the two of you were involved in a budding romance, even though you *know* the relationship is not really a romantic one.

A Glamour Gaslighter friend may draw you into the feeling that it's the two of you against the world, comforting you with the promise of "friends forever," or flattering you by insisting how special you both are: That's the bait she uses to get you to put up with her gaslighting. Then, when you have to cancel your regular Sunday brunch because of a family emergency, she accuses you of deliberately undermining her and not respecting the friendship. If you, too, are deeply invested in the "friends forever" ideal, you may be convinced by her attempts to gaslight you; you *thought* you were attending to another priority, but perhaps you *were* undermining her.

Likewise, Glamour Gaslighter relatives might romanticize the family, encouraging you to feel like a part of the special clan. That doesn't necessarily stop them from trying to get you to go along with their distorted view of who you are. Maybe they'll make statements such as, "Oh, you're always making such a fuss!" or "I don't know why you can't be creative, like your sister," and instead of calling them on it or silently disagreeing, you buy into their view of you because you so desperately want to be "one of the family" and your agreement seems to be the price of admission. Or you may be invited to bond with a sibling, parent, or other relative against the rest of the family, as though the two of you share a special world that no one else understands. Again, that's the bait that keeps you hooked, so when your gaslighter insists that you see things *her* way, you try to accommodate her. "You're always such a scatterbrain," your mother or sister or special cousin might say. You don't agree with this assessment and actually feel quite insulted by it. But you so love the way it's you and her against the rest of the family that you start to think perhaps you *are* a bit scattered in order to keep that special bond.

As you can see, in all these cases, the basic formula for gaslighting is the same: Someone else insists that you go along with a point of view you *know* isn't true, but you try to convince yourself it is in order to win that person's approval and preserve a relationship that makes you feel good, special, loving, capable. Your need for outside validation keeps you in the gaslighting relationship.

The Good-Guy Gaslighter:
When You Can't Quite Say What's Wrong

My coaching client Sondra was confused. A red-haired woman with striking green eyes, Sondra was in her mid-thirties, and at first glance, she seemed to have the perfect marriage, and the perfect life. She and her "perfect husband," Peter, had three beautiful children, she loved her job as a social worker; and she was part of a warm and loving network of friends and colleagues. Although she and, Peter—also a social worker—were as busy as young professional parents usually are, Sondra had always been proud of the way they shared everything, including the housework and child care.

Yet Sondra had been feeling increasingly dissatisfied—for no particular reason, she assured me. In fact, she described her emotional state as "numb." For the past three years, she'd been feeling "cooler and cooler," as though nothing mattered very much. When I asked her to tell me the last thing that had made her feel genuinely joyful, she looked distressed—a look she quickly covered as her face returned to its previous mask of calm. "I honestly can't remember," she told me. "Is that a bad sign?"

As Sondra and I worked together, she began to talk a bit differently about her husband. I could see that he did many nice things for her and the children, and that on many issues, Sondra could say she'd gotten her way. But I could also see that Peter had a hot, hasty temper, which his family went to great lengths to avoid provoking. Although Sondra was willing to take him on, she never knew what would become a battle and what wouldn't, and the effort to be continually "battle-ready" kept her exhausted even when Peter didn't actually get mad. Although she insisted that she and her husband had a perfect marriage, she seemed to feel drained and depressed by her encounters with him.

"Let's say I want a night out of the house to go to a staff meeting," she told me. "Peter needs the same night out for a meeting at *his* job. And we just can't find a sitter. We'll discuss for hours whose meeting is more important. I just end up feeling exhausted by the whole thing. Peter will keep saying things like, 'Are you sure you need to go? You know how you tend to worry too much about little things' or 'Remember that other meeting—you thought you needed to go and you didn't. Are you sure this isn't another case of that?' In the end, I might even 'win' and get to be the one to go. Then Peter will look at me like 'Aren't you happy now? You won!' But somehow I never feel satisfied. I just feel exhausted."

Sondra, it seemed to me, was involved with a Good-Guy Gaslighter, a man who needed to appear reasonable and "good" but who was nonetheless deeply committed to getting his own way. My longtime friend and colleague the psychotherapist Lester Lenoff aptly labels this "disrespectful compliance," when the façade is one of acquiescence but the real agenda is disregard. Peter *seemed* to be respecting Sondra, but all the time he kept suggesting that maybe she didn't know what she was talking about, or that maybe she was worrying too much. In the end, that disregard and disrespect were what Sondra took away from the discussion—and that's what made her feel frustrated whether she "won" or "lost."

If you're involved with a guy like this, you may often feel confused. You may sense on some level that you're being dismissed or disrespected—that your wishes and concerns never really get through—but you can never quite put your finger on what's wrong.

We've all had dealings with people when something felt "off," even if we could never quite say why. The boss who called us in for an apparently positive job evaluation only to leave us feeling shaky and insecure. The friend who has done so much for us—but somehow we never quite find the time to meet her. The boyfriend we "should" adore, who looks so good on paper— yet we just can't bring ourselves to commit to him. The relative who's such a saint—yet we always return from her house bad-tempered and depressed.

Often these confusing experiences indicate gaslighting—the undermining or denial of your sense of reality by a gaslighter who needs to be right.

What you take away from the conversation is not what actually happened but the covert message "You're wrong and I'm right!" So you find yourself giving in without knowing why and getting what you want without feeling satisfied. While you aren't sure what to complain about, you can tell something is wrong. Like Sondra, you feel numb, disempowered, joyless—and all the more depressed for not knowing why.

The problem, quite simply, is that your gaslighter is caught up in his need to bolster himself and his sense of being right. He *needs* to do nice things, but not because he cares about *you;* he's just desperate to prove what a good guy he is. That leaves you feeling lonely, even if you don't know why. But you're desperate to think well of him and to have him think well of you, so you ignore your frustrations. Like Sondra, you may even "numb out."

Are you involved with a Good-Guy Gaslighter? See if any of these situations feel familiar.

Are You Involved with a Good-Guy Gaslighter?

- Is he constantly working at pleasing you and other people?
- Does he offer help, support, or compromises that somehow leave you feeling frustrated or vaguely dissatisfied?
- Is he willing to negotiate household, social, or work arrangements with you, but you still never quite feel as if you were "heard," even though you've presumably gotten what you asked for?
- Do you feel as though he always gets his way in the end, but you can never quite figure out how that happened?
- Do you feel as though you never quite get what you want, but you can't quite put your finger on what you have to complain about?
- Would you describe yourself as perfectly happy in your relationship but somehow feeling numb, disinterested, or discouraged about life in general?

(continued)

> • Does he ask you about your day, listen attentively, and respond sym-
> pathetically, yet somehow, you end most such conversations feeling
> worse than before?

The Intimidator: When He Bullies, Guilt-trips, and Withholds

Glamour Gaslighting and Good-Guy Gaslighting are often hard to spot because so much of the behavior involved might be so desirable under other
circumstances. But some gaslighting behavior is more obviously problematic: yelling, put-downs, freeze-outs, guilt trips, and other types of punishment and/or intimidation. You may have all sorts of reasons for putting up
with this unpleasant behavior—you see this man as your soul mate; you
think he's a good father to your children; you believe that his criticisms of you
are correct—but you also know on some level that you don't like being
treated this way.

In some cases, these problematic actions alternate with Glamour or
Good-Guy behavior. In other cases, they characterize so much of the relationship that it would be correct to call your gaslighter an Intimidator.
Melanie's husband, Jordan, for example, was a classic Intimidator. When
Melanie hadn't been able to find the wild salmon for their dinner party, Jordan had put her down, yelled at her, and battered her with a hundred questions she couldn't answer. Then he stopped speaking to her for several hours.
That was how he always responded when he didn't like something she did,
and by now Melanie felt worn down by his attacks. She had long since
stopped trying to defend herself, though she had never stopped trying to win
his love. She still thought that Jordan's approval would prove she was a
strong, smart, competent woman who deserved to have a good and happy
life, and that Jordan's rejection was the ultimate proof of her worthlessness.

Are you involved with an Intimidator? See if you recognize any of these
situations.

Are You Involved with an Intimidator?

- Does he put you down or find other ways of treating you with contempt, either in front of other people or when the two of you are alone?
- Does he use silence as a weapon against you, either to get his way or to punish you when you displease him?
- Does he frequently or periodically explode into anger?
- Do you find yourself feeling fearful in his presence or at the thought of him?
- Do you feel that he mocks you, either openly or as under the guise of "just kidding" or "just teasing"?
- Does he frequently or periodically threaten to leave if you displease him, or does he suggest or imply that he may leave?
- Does he frequently or periodically invoke your worst fears about yourself? For example, "Here you go again—you're so demanding!" or "That's it—you're just like your mother!"

Being involved with an Intimidator can be challenging to say the least. To make your relationship more satisfying, both of you will need to work on two areas: the gaslighting and the intimidation, which is unpleasant even when it's not part of gaslighting. The Intimidator may need to alter his way of relating—but you'll also need to work on your own ability to withstand his intimidating actions, so that you don't give in immediately to avoid the unpleasantness.

Gaslighting: A New Epidemic

Why is gaslighting such a widespread problem? Why are so many smart, strong women caught in debilitating relationships that would have made

1950s-sitcom marriages seem enlightened? Why are so many men and women struggling to disentangle themselves from employers, family members, spouses, and friends who are clearly manipulative and often cruel? Why has the truth of these relationships become so hard to see?

I believe there are three major reasons for the Gaslight Epidemic, a powerful set of messages in our culture that go beyond any of our individual reasons for remaining in gaslighting relationships.

The Profound Change in Women's Roles — and the Backlash Against That Change

With regard to male-female romantic and professional relationships, it's important to remember that women's roles have changed swiftly and suddenly. The last time women's roles changed dramatically was during World War II, as large numbers of women suddenly entered the workforce to take the jobs that all the men had left when they entered the armed forces. Hollywood's response to women's new economic power was to produce several "gaslight" movies, including the original *Gaslight,* itself, with Ingrid Bergman and Charles Boyer. In these films, powerful, charming men managed to deceive strong but vulnerable women into giving up their own perspectives, a type of relationship that seemed related to the abrupt shifts in the expectations and experiences of both sexes. In both the 1940s and our own era, women suddenly took on new power in their work lives and personal lives—a transformation in roles that both they and their men may have found threatening. Despite their newfound freedom to work, run for office, and generally participate in public life, many women still wanted some version of a traditional relationship—a strong man on whom they could rely for guidance and support. And many men, on some level, were threatened by women's new demands for an equal voice in both public and private realms.

As a result, I think, some men responded by trying to control the same strong, smart women to whom they were attracted. And some women responded by actively "reprogramming" themselves to lean on their men, not just for emotional support but for their very sense of self—"Who am I in the world?" A whole new generation of gaslighters and gaslightees had been created.

Paradoxically, too, the very feminist movement that gave women more options also helped create pressure on many of us to be strong, successful, and independent—the kind of women who would theoretically be immune to any form of abuse from men. As a result, women who are in gaslighting and other types of abusive relationships may feel doubly ashamed: first, for being in the bad relationship, and second, for not living up to their self-imposed standards of strength and independence. Ironically, women may use the very ideas intended to support them as a reason *not* to ask for help.

Rampant Individualism—and the Isolation That Goes with It

Traditional societies may not have offered much scope for individual development, but they were very good at grounding most people within a secure network of relationships. I'm not saying women were never isolated in their marriages, but they did tend to have access to a wider set of family relationships, as well as social rituals that made them part of a larger whole. Even in our own modern industrial society, both men and women had much wider access to social networks—unions, churches, community groups, ethnic groups—as recently as a few decades ago. At least to some extent, people were part of a larger world in which any one individual—even a spouse or employer—could be seen in a broader context.

Now, with our high level of individual mobility and our society's focus on consumerism, we tend to be far more socially isolated. We spend long hours at work, often with a changing cast of characters, and our leisure hours are generally spent in private situations—with a partner or with a few friends, rather than as part of a church group, union, or community organization. In such a context, any one individual can take on enormous influence, as we become isolated from other sources of information and response. A partner comes to seem like the sole source of emotional support; an employer seems to have almost unlimited power over access to professional self-esteem; a friend may be one of the few human connections in a busy and isolated life. As a result, we focus all our need for approval on these relationships, which we expect to complete or define our sense of what we are. In traditional cultures, we'd have a broad range of emotional connections that might help us feel stable and grounded; in modern society, we often have only one person— a partner, friend, or family member—to turn to when we're looking for a depth of understanding and connection that no single relationship can really satisfy. Hungry for reassurance that we are good, capable, and lovable, and increasingly isolated from other connections, we are prime candidates for gaslighting.

The Gaslight Culture

The problem goes deeper, though. As I look around my own work and family life, I am struck by the frequency with which I am told—by "experts," politicians, or the media—to believe something that is obviously not true. Advertising insists that no man can love a woman who doesn't have a perfect size 2 body and a beautifully made-up face; but I know from my own experience and observation that isn't so. School officials tell my children that learning is valuable for its own sake while reminding them that if they don't have the grades and the SATs, they won't get into the colleges they want. Politicians give us one reason for their actions, then switch ground midstream and offer another, without ever acknowledging that the new "party line" isn't the same as the old one. In that sense, I believe, we are living in a Gaslight Culture. Rather than being encouraged to discover or create our own reality, we are bombarded with a million different powerful demands to ignore our own responses and accept as our own whatever need or view is currently being marketed.

Finding a New Way

Fortunately, there is a solution to the problem of gaslighting. The key to freeing yourself from this crippling syndrome isn't easy, but it is simple. All you have to do is understand that you are already a good, capable, and lovable person who doesn't *need* an idealized partner to provide approval. Of course, this is easier said than done. But when you realize that you alone can define your sense of self—that you are a worthy person who deserves to be loved, regardless of what your gaslighter thinks—you've taken the first step toward freedom.

Once you understand that your entire sense of self doesn't depend upon your gaslighter, you become willing to insist that the gaslighting end. And because you know you're entitled to love and to a good life, you're able to take a stand: Either your gaslighter treats you well, or you'll walk away. That's the leverage you need to step back, look clearly at reality, and refuse to give in to your gaslighter's relentless criticism, demands for perfection, and manipulative behavior.

I know this sounds daunting right now, but don't worry. I'll talk you through the entire process and show you how to turn off the gas. Once you're *willing* to leave your relationship, you can decide whether or not you *want* to leave it.

That's how it worked for Melanie. Little by little, she learned to see herself as the smart, kind, and competent woman she really was. She learned how to opt out of the devastating arguments she could never win and how to turn off her husband's nagging, critical, demeaning voice when she started to hear it inside her own head.

As Melanie grew stronger, she realized that Jordan was deeply committed to gaslighting. He really needed to be right—all the time—even at Melanie's expense. After a while, she stopped idealizing him and ceased to care so deeply about his approval. And when that happened, she realized that she wasn't getting enough love, affection, or companionship from Jordan to make the marriage worthwhile. She left her husband and eventually began a new, more satisfying relationship.

That was Melanie's choice; it may not necessarily be yours. You may discover that once you no longer need your gaslighter's approval, you can respond to him differently. And perhaps his behavior, unlike Jordan's, will change as well. If your gaslighter is a family member or an employer, you may find ways to limit the relationship while staying in it—visiting your mother only when you can bring a friend along, for example, or finding ways to work less closely with your abusive boss. Or, like Melanie, you could decide to terminate the gaslighting relationship once and for all.

Whatever decision is right for you, you have a deep source of power within you to free yourself from the Gaslight Effect. The first step is to become aware of your own role in gaslighting, the ways in which your own behavior, desires, and fantasies may be leading you to idealize your gaslighter and seek his approval. So let's move on to Chapter 2 and a closer look at the Gaslight Tango.

The Gaslight Tango

T rish was a tall, athletic woman in her late twenties with long, blonde hair. Feisty and energetic, Trish would be the first to admit that she lived to argue. She'd been on the debating team in high school, she'd run for student council in college, and she'd gone on to become a top litigator, arguing, as she put it, for a living. Now, however, the constant arguments in her marriage had become a cause for concern, and she'd come to my office hoping that I could help her find another way of dealing with her increasingly contentious husband, Aaron. "He thinks he's always right," Trish told me, with what I soon came to recognize as a characteristic toss of her head whenever she started to complain about her spouse. "He doesn't realize that of course *I'm* always right!"

Trish laughed when she said it, to make sure I knew she was joking. I sensed, however, that there was more than a grain of truth inside the joke. Trish was very concerned about being right—and about having others know it. The notion of "agreeing to disagree" or "walking away from a fight" was totally foreign to her.

As Trish and I continued to work on the issues that had brought her through my door, I began to realize that she was almost certainly being gaslighted. Her husband, a high-powered lawyer like herself, also lived to argue, and whenever they disagreed, he'd marshal an enormous body of facts to bend her to his will. Indeed, when they'd first gotten together, they'd both seemed to enjoy the crackling arguments and the "makeup sex" that followed. Now, Trish confessed, she was starting to feel worn down. "I can't *always* be wrong," she told me once, in an uncharacteristically small voice. "I can't be *that* stupid."

Gradually, it emerged that Trish wasn't merely the victim of Aaron's high-pressure arguing style. She herself, it turned out, was an active—if unconscious—participant in the Gaslight Tango. As much as her husband needed to "squash her," with facts and figures, as she put it, she needed to undermine him with counterarguments and emotional appeals. When I asked her what would happen if she simply cut an argument short by saying, "Well, I don't see your point yet, but I'm willing to think about it," she nearly went through the roof.

"You don't understand!" she said passionately, suddenly turning all the force of her need to be right on *me*. "I can't *stand* it when Aaron thinks I'm some dumb blonde—I can't *stand* it! It's the most awful feeling—I feel as though I'm going to jump out of my skin—I feel like I'd jump off a cliff or smash the house down or do *anything* to get him to change his mind. I *can't* walk away when he's like that—I really *can't*."

"You can't?" I asked her.

"*No!*" Trish said, her voice higher and more strained than ever. "If he thinks *that* about me— I mean, he's my *husband*. Why did he *marry* me if that's what he thinks? What if it's *true*?"

Trish's situation was a perfect example of how many of us get caught within the Gaslight Tango. People who become gaslightees are often terrified of being misunderstood. Despite the confidence and forcefulness they frequently display, they are in reality extremely vulnerable to the opinions of their loved ones and associates. In intimate relationships, especially, they tend to give away a lot of power to the man or woman they love, investing their partners with an almost magical ability to "see" them and "understand them truly."

In this setup, being misunderstood can feel like a death blow. For Trish's husband to see her as "wrong" felt far more extreme to her than a simple disagreement or a minor divergence of opinion. It felt like a major wound to her sense of self. And if Aaron actively disapproved of her, she felt as though the bottom had dropped out of her world. Having idealized Aaron, she had become desperate for his approval and affirmation of her as an intelligent, competent person—leaving herself vulnerable to gaslighting.

One of the couple's running arguments was over Trish's use of her credit card, which she paid for entirely out of her own earnings. She was an impulsive shopper and liked to pick up clothes on her way home from work. She'd always pay her bills on time, but she would run up some debt each month. Aaron, a more frugal type who had grown up in a low-income family, insisted that what Trish saw as a reasonable use of funds was actually a dangerous extravagance. When I pointed out that in practical terms his opinion didn't really matter because Trish controlled her own credit card, she stared at me in disbelief. "But how can I live with a man who thinks so badly of me?" she protested. Winning the argument with her husband—insisting that he agree with her self-concept—was even more important to her than the actual issue of him trying to control how she spent her money.

As we saw in Chapter 1, the gaslighter is someone who desperately needs to be right in order to bolster his own sense of self and hold on to his own sense of power. The gaslightee tends to idealize her gaslighter and to long for his approval. Trish's need for Aaron's approval led her to argue with him endlessly, trying to get him to share her views, especially her views of herself. Maybe he couldn't let anything go, but neither could she. Even though Aaron usually won their arguments, the two of them were equally committed to arguing because Aaron needed to be right and Trish needed to be approved of. This made their arguments supercharged—and left Trish feeling superdefeated.

Dancing the Gaslight Tango

Although from the outside gaslighting can look like the work of a single, abusive gaslighter, a gaslighting relationship always involves the active participation of two people. That is, in fact, the good news. If you're caught in a gaslighting relationship, you may not be able to change the gaslighter's behavior, but you can certainly change your own. Again, it's not easy, but it is simple: *You can end the gaslighting as soon as you stop trying to win the argument or convince your gaslighter to be reasonable. Instead, you can simply opt out.*

So let's take a closer look at the intricate steps of the Gaslight Tango. The dance usually begins when a gaslighter insists that something is true, despite your "deep knowing" that it is false. Remember Katie from Chapter 1? Her boyfriend, Brian, insisted that she was surrounded by leering, mocking men, even though she thought of most people as simply friendly. Likewise, Liz's boss insisted he was on her side, despite all the evidence that he was trying to sabotage her. And Mitchell's mom said she wasn't insulting him, although the knot in his stomach was powerful evidence to the contrary.

Now, people disagree, distort the truth, and insult each other all the time, so these experiences are not in themselves gaslighting. In theory, Katie could simply shrug and say, "Well, you may see those guys as ogres, but I think they're just being friendly, and I don't intend to change." Likewise, when Liz's boss turned on the charm, she might have given him a long, hard look and thought, "Okay, something fishy's going on here—I wonder what." By the same token, Mitchell could have said, "Mom, your laughing at me hurts my feelings, and while you're doing it, I won't talk to you." If any of our gaslightees had been able to respond in this way, there would have been no Gaslight Effect.

That's not to say that Katie's boyfriend, Liz's boss, or Mitchell's mom would have acted any differently. They might have changed, but they might also have dug in their heels and become even more stubborn. Then Katie, Liz, and Mitchell would all be facing difficult choices about what to do next. But they wouldn't be involved in gaslighting.

Gaslighting can occur only when a gaslightee tries—consciously or not—to accommodate the gaslighter, or to get him to see things her way, because she so desperately wants his approval so she can feel whole. Katie argues with Brian, insisting that she really *isn't* flirting. Then she tries to see things from his point of view so she'll feel like a good, loyal girlfriend—someone who would never flirt in front of her boyfriend. Liz tries to explain to her boss all the bad things that have been happening to her. Then she tries to convince herself that her boss is right—she's just paranoid. That way she can feel like a good, competent employee who has it within her power to make her professional situation work out. Mitchell attempts to talk back to his mother, trying to get her to speak to him more kindly. Then, when she calls him rude, he worries that maybe she's right. All three gaslightees *know*, deep down, that their gaslighters are telling them something that doesn't ring true. But rather than stick with their own perceptions, they try to win the gaslighters' approval by finding a way that the two of them can agree. Most often, they try to change themselves by giving in.

Why Do We Go Along with It?

Why do we bend ourselves out of shape to fit a gaslighter's vision? I believe there are two reasons: fear of the Emotional Apocalypse and the Urge to Merge.

Fear of the Emotional Apocalypse

Most gaslighters seem to hold in reserve a secret weapon, an emotional explosion that flattens everything in its vicinity and poisons the atmosphere for weeks afterward. A person in a gaslighting relationship fears that if the gaslighter is pushed too far, he'll invoke this Emotional Apocalypse, something even worse than the ongoing attrition of annoyed questions and cutting remarks. This apocalypse is such a painful experience that, eventually, she'll do anything to avoid it.

The Emotional Apocalypse might happen only once, or it might never happen, but the fear of the Emotional Apocalypse is sometimes even worse than the event itself. The gaslightee is terrified that her partner might yell, or criticize her, or even leave her, and she's sure that if her fear is realized, she'll be completely overwhelmed. "You feel like you're going to die," one of my patients told me once, and she wasn't much comforted by my replying, "But you *won't* die."

The Emotional Apocalypse for Katie was Brian's anger. She never knew when he might simply explode in rage. His particular version of anger involved a lot of yelling, which Katie found especially frightening. She knew he'd never actually hit her; still, just the sound of his loud, angry voice was enough to make her anxious. After a while, she found herself giving in to whatever he said, just to keep the yelling at bay.

If Katie had been able to give in on the surface while holding fast to her inner knowing that she *wasn't* being flirtatious, she might have escaped the worst effects of gaslighting—the loss of confidence, the disorientation, the mounting depression. But she thought if she gave in that way, she'd be little better than a coward who was continually placating her boyfriend. Nor did she want to face the fact that her boyfriend was so bad-tempered—so far from the ideal guy she had once believed him to be. So she had powerful reasons for believing that Brian was right; that way, she wouldn't be a coward and he wouldn't be a bad guy. On some level, Katie preferred to see the situation as agreeing with a perceptive boyfriend rather than giving in to an unreasonable one. And so every time she gave in to Brian to prevent an explosion, a part of Katie wondered whether he was right. The price she paid for holding on to these ideas was being gaslighted—allowing her boyfriend to define her view of the world and her concept of who she was.

Liz's boss threatened another sort of apocalypse—professional defeat. Liz was invested in her high-powered job, and she couldn't bear the thought of losing it. She feared, too, that her entire professional reputation was at stake. What if her boss fired her and then spread nasty rumors about her incompetence and her "paranoid" personality? Who would hire her then? Just as Katie didn't want to face her boyfriend's bullying, Liz was afraid to think clearly about how much power her boss really had and what her options really were. So the worse her employer's behavior got, the more she doubted herself.

The apocalypse that paralyzed Mitchell was guilt. For as long as he could remember, Mitchell had worried about letting his mother down and had hoped to make up for all the other disappointments in her life. As a result, he was vulnerable to her gaslighting. Although she rarely accused him of anything directly, her hurt looks were more powerful than words. "I feel like I've broken her heart," he told me in one especially painful session. "I'd do anything to keep her from looking that way and knowing that I caused her pain." Rather than ask himself what, realistically, were his chances of making his mother happy and how willing he was to sacrifice himself to do so, Mitchell insisted that his mother *could* be happy   if only he could be a better son.

Sometimes the gaslighter progresses to increasingly painful responses—from cutting remarks to outright yelling, from implied guilt to explicit accusations. And if a gaslightee resists, the behavior may become still worse—daily yelling, broken dishes, threats of abandonment. She may start to feel as though even thinking about resisting provokes an escalation, as though it's not safe to disagree even in her own thoughts. Giving in completely—in thought and emotion as well as action—may come to seem like the only safe course.

When gaslightees try to tell me about their apocalyptic fears, they often have two contradictory positions. On the one hand, putting these fears into words may make them seem trivial, so my patients express a lot of shame and self-doubt. "I know it doesn't sound like much . . . ," they'll say. "Only an idiot would get upset about such a little thing." Or "I'm sure it's not that big a deal. It's just that *I'm* such a wimp. He's always telling me I'm too sensitive."

On the other hand, if I ask a gaslightee to wonder what might happen if she responded to the Emotional Apocalypse with a shrug or by walking out of the room, she may desperately insist that I don't understand how bad it really is. "But he'll *keep* yelling," she might say. "And if I leave, or ask him to stop, he'll yell *more*." If I ask what makes the yelling so frightening, I get a stare of disbelief. It's as though the gaslighter's secret weapon—whatever it might be—really did have the power to annihilate the gaslightee and destroy her entire world.

I know when the Emotional Apocalypse threatens, it can be truly frightening. But in fact, the yelling will *not* destroy your world. The criticism will *not* end your life. The insults—however painful—will not actually bring your house crashing down in ruins around you. I know it *feels* as though the Emotional Apocalypse will literally destroy you—but it won't. And when you're able to see past the fear that is choking you and clouding your mind, you may be able to shrug off your gaslighter's point of view and refuse to engage with it—neither believing it nor arguing with it, but simply holding on to your own inner truth.

Apocalypse Now: The Gaslighter's Secret Weapons

What do *you* find most painful? Your gaslighter is an expert at using that sore spot as his secret weapon. He may

- **Remind you of your worst fears**
   "You really are too fat / frigid / sensitive / difficult . . ."

- **Threaten you with total abandonment**
   "No one will ever love you again."
   "You'll be single for the rest of your life."
   "No one else would put up with you."

- **Invoke other troubled relationships**
   "No wonder you can't get along with your parents."
   "Maybe this is why your friend Suzi has dropped you."
   "Don't you see, this is why your boss doesn't respect you."

- **Use your ideals against you**
   "Isn't marriage about unconditional love?"
   "I thought friends were supposed to be supportive."
   "A true professional would be able to take the heat."

(continued)

- **Make you doubt your own perceptions, memory, or sense of reality**

    "I never said that—you only imagined it."

    "You promised to take care of that bill; don't you remember?"

    "My mother was really hurt by what you said."

    "Our guests thought you were ridiculous—everyone was laughing at you."

One of the first steps in freeing yourself from a gaslighting relationship, then, is to acknowledge how unpleasant and hurtful you find this Emotional Apocalypse. If you hate being yelled at, you have the right to insist that yelling not be a part of your disagreements. Maybe some other woman wouldn't mind the loud voice, but you do. If that makes you too sensitive, so be it. You have the right to set limits where *you* want them, not where some mythical other, "less sensitive" woman wants them.

At the same time, it's useful for you to realize that being yelled at won't bring your entire world crashing down—not so that your gaslighter feels entitled to keep yelling at you but so that you don't feel compelled to give in every time he threatens to yell. It may not be fun to walk away from a loudly yelling man, to shut the door of your study behind you, or even to leave the house. And your disengaged response may indeed provoke ever-greater retaliation. But it's important not to feel that your partner has such a massive weapon that he can always ultimately compel you to give in.

In Chapter 6, we'll look more closely at some techniques for setting these limits and for strengthening your internal core of self-respect—the first steps to turning off the gas. First, though, I want to look at the second reason why so many of us give up our own perceptions to join in the Gaslight Tango.

The Urge to Merge*

Those of us who are prone to being gaslighted seem to have one thing in common. No matter how strong, smart, or competent we are, we feel an urgent need to win the approval of the gaslighter whom we've idealized. Without that approval, we feel unable to see ourselves as the good, capable, and lovable people we so desperately want to be. Needing our gaslighters' validation, we're terrified to feel divided from them in any way. So it makes us nervous to see things differently from our loved ones, or to have preferences that are different from theirs.

Mariana was a voluptuous woman in her early forties with pale blond hair and wide blue eyes. A supervisor in a small office, she'd been involved for several years in a gaslighting relationship with her friend Sue. I once asked Mariana to describe a disagreement with Sue, and I almost provoked an anxiety attack. "Just thinking about when we disagree," Mariana told me, "I feel as though I've fallen off the planet. It's like I'm spinning out there in space with no gravity, nothing to hold me down to earth."

Once again, people's responses may vary. Mariana and Sue had a lot of trouble tolerating any difference of opinion, whether the topic was fashion, politics, the people they knew, or even their own families. They once spent several hours arguing over whether Mariana was being too critical of her mother, who lived in another state and whom Sue had never even met. Yet both women found it a matter of supreme urgency to come to some common understanding on this issue, unable to bear the thought that they saw Mariana's behavior differently.

In some gaslighting relationships, it may be all right to disagree about some topics but not others. Sometimes, disagreements that feel safe one day become fraught with danger the next. In many cases, the tolerance for difference varies according to each partner's degree of stress and security. If both partners are doing well, they may allow each other more room. If one or both

---

*Although the term *merge* has a very specific meaning in psychoanalysis, I'm using it here in its more colloquial sense, as a desire for a conflict-free state of total agreement.

are feeling vulnerable, they may require greater "loyalty"—that is, unconditional agreement—from each other.

When gaslightees do feel anxious about disagreement or disapproval, they tend to respond in one of two ways. They might quickly align themselves with a partner, spouse, friend, or boss, giving up their own perception as quickly as they can in order to win the other person's approval and thereby prove to themselves that they're good, capable, lovable people. Or they might try to induce their gaslighter—through argument and/or emotional manipulation—to come around to their own point of view in order to feel secure and valued.

Trish, for example, was desperate to convince her husband, Aaron, that she really *was* competent with money. She couldn't bear the thought that he saw her as financially incompetent, and she was willing to argue endlessly with him, unable endure his negative view of her. She used arguments to get her husband to agree that she was right after all.

Mariana, by contrast, used emotional manipulation. She might start crying in the midst of a discussion, telling Sue how lonely she felt. Or she might burst out with a strong statement about how much Sue meant to her and how much she counted on the friendship, as though any disagreement were a threat to their bond.

Although they expressed their anxiety differently, both Trish and Mariana feared that seeing things differently from a loved one meant losing the approval and losing the connection, becoming isolated and alone. Each was willing to do almost anything to protect her sense of being close to another person, even if it meant annihilating herself in the process.

Your Part in the Tango

Are you dancing the Gaslight Tango? See what you learn by taking the following quiz.

It Takes Two to Tango: Are You Becoming a Gaslightee?

1. Your mother has been calling for weeks to try to get you to make a lunch date, but you're really swamped. Between your new boyfriend, your recent bout with the flu, and your mounting deadlines at work, you just couldn't find the time. She says, "Well, I can see that you don't care about me at all. It's nice to know I raised such a selfish daughter!"

   You say:

   a. "How can you say I'm selfish? Can't you see how hard I'm working?"

   b. "Gosh, I'm so sorry. You're right. I'm a terrible daughter. I feel awful."

   c. "Mom, I have a hard time talking to you when I feel like you're putting me down."

2. Your best friend has just canceled on you at the last minute—again. You screw up your courage and say to her, "It really drives me crazy when you cancel on me like that. I end up alone on a weekend night, feeling lonely and abandoned. I'm frustrated because I could have made plans with somebody else. And frankly, I miss you!" In a warm, concerned tone, your friend says, "Well, I've been meaning to tell you, I think you're becoming a little too dependent on me. I'm a little uncomfortable spending time with someone who is so needy."

   You say:

   a. "I'm not needy. How can you say I'm needy? I do things by myself all the time! I just don't like it when you cancel on me—*that's* the problem!"

   b. "Wow, is *that* why we don't spend time together? I guess I'd better work on that. I'm so sorry to be a burden."

   c. "I'll think about that. But how did we get from you canceling on me at the last minute to me being needy?"

3. Your supervisor is under a lot of pressure lately, and you think she's taking it out on you. Although there are times when she praises you to the skies, there are other days when you walk into her office and she

reads you the riot act for minor infractions. She's just spent ten minutes pointing out that your choice of typeface on your latest market analysis has violated the company's standard format. "Why do you insist on making my job so difficult?" she asks you. "Do you think you deserve some kind of special treatment? Or it is some kind of problem with authority?"

You say:

a. "Oh, get *over* yourself, it's only a typeface!"

b. "I don't know what's wrong with me lately. Maybe I do have some issues to work on."

c. "I'm sorry I didn't follow procedure" (*Thinking: "I really hate being yelled at."*).

4. Your boyfriend has been moody and withdrawn all evening. Finally, he snaps, "I don't see why you have to spill my secrets to the whole world." As you prod him for details, the story emerges: You told someone at his office party about the Caribbean vacation that the two of you are planning. "It's nobody's business where we go!" he insists. "People get all sorts of clues from information like that—how much money I'm making, how my sales have been going—things I don't want them to know. Obviously, you have no regard for my privacy, or my dignity."

You say:

a. "Are you nuts? It's a simple vacation. What's the big deal?"

b. "I had no idea I was so insensitive. Now I feel terrible."

c. "I'm sorry you feel bad about this. But wow, we do tend to see things differently, don't we?"

5. You and your husband have been locked in the same conversation for hours. You've failed to pick up his dry cleaning, as you had agreed to do, and now he has no clean suits to take on his business trip tomorrow. You apologize but insist it wasn't intentional—you simply got to the cleaner's five minutes after it closed. He points out that you're always late when it comes to doing him favors; this isn't the first time you've

screwed up. You agree that you are chronically late but insist that it's not directed against him personally. He accuses you of trying to sabotage the trip so he'll have to stay home with you. Or maybe you're jealous of his new co-worker. Or maybe you're just tired of your own job and envious of how much he likes his.

You say:

a. "How can you say these terrible things about me? Can't you see how hard I'm trying? If I were trying to sabotage you, would I have left work an hour early just to help you out?"

b. "I don't know, maybe you're right. I probably was trying to get back at you for something."

c. "You have your perception about what I did, and I have mine; and at this point, we're going to have to agree to disagree."

ARE YOU DANCING THE GASLIGHT TANGO?

IF YOU ANSWERED (A): You're locked into an ongoing argument with your gaslighter—an argument you can never really win. By needing to win your gaslighter's approval, you give him the power to "make you crazy." Even if you're right, you might consider ways to opt out of the arguing so you can end the dance.

IF YOU ANSWERED (B): Sounds like your gaslighter has already convinced you to see things his way. Because you want his approval so much, you're willing to agree with him—even at the expense of your own self-esteem. But even if you've made a mistake, you don't need to agree to your gaslighter's negative view of you. Keep reading. I'll help you work on reclaiming your own point of view and restoring a healthy, positive sense of yourself.

IF YOU ANSWERED (C): Congratulations! Every one of these answers is a terrific way to step gracefully out of the Gaslight Tango.

Because you're more committed to your own sense of reality than to winning your gaslighter's approval, you have the power to opt out of arguments and interrupt the gaslighting. You're well on your way to freeing yourself from the Gaslight Effect.

Whether you answered (a), (b), or (c) to most of the questions, don't worry. In the rest of the book, I'll be giving you lots of specific suggestions for ways to opt out of the Gaslight Tango. Remember: As long as there's any part of yourself that believes you need your gaslighter to feel better about yourself, to boost your confidence, or to bolster your sense of who you are in the world, you'll be leaving yourself open for gaslighting.

So let's look at one more aspect of the Gaslight Tango that often lures us into that dangerous dance.

The Empathy Trap

Empathy is the ability to imagine what another person is feeling by putting yourself in his or her place. When I hear that my friend had a problematic mammogram, that my child was teased in school, that my partner got turned down for a grant, I don't just feel sorry for them. I share in their fear, hurt feelings, and frustrations by connecting to the way I felt when I was afraid, frustrated, or disappointed. And when I hear that my friend's health is fine, that my child has a new friend, or that my partner just got a promotion, I participate in their joy as well.

In many situations, empathy is the most wonderful quality I can think of: the balm that makes sorrow bearable, the gift that multiplies joy. Ideally, empathy is the current that flows between two people in a close relationship, helping us to feel less alone, reassuring us that we are loved and understood. But sometimes, sad to say, empathy can be a trap, and never more so than in a gaslighting relationship. Your very ability to offer empathy—and your own need to receive it—can make you prone to the Gaslight Effect.

Katie, for example, was one of the most empathic people I had ever met.

She seemed remarkably tuned in to what all her loved ones were feeling, able to imagine with remarkable accuracy how any given event might affect them. When she asked me to reschedule an appointment, she apologized for inconveniencing me in a way that showed me how aware she was of my needs as well as her own. I could see how this quality would make her an excellent friend and partner.

But I also saw how Katie's empathy made it hard for her to choose her own worldview over that of her boyfriend. "I can see how upset Brian gets when I chat with the guy at our deli," she'd say. "It's as though he's afraid I'll leave him and never come back. I feel so bad for him when I see how scared he is. I can't stand it." Katie often got so caught up in her boyfriend's fear that she forgot her own perceptions about what happened during that chat and what it meant. She was so compelled to see things from Brian's point of view that she lost sight of her own perspective.

Unfortunately, Brian didn't extend the same empathy. He appreciated Katie's response; her depth of understanding was part of the reason he was so attached to her. But he didn't respond in kind. Rarely, if ever, did Brian think, "I see how pleased Katie is when someone smiles at her—it makes her feel happy and secure" or "I see how upset Katie gets when I yell at her—how unsafe she feels, how uncomfortable." Most of the time, Brian was aware only of his own needs and feelings. Indeed, from his point of view, to focus on Katie's feelings would be to give up his own. Acknowledging that she might feel differently than he did was like admitting that his feelings were invalid. He *couldn't* emphatize with her without feeling defeated, as though he had given up all hope of having his own point of view understood and respected.

Brian may have genuinely lacked the ability to imagine another person's feelings. Or he may have feared his own capacity for empathy, seeing it as a quality that might defeat him. Indeed, when I saw them briefly in couples counseling, he said, "I don't see why I have to see it *her* way all the time—it's never *my* way! And every time I see it her way, I end up giving in."

In this gaslighting dynamic, then, Katie's empathy created a kind of trap. She wanted to see her boyfriend's point of view, but he didn't want to see hers. When they argued, she gave a lot of room to his side of the argument, while he never gave any ground to her. Empathizing with Brian made Katie feel sensitive and loving. But when Brian was asked to empathize with Katie, he felt weak and defeated. Meanwhile, Katie's compulsive empathy led her to disregard her own feelings and perceptions in her effort to see things as Brian saw them.

Katie didn't only give empathy, though; she desperately wanted to receive it—along with the approval she wanted so badly, after all, that approval was the only way she could prove to herself that she was a good, loyal girlfriend instead of the flirtatious, disloyal woman Brian had insisted she was. Her need for Brian's empathy and approval was so great that it threatened to overwhelm her ability to think clearly. Longing for Brian to see her point of view and to approve of her, she found it very difficult to tolerate their disagreement. For her, love meant total understanding and unconditional acceptance—nothing less—and without that love, Katie felt that she would be completely worthless, abandoned, and alone. This desperate need for approval, understanding, and love kept Katie continually open to Brian's gaslighting.

I once asked Katie if she could accept the fact that her boyfriend would never be able to grasp why being friendly and open meant so much to her. Maybe he could stop insulting her, I suggested. But he might continue to *think* differently.

Katie's jaw dropped. "But Brian loves me," she protested. "He'd do anything for me."

"Maybe so," I responded. "But feelings and acts of love are not the same things as understanding. Sometimes we love people without being able to feel what they're feeling. Sometimes we don't approve of someone's actions, decisions, or opinions, even within a loving relationship."

Katie stared at me as though I were speaking Greek. "That's not love," she said finally. "If you love someone, you understand them; you feel what they feel. And you think they're wonderful! And Brian *does* see me that way—just not all the time." She went on to recount the time she came home from work exhausted and he gave her a foot rub—a story she had told me several times. "He knew just what I needed—and he gave it to me!" she would repeat with every retelling. "That was when I knew how much I meant to him—and how he would always take care of me." That memory was so precious to Katie that she was willing to endure Brian's insults and yelling in the hope of someday recapturing those few special moments when she was able to imagine that he "understood" her and would always be there for her.

How can you break out of the Empathy Trap? Try the following suggestions.

Freeing Yourself from the Empathy Trap

Clarify your own thoughts and feelings Often when we're involved in a gaslighting relationship, we get completely focused on our partner's point of view, so much so that we can no longer remember our own perspective. Try completing the following sentences about a relationship that you find troubling, sticking entirely to your own point of view. I suggest writing down your answers, speaking them aloud, or both. You may find it helpful to *hear* and *see* your own perspective, not just think it!

In this relationship, I want _____.
Something I would like to change is _____.
I can't stand it when _____.
I see myself as basically _____.
I like it when people _____.

How did it feel to complete those sentences? If you found yourself panicking, don't worry. That's just evidence of how new it is for you to focus so completely on your own perspective. Try sitting with the feelings and seeing what emerges. You might also find it easier to think of these big questions in more simple, concrete ways.

This week, one thing I would like my boyfriend to do is _____.
Tomorrow, one thing I wish could be different would be _____.
One thing I like about myself is _____.

You can also draw your feelings if you prefer, or use a combination of words and images. (For a list of "feelings words," see Appendix A.)

Access your "ideal adviser" Visualize a wise person whom you trust entirely. This might be a person you actually know or the perfect adviser you wish you had. You can visualize a real human being, a magical or spiritual guide, or even an animal. Picture this guide witnessing a recent troubling incident with your gaslighter. He or she sees everything that happens with perfect clarity. Imagine going to visit this guide after the incident. What does he or she say to you about what happened? What is your guide's advice?

Talk to someone you trust If you've got a friend or relative whom you really trust, explain that you're doing an exercise in discovering your own point of view. Try telling this person exactly what you think about a troubling situation that involves your gaslighter. Ask the person to interrupt you gently—perhaps simply by holding up a hand—whenever he or she hears you slipping out of your own point of view into anyone else's, especially your gaslighter's. The goal is for you to clarify your own thoughts and feelings, without reference to anyone else. Make sure this person doesn't insert his or her own opinion! If you can't stand not knowing what your friend or relative thinks, make a date to discuss this exercise in a day or so. Then try living for twenty-four hours with only your own opinion in your head.

THE GASLIGHT TANGO can be a seductive dance, but as we've seen, it takes its toll. Whether gaslighting is a minor part of your life or a central dynamic in your relationships, you'll benefit from finding ways to step out of the dance. In the next three chapters, we'll look at some specific ways you can free yourself from all types of gaslighting, from the apparently trivial to the seemingly overwhelming, as we explore Gaslighting Stages 1, 2, and 3.

chapter 3

Stage 1: "What Are You Talking About?"

Y ou're at the movies with a date, waiting for the film to start, and you suddenly feel thirsty. "Excuse me," you say. "I'm dying of thirst. I'll be right back." You go out to the lobby, get a drink from the water fountain, and return. When you ease back into your seat, your date is glaring at you. "What's the matter?" you ask.

"What were you doing out there?" he fumes. "How could you be so inconsiderate? I'm sitting alone here for nearly twenty minutes. What am I supposed to do with myself?"

"Was it really that long?" you respond, slightly surprised. The movie hasn't even started yet, and the two of you didn't arrive *that* early.

"Maybe you weren't keeping track of time, but I was," your date says. Then the lights dim, and he puts his arm around you in that affectionate way you always love. "Whatever perfume you're wearing tonight, you should *always* wear it," he murmurs romantically into your ear. The rest of the evening goes so well, you remember all over again why you like this guy so much. And the next day, when you tell your best friend about the date, you don't even mention the drinking-fountain incident.

YOU'VE JUST MET your new boss, and she seems perfect. She takes you out to lunch during your first week and spends the entire time compli-

menting you on the great job you've been doing. You've never felt so appreciated, and you can't wait to show this woman what you can *really* do now that
you've got the chance.

Then one day, you oversleep and come in forty-five minutes late. You apologize profusely, but your new boss smiles and says she understands. "Sometimes, when we feel threatened, we tend to want to avoid whatever makes us
feel that way," she says sweetly. "So please, tell me, what exactly do you find
threatening about your current job situation? I'm happy to work with you to
make this a more comfortable place."

You insist that you simply screwed up in setting your alarm (you don't
want to admit you were out late partying the night before), but no matter
what you say, she only smiles.

"I'm sorry you feel you can't be honest with me," she says as she finally
sends you back to your desk. "If you change your mind, please, my door is always open."

She couldn't have been nicer, but you find yourself feeling extremely uncomfortable, though you're not sure why. And when later that day your boss
hands you an assignment you've been coveting for the past six months, you
promise yourself never to be late again and put the incident out of your mind.

YOUR FAMILY IS planning an eightieth birthday party for a favorite
uncle, and you're calling Aunt Jean to find out what you can bring. "Oh,
you're such a busy career girl," she says. "Why don't you just bring some
bread from a nice bakery? Then you won't have to cook."

You insist that you'd love to cook for Uncle Ira, but Aunt Jean won't hear
of it, and you agree to bring the bread. Then, the day before the party, Aunt
Jean calls you at the office. "Your mom was just telling me about the fabulous
chocolate-hazelnut cake you made for your father's birthday," she says. "Ira
loves chocolate. Why don't you bring that?"

You point out that the cake requires an elaborate set of ingredients and
several hours to make. You've just been hit with a monster deadline at work,
and at this point, you have no time left either to shop or to cook.

"But you *said* you wanted to make something!" Aunt Jean says plaintively. And when you offer to pick up a bakery cake, she just sighs. "Well, go ahead and buy the cake then," she says finally. "I'm sure it won't be as good as your own special recipe, but never mind. I would never have bothered you if I'd known how busy you were."

You hang up the phone feeling confused. You *did* offer to bring something homemade—and you would have loved to cook something special for your beloved Uncle Ira. How have you ended up failing both him and Aunt Jean?

Entering Stage 1: A Crucial Turning Point

The tricky thing about Stage 1 gaslighting is that it seems so minor. Just a little misunderstanding, just a moment of discomfort, just a tiny loss of temper or petty disagreement. If you've never thought of gaslighting as a category, you might not even notice these seemingly trivial incidents. Even if you're highly aware of gaslighting, it may be hard to tell whether incidents like the ones above are little annoyances to be dismissed, problems for which you're to blame, or the warning signs that herald a destructive pattern.

Yet the gaslighting that takes place at Stage 1 often proves to be a crucial turning point in a relationship. Sometimes a relationship can go either way—into gaslighting or away from it—depending on the gaslightee's response. So a clear, decisive refusal of Stage 1 gaslighting may enable you to nip those tendencies in the bud and go on to a healthier relationship. (Don't worry. I'll show you exactly how to opt out of Stage 1 gaslighting later in this chapter.)

Sometimes, too, gaslighting will begin in a relationship that has been relatively healthy for weeks, months, or even years. Your mutual history may make it that much harder to realize that your spouse, friend, or boss is gaslighting you. Yet the sooner you realize it and stop playing into the pattern, the better chance you have of restoring your previously healthy relationship.

Alternately, your recognition of Stage 1 gaslighting might help you decide much sooner—and with far less pain—that a new or ongoing relationship is never going to work for you. You might choose to break off the romance or ease out of the friendship, or at least dial down the intensity. If your gaslighter is someone you can't avoid dealing with—a relative, boss, or colleague—you can make sure to limit your contact with the person and cut back on your emotional involvement.

Finally, identifying gaslighting at this early stage will help make you aware of your own tendencies to dance the Gaslight Tango. Now is the perfect time to practice rewriting your own gaslight-prone responses, while the gaslighting is still at a manageable level and your sense of self is relatively intact.

So let's start by looking at some telltale signs that you have entered Stage 1 gaslighting. As you'll see, some of these signs contradict one another, and they can all be explained in many different ways. But if you feel an anxious or sad sense of recognition as you read through these lists, or if any of the signs rings a very loud bell with you, pay attention. Your intense response may be your way of letting yourself know that you've entered the first stage of gaslighting.

Signs That You Have Entered Stage 1

With a Lover or Spouse

- You often argue about who's right and who's wrong.
- You find yourself thinking less about what you like and more about whether he is right.
- You can't understand why he so frequently seems to be judging you.
- You often have the sense that he's distorting reality—remembering or describing things very differently from how they actually happened.
- The way he sees things often makes no sense to you.
- Your image of the relationship is that it's going really well—"except for" these isolated incidents that keep sticking out in your mind.
- When you describe your guy's point of view, your friends look at you like *you're* crazy.

(continued)

- When you try to describe what's bothering you about the relationship—to others or yourself—you find yourself unable to convey the problem.
- You don't tell your friends about those small incidents that disturb you; you'd rather just ignore them.
- You actively cultivate friends who think you're in a good relationship.
- You think of him as masterful and in charge rather than controlling and demanding.
- You think of him as glamorous and romantic rather than unreliable and unpredictable.
- You think of him as reasonable and helpful—then wonder why you don't feel better about the relationship.
- You feel protected and safe with him, and unwilling to give up that safety just because of some occasional bad behavior.
- When he's possessive, moody, or preoccupied, you see how troubled he is, and you want to make things better for him.
- You call him on his stuff, and it goes nowhere. But you keep hoping it will.

With a Supervisor or Boss

- Your boss is telling you about yourself all the time, and most of it is negative.
- Your boss praises you to your face, but you have the feeling that he's undermining you behind your back.
- You feel there's nothing you can do to please your boss.
- You used to feel competent at work and now you don't.
- You're always checking out perceptions with your co-workers.
- After you leave work, you're constantly replaying conversations you had with your boss.

(continued)

- When you replay conversations with your boss, you can't quite figure out who's right.
- When you replay conversations with your boss, you can't quite remember what he said—but you know you felt attacked.

With a Friend

- You're frequently in disagreements.
- Every disagreement seems to become personal, even if nothing is actually said about you.
- You often don't like the way your friend appears to regard you and are frequently trying to change her opinion.
- You avoid certain topics of conversation.
- You feel put down by your friend.
- You find yourself not wanting to make plans with this friend.

With Family

- Your parents' or relatives' perception of you doesn't match your perception of yourself, and they're happy to tell you about it.
- Your siblings are constantly accusing you of behavior or attitudes that you don't believe you have.
- Your siblings have an image of you and of themselves that you just don't see, and they insist that you share it.
- Your siblings insist on treating you as though you were stuck in your childhood role; if you're the youngest, they treat you as if you were still acting like a baby; if you're the oldest, they behave as though you were still bossing them around.
- You're frequently defending yourself.
- You feel like you're never doing enough.
- You feel like a bad kid for asking for something.
- You find yourself feeling guilty more often than not.

Who's Crazy: Me or Them?

I often feel anxious when I fly, even though I know intellectually that the statistical chances of being in an airplane accident are less than the chances I take driving out of town in my car. Still, a little turbulence and I immediately become absolutely certain that the plane is going down. I *know* this is highly unlikely—but what if it's true? When do I listen to my feelings, and when do I tell myself to ignore them?

Caught in this dilemma, I was extremely grateful, years ago, to get some comforting advice from an old friend. "Look at the flight attendants," she told me. "They always know what's going on. If they're calm, you can relax and ignore that nervous feeling in the pit of your stomach. But if the flight attendants keep looking at one another or having those little whispered conferences, then you can start to worry."

I've often thought of my friend's advice when my patients ask me how they can tell whether or not they're being gaslighted. After all, every relationship has some uncomfortable moments, and every person has flaws. So what if your boyfriend hates to be left alone in a movie theater, or your boss gets a bit out of line when you're late, or your elderly Aunt Jean vents her nervousness about her husband's birthday on you? Taken by themselves, none of the incidents with which I started this chapter is all that big a deal—just a little turbulence and a few bumps.

Sometimes, though, a warning signal *does* indicate danger, and then you'd be foolish to ignore it. So my advice is, look at your Flight Attendants. Find some trustworthy indicator—other people, gut feelings, or your inner voice— to help you sort out when your anxiety is warranted and when it's just a feeling that you may want to put on hold.

Some Flight Attendants Who Might Signal Danger

- Frequent feelings of being bewildered or confused
- Bad or restless dreams
- A troubling inability to remember details of what happened with your gaslighter
- Physical indicators: sinking stomach, tight chest, sore throat, intestinal difficulties
- A sense of dread or hyperalertness when he calls or comes home
- An extra effort to convince yourself or your friends of how good the relationship with your gaslighter really is
- The feeling you're tolerating treatment that compromises your integrity
- Trusted friends or relatives who frequently express concern
- Avoidance of your friends, or refusal to talk with them about your relationship
- A loss of joy in your life

Stage 1 gaslighting is insidious. It may not involve any of the signs we traditionally associate with emotional abuse—no insults, cutting remarks, put-downs, or controlling behavior. There may not even be an Emotional Apocalypse in Stage 1—that may come later. But gaslighting, even in this early phase, is profoundly destabilizing and undermining, because we are eager to win our gaslighter's approval, and we may already have started to idealize him. We have decided that *this* man knows "who we really are," and if he thinks badly of us, he must be right. So we argue with him—in person or in our heads—hoping desperately to prove that his criticisms aren't true and that we really *are* good people after all. With all this focus on winning our guy's approval, we may not be able to see clearly that he's behaving badly.

That vague sense that something is wrong—something you can't quite put your finger on—might be your only clue that there is a problem. Thus, in the example about your date at the movies, you *know* you were gone only a few minutes—otherwise the movie would have started—and even if you'd been gone longer, you'd have done nothing wrong. Yet your date's extreme annoyance communicates the message that you behaved badly. So you've got two choices:

Gaslight-Free: If you are able to stay strong and centered, uninterested in your date's approval and grounded in your own reality, you may be able to see his annoyance as a reflection of his own anxieties. "Oh, he's nervous about the date," you may think, "or maybe he really just gets anxious when he's left alone for five minutes." Either way, you know it's *his* problem, not yours, and you've refused the opportunity to be gaslighted. (You can then decide whether you *want* to keep seeing a guy who's so easily annoyed!)

Gaslight-Prone: If you're already invested in thinking that this is a great guy and you want him to love you, you're likely to strive for his approval, even at this early stage. In that case, you may blame yourself for his annoyance. You might start thinking that perhaps you *were* insensitive, or asking yourself why you behaved so badly, or questioning your sense of time. You fear that if this wonderful guy thinks you're insensitive, maybe you are. And the way to prove you're *not* insensitive is to win his approval. So the Gaslight Tango begins.

Likewise, in the story about your new boss, you *know* you were late to work because you'd partied too hard the night before. Yet your boss insists on explaining your lateness in terms you don't accept. So once again, you can choose between two options:

Gaslight-Free: If you are relatively confident about yourself and your work, you may not be overly concerned about winning your boss's approval. Sure, you want her to like you and give you good assignments, but what she thinks about you doesn't really penetrate deep into your sense of who you are. With that kind of self-esteem, you may be able to shrug off her odd interpretation and avoid the gaslighting. "Wow," you may think. "This woman really has some weird theories. Guess I'd better not be late again, or I may have to hear some more!"

Gaslight-Prone: If your sense of yourself as a good worker and a smart, competent person depends upon your boss's approval, you might start to wonder if maybe she has a point. Maybe you *were* avoiding something. Maybe you *are* feeling threatened. Maybe you were sabotaging yourself by staying out late. As soon as you begin giving space to her theories, *knowing* they are not true, you've opened yourself to further gaslighting.

In the encounter with Aunt Jean, you may also emerge feeling frustrated and confused. Aunt Jean implies that first you offered to prepare food and then you refused to do so—and there's just enough truth in that version of events to throw you off course. The reality is that you *did* offer to cook, but when Aunt Jean refused your offer, you went on to other commitments. So what are your two choices here?

Gaslight-Free: If you've got a good sense of yourself as a kind, loving, generous person, you'll *know* what really happened and Aunt Jean's distortions of reality won't bother you too much. You may even be able to view her with compassion, reminding yourself that she's probably nervous about the party as you shrug off her inaccurate account of your actions.

Gaslight-Prone: If, like so many of us, you have a big investment in your family thinking well of you, Aunt Jean's distortions might throw you for a loop. It's not enough for you to know what happened; you have to get Aunt Jean to see it, too. Otherwise, maybe it's true, maybe you are a bad, selfish person who neglects your family. So you try desperately to convince her of your good intentions or argue with her passionately about what really happened. You might even stay up all night to bake that cake! Now you're dancing the Gaslight Tango.

Stage 1 Gaslighting Occurs More Easily . . .

- if you are easily swayed by people who seem certain.
- if you are very responsive to people who seem hurt, frustrated, or needy.
- if you have a strong need to be right and to be seen as right.
- if you have a big stake in being liked, appreciated, or understood.
- if it's very important to you to be able to fix things and make everything come out well.
- if you have a huge capacity to feel for others and find that you can shift all too quickly to your gaslighter's point of view.
- when you want very much to preserve the relationship.
- if you want generally to keep relationships going—you have a hard time letting go of people.
- when you want very much to preserve your good opinion of the gaslighter.
- if you have a hard time acknowledging that someone is treating you badly.
- if you feel very uncomfortable with disagreement or conflict.
- if you are more comfortable relying upon another person's opinion than upon your own.
- if you worry frequently about not being good enough, capable enough, or lovable enough.
- *if you want to win your gaslighter's approval, especially because you have idealized or romanticized him, or because you're very invested in preserving the relationship.*

When Criticism Becomes a Weapon

Suppose you've gotten involved with a man who occasionally loses his temper and yells. You hate being yelled at, but you're willing to tolerate it. So when your guy bursts forth in a loud voice, you say calmly, "Please don't yell at me. Let's put this whole argument on hold and just go to bed."

So far, so good—no one is being gaslighted, and the argument may well dissolve. But what if your boyfriend says, "I don't see why you have to be so sensitive!" or "I wasn't yelling. I was speaking in a normal voice"?

Now you have a few choices. If you say, "I don't want to continue this conversation," or "I guess we see things differently," or even "You may be right," you may still be able to end the argument with your sense of self intact. Note that you haven't said your boyfriend *is* right, only that he might be. You're acknowledging that you are two separate people with two distinct points of view—a refusal of the Urge to Merge that is a terrific protection against gaslighting.

But what if you find yourself wondering whether you really are too sensitive or whether your boyfriend's loud voice really was normal? Are you being "open to criticism"—which is usually a good thing—or are you simply opening yourself up to Stage 1 gaslighting?

Once again, it's a fine line. Sometimes our loved ones *do* operate differently than we do, so that our "yelling" is their "passionate but normal voice." Sometimes, too, they have insights and perceptions that challenge our own but might indeed be helpful to us. Learning to see yourself through a loved one's eyes can be a tremendous spur to growth, just as being receptive to criticism is part of any important relationship.

Sometimes, though, a gaslighter will use criticism as a weapon—criticism that makes you feel so anxious and vulnerable, you're sure it will reduce you to a puddle on the floor. You can't bear that he thinks so badly of you, you fear that if he thinks you're insensitive or unreasonable or incompetent, he may be right, and you desperately don't want to be those "bad things." That criticism becomes his Emotional Apocalypse, because you're so vulnerable to it.

A gaslighter's criticism may even be partly true, but its intention is to undermine, not to help. Aaron, for example, pointed out to Trish that she was often late paying her credit-card bills and incurred several late fees as a result. He was probably right that she could stand to be more careful and timely in her bill paying. And if he'd made those points in a loving, helpful way, Trish might have followed his advice and benefited accordingly. But Aaron was using those grains of truth to make a bigger case that wasn't true: that Trish was a childish, irresponsible person who couldn't be trusted to handle her own money, an extravagant spendthrift who was going to bring them both to the brink of ruin. That *wasn't* true. But Trish feared secretly that if Aaron thought she was "that bad," maybe she *was* "that bad." Her desperate attempts to argue him out of this position were really efforts to prove to herself that she wasn't as irresponsible and childlike as Aaron seemed to think she was.

So if someone is criticizing you and you're feeling anxious and undermined, you might look to your Flight Attendants. Your good friends and trustworthy intuitions can help you decide whether to listen with an open heart or protect yourself with a strong resistance to any negative opinions. The minute you sense that you're being undermined or attacked, you should stop listening to the words and focus on the main point: You don't deserved to be treated this way, no matter what you have or haven't done.

Some Flight Attendants Who Might Signal Danger

- Frequent feelings of being bewildered or confused
- Bad or restless dreams
- A troubling inability to remember details of what happened with your gaslighter
- Physical indicators—sinking stomach, tight chest, sore throat, intestinal difficulties
- A sense of dread or hyperalertness when he calls or comes home

(continued)

- an extra effort to convince yourself or your friends of how good the relationship with your gaslighter really is
- the feeling that you're tolerating treatment that compromises your integrity
- trusted friends or relatives who frequently express concern
- avoiding your friends, or refusing to talk about your relationship with them
- a loss of joy in your life

I think this point is so important, I'm going to repeat it: You should *never* listen to criticism that is primarily intended to wound, even if it contains more than a grain of truth. If your Flight Attendants tell you that someone is using truth as a weapon, *stop listening* and remove yourself from the conversation. Otherwise, you risk being drawn into the Gaslight Tango.

Criticism That Is Intended to Undermine Often . . .

- includes name-calling, exaggeration, or insults
- comes in the midst of a fight or an angry exchange
- is presented as part of a person's efforts to win an argument
- is made over your objections or your wish to end the conversation
- seems to come out of nowhere
- changes the focus from the other person's behavior to yours
- is given in a context where you cannot easily respond

The Explanation Trap

My friend Leah is a small business owner in her late fifties. A petite, silver-haired woman with a straightforward manner and a surprising sense of humor, Leah was widowed after a long marriage, and now she's tentatively reentering the dating scene. Recently, at a friend's dinner party, she ended up sitting beside a man named Matt. She had some major reservations about him—he seemed both a bit arrogant and somewhat reserved—but she was willing to make plans with him when he asked her out for Saturday night.

Throughout the week, Matt kept e-mailing to say how eager he was to see her, but he never quite made a definite plan. Then, on Saturday afternoon, he called to say that a family emergency had come up and he'd have to break the date. He apologized several times, but Leah was still stranded on a Saturday night.

Matt called Leah on Monday to make another date, but between her schedule and his, the next available time to get together was three weeks later. "Hey, this is terrible," Matt told her. "Now I feel even worse about canceling. Are you *sure* you can't squeeze me in? I'd really like to see you as soon as possible."

Leah told him no, and they made plans for the later time, but it was clear that Matt wasn't pleased. So Leah began to have second thoughts. What if he had picked up on her reservations and that was why he had canceled? What if, by not finding a way to see him sooner, she was sabotaging any chance the relationship had of getting off the ground? Clearly Matt was upset about having canceled; he kept saying how bad he felt. Didn't he deserve a second chance? Maybe if she had been more compassionate, he would have been more forthcoming.

By the time she spoke to me about it, Leah had come up with an explanation for the entire incident. She decided that, since she'd had reservations about dating Matt, she had somehow pushed him away, which had caused him to cancel the date. By not rescheduling with him sooner, she had continued to distance him. Any bad temper or displeasure he was expressing was clearly warranted by her distancing behavior.

"But, Leah," I told her, "you're leaving out one very important part of the story: Matt broke a date with you at the last minute. Even if you understand why he did it—even if all your explanations for his behavior are correct—he still did what he did. You're trying to pick and choose, deciding which part of his behavior to respond to and which part to ignore. But explaining something doesn't mean it didn't happen." Leah's efforts to explain away Matt's bad behavior were involving her more deeply in his gaslighting. Instead of seeing Matt as he really was, she used her explanations to see him as he wanted to be seen.

As I saw it, Leah was falling into the Explanation Trap, the effort to explain away behavior that disturbs us, including gaslighting. Instead of letting these early signs set off the warning bells they are meant to, we find seemingly rational explanations to prove to ourselves why these danger signals aren't really dangerous. As with all gaslighting, the Explanation Trap affects us because, on some level, we desperately want a particular relationship to work out; we think this relationship may finally win for us the approval of a man who makes us feel good, capable, and lovable. And so we look for reasons to ignore the unpleasant truth and idealize the gaslighter. Here are three ways you might imprison yourself in the Explanation Trap.

"It's Not Him, It's Me."

In this version, we interpret everything that happens in the relationship as our own doing. Thus, Leah insisted that Matt hadn't canceled the date because he was anxious, rude, or actually had a family emergency; instead, she had pushed him into this unpleasant behavior by her own thoughts, feelings, and actions. This kind of explanation attracts many of us because it's a sneaky way of saying that we're all-powerful. If our gaslighter's bad behavior is all our fault, then we've got complete control of the situation. All we have to do is try harder, and the relationship is sure to improve.

"He Feels So Bad."

Here, we confuse the other person's sorrow, anger, or frustration with genuine regret. So Leah kept telling me how terrible Matt felt about canceling their date. Indeed, when Matt saw that rescheduling would be difficult, he may well have felt sorry that he'd canceled. But his bad feelings were all about himself, about how hard he was finding it to make the plans he wanted. He never expressed any awareness that Leah might have felt lonely, hurt, or confused by his canceling the date, only that he had inconvenienced *himself* by doing so. By focusing on his bad feelings, Leah was deceiving herself into believing that Matt really did care about her, and that he actually was good relationship material. Through the power of fantasy, she saw not a self-absorbed man who was barely aware of her feelings but a sensitive, caring guy who was upset about what he had done.

"No Matter How He Behaves, I Should Rise Above It."

If all other explanations fail, we can always try to convince ourselves that we are—or should be—unaffected by another person's bad behavior. In the end, Leah couldn't stop Matt from canceling the date, but she could try not to mind. Sometimes we simply "decide" not to mind a certain action; sometimes, like Leah, we basically forget it happened. Either way, we're trying to make ourselves seem so strong that the gaslighter's behavior cannot affect us. "No matter what he does, I should love him in exactly the same way," a patient once told me. "Isn't that the meaning of unconditional love?"

That, to me, is the problem with "unconditional love"—it's an ideal that stands *outside* of relationships. What is this unconditional lover really saying? "No matter how you treat me, no matter what you do, I'm going to feel the very same way about you. So don't even try to change my feelings! You can break a date, and I'll feel exactly the same way about you as if you had kept it. You can ignore my feelings to focus on your own, and I won't feel any differently about you than if you had showered me with love and affection. You can insult me, ignore me, or make unreasonable demands, and I won't be affected in the least. *That's* how good a person I am, and how much I love you. In the end, you and your behavior don't really matter, all that matters is me and my love."

Now don't get me wrong. I'm all for people sticking out the bad times in a relationship. I believe that any loving relationship requires a certain amount of self-sacrifice. And I know love isn't always easy. But the essence of love is that it's a *relationship*. What each partner does affects the other—that's both the good news and the bad news, love's sorrow and its joy. It's not possible to remain unaffected by the other person's behavior; if it were, we could just have the entire relationship by ourselves.

So why are we so attracted to this idea of unconditional love? Well, many of us have found love a disappointing experience. Our family members, friends, and lovers haven't always treated us so well. We may have grown up with parents who failed us, or had a series of lovers who betrayed us, or found ourselves repeatedly let down by colleagues and friends. We may come to feel, consciously or unconsciously, that love really isn't an option for us, that we'll never meet anyone who's actually capable of giving to us generously and caring for us with empathy and support.

Out of this painful fear, we may try to solve the problem all on our own by re-creating ourselves as strong, self-sufficient, and all-powerful. In effect, we try to short-circuit our loved ones' shortcomings by becoming better people ourselves. Instead of looking clearly at a parent, lover, or friend and asking ourselves what this person is really capable of, we hold on to a fantasy of what the relationship could be, with all the focus on our own part in it. Instead of looking at how we actually feel in a relationship—satisfied or empty? loved or neglected?—we cling to a fantasy of how we *would* feel if only we were less selfish, more giving, more loving. And so we leave ourselves wide open to gaslighting. As long as there is any part of us that believes we need our gaslighter to feel better about ourselves, to boost our confidence, or to bolster our sense of who we are in the world, we're gaslightees just waiting for our gaslighters.

Remember what goes on during gaslighting: Your gaslighter—even if he's capable of genuinely relating to you some of the time—becomes overwhelmed by his own need to restore his sense of self and his sense of power by proving to you that he's right and insisting that you agree. No matter how much he talks about you and your feelings, he's really concerned with only one thing: getting you to agree he's right.

But if you're falling into the Explanation Trap, you may try to find some way to explain this behavior away. You are so eager to win your gaslighter's approval and see him in an idealized light that you ignore his actions and focus on his words.

Matt, for example, insisted that he wanted to go out with Leah. But at the same time, he had failed to make specific plans with her and had actually broken the date. He never gave any evidence of caring about Leah's feelings; his only concern was about his own convenience. Instead of realizing how much she didn't like Matt's behavior, Leah took the problem on herself, crafting a reassuring explanation that made her entirely responsible for everything that went wrong, and so, presumably, entirely capable of fixing it.

In her own way, Leah had disregarded Matt as much as he'd ignored her. Instead of focusing on the real-life guy who had broken a date and then grumbled about rescheduling, she imagined a sweet, lonely guy who would treat her well once she assured him of her affection. Then she blamed herself for not being affectionate enough.

How can you escape the Explanation Trap? Just stay in touch with your Flight Attendants. They will help you see the difference between explanations that genuinely illuminate a situation and those that help you ignore reality. If you're feeling anxious, unsettled, or disturbed and have to keep repeating your explanation over and over again—to yourself or to a friend—that's a pretty good sign you're trying to explain something away. A genuine explanation brings the relief of understanding and compassion; an Explanation Trap often feeds the very anxieties it's meant to squash.

Some Ways to Access Your Flight Attendants

*As you do any of these activities, feelings may come up that make you un-
comfortable. That's okay—in fact, it's a sign that you're accessing the
very internal wisdom you need to solve the problem. Just hang in there,
observe the feelings, and see what they have to teach you.*

• *Keep a journal.* If you are feeling troubled or uncertain, commit to
  filling at least three pages daily for at least seven days. Write as
  quickly as you can, without pausing to censor yourself or consider
  your thoughts. Allow the truth to emerge.

• *Meditate.* Meditation is the practice of clearing and quieting your
  mind. Many people report that after meditating only fifteen minutes or so each day, they discover an inner clarity in which their
  deepest thoughts and feelings come to the surface, either during
  meditation itself or at other times of the day. Most yoga centers offer classes in meditation. I also recommend Sharon Salzberg's excellent book *Lovingkindness.*

• *Moving meditation.* Forms of exercise that integrate mind and
  body—yoga, tai chi, and many forms of martial arts—are often a
  kind of moving meditation. These disciplines will make your body
  more flexible while helping to open your mind, heart, and spirit.
  They are an excellent way to recover your unique vision and reconnect to your deepest, truest perceptions.

• *Spend some time alone.* Often, our lives are so busy and scheduled
  that we don't have time to connect to our selves. The psychologist
  Thomas Moore compares the soul to a shy creature of the wild, suggesting that we must wait patiently by the side of the forest for it to
  emerge and share its wisdom. If you're feeling disconnected or confused, maybe all you need is some time to reconnect.

• *Spend some time with friends or family.* Sometimes, even in Stage 1

(continued)

gaslighting, we find ourselves becoming increasingly isolated from everyone but our gaslighter. Even when we're not with that troubling boyfriend, girlfriend, colleague, or boss, we allow ourselves to become preoccupied with what he or she might say, think, wish, demand. Hanging out with a person who sees you as you see yourself can be an excellent way to regain your own perspective.

Avoiding the Gaslight Tango

Stage 1 gaslighting is a special time—it's the only one of the three stages when you have the opportunity not just to stop the Gaslight Tango but to avoid it altogether. How can you avoid the Gaslight Tango? Here are some suggestions.

With Your Date

- *Pay attention.* Be on the lookout for gaps between what you think is important and what he thinks is important.
- *Clarify your own thoughts and judgments.* If he seems to accuse you of something, ask yourself whether you agree with that assessment of your behavior.
- *Keep your sense of humor.* If he seems to be taking something far more seriously than you do, hang on to your own sense of what's trivial, perhaps even *absurdly* trivial.
- *Stand up for yourself without engaging in an argument.* Often, when someone accuses you of something you find ridiculous, not saying anything is the best response. Trying to prove how right you were is almost guaranteed to get the tango going, because that tango is driven by the need for approval.
- *Check in with your own feelings.* As the date proceeds, do you find yourself feeling annoyed? Anxious? Swept off your feet with delight? It may

be too soon to tell what any of these feelings mean, but at least you can notice that you have them.

- *Maintain a sense of perspective.* At the end of the date, check in with yourself again to get your overall sense of how things went. If the good outweighs the bad, you may well want to see this guy again, but allow yourself to remember anything that troubled or puzzled you.

With Your Boss

- *Identify the pattern.* Although your boss has gaslighted you, suggesting that you're emotionally unstable and unable to handle pressure, you don't yet know whether he engages in this type of gaslighting all the time or only in response to certain situations, such as when you make a mistake, do exceptionally well, or seem to be having difficulties. Knowing your boss's gaslight pattern can help you figure out what you can and cannot tolerate.

- *Find out how far your boss will go.* Does the gaslighting inevitably result in punishment—altered work assignments, docked pay, dismissal—or is it only a psychological game? Again, when you see the situation clearly, you can figure out your own limits.

- *Figure out how much contact you really need to have.* Some bosses are central parts of our working lives; others function more as offstage figures. No one likes to be gaslighted by her boss, but the behavior may be easier to endure if your boss plays a relatively minor role in the day-to-day performance of your job.

With Your Family

- *Refuse to engage.* This is one of those "easy to say, hard to do" pieces of advice that you've probably heard many times before. Nevertheless, it's still the best way to keep from doing the Gaslight Tango with your mom, dad, brother, sister, or crabby Aunt Jean. With family, especially, the patterns have been so well-established that they're very difficult to break. Refusing to engage in a gaslighting conversation is often the most powerful response of all.

- *Give up your investment in being seen as right.* If you need to be seen as right, you're open to being gaslighted. I'm not saying you have to give up your deep, inner certainty that you *are* right. But as soon as you honestly don't care what your relatives think about your rightness, you'll be well on your way to freeing yourself from family gaslighting.

- *Let go of your commitment to being understood.* "I understand their point of view, why can't they understand mine?" a patient once asked me. It's hard to feel misunderstood, and even harder when it's your own family who misunderstand you. But again, wanting to be understood leaves you wide open for gaslighting.

Stopping the Dance

Even Stage 1 gaslighting can draw us in to the point where we start to participate in the Gaslight Tango. So once the dance has begun, how do you stop it? Here are some suggestions that are useful at any stage of gaslighting but are especially effective at Stage 1.

Don't Ask Yourself "Who's Right?" Ask Yourself "Do I Like Being Treated This Way?"

As we've seen, one of the biggest hooks that keep us in gaslighting relationships is our need to be right. Worrying that we're not being fair, that we're too sensitive, or that we're making too big a deal of something can be a powerful silencer, leaving us vulnerable to another person's manipulations. But if we focus on how we're being treated, we cut through a lot of the confusion. Returning to the example that began this chapter, suppose, when your boyfriend complains about your leaving him alone in the movie theater, you don't ask, "Does he have a point?" Instead you ask, "Do I like being with a guy who talks to me this way?" If you feel pleased that he's sharing his feelings with you, rueful about the way he's accurately called you on your stuff, or genuinely indifferent to the incident, then there's no problem, especially if you enjoy his company the rest of the time. If the incident leaves you feeling stung, angry, trapped, or confused, then allow yourself to have these negative feelings—and let that unpleasant experience form part of your judgment about whether you want to keep seeing this guy.

Don't Worry About Being "Good"—Just About Being "Good Enough"

Many of us are preoccupied with being a "the good girl" or "a good person." Seeing ourselves as good—however we define that word—is supremely important to us. We desperately want to be seen as nice, kind, generous, nurturing, understanding, or responsive to a partner's need. Instead of thinking about how our partner is treating us, we put all our attention on how we ourselves behave. That can be a useful way to take responsibility in a relationship, but it can also be a way to avoid seeing that, in fact, our partner is treating us badly and we really shouldn't put up with it. If you find yourself worrying constantly about being "a good person," you might try to switch the focus to whether you believe your own feelings and behavior have integrity, and ask yourself whether you are taking on all the responsibility for "good behavior" in the relationship. If your partner really is gaslighting you, the relationship won't improve by your being "good"; it will only get better by your opting out of the Gaslight Tango, whether you are "good" or not.

Don't Debate What You Know to Be True

If you *know* what happened, you don't need to argue about it. In fact, arguing about it will only make you feel crazy. Debating something basic—"I was *not* gone for twenty minutes"; "I am *not* threatened by this job"; "I never agreed to make a cake *at the last minute*"—suggests that reality is in fact open to debate, and that you'd change your position if you heard a good argument. It's an invitation to your gaslighter to batter you with facts or emotional statements until you finally give in. Would you argue with a four-year-old about whether the moon can fall onto the earth, or whether candy is a good substitute for vegetables, or whether he can stay up all night and never get tired? No, because you know you're right, and nothing the four-year-old can say will change your mind. More important, you want *him* to get the message that you're not open to argument about these topics; *you* know what's true, and that's the end of it. Even though your gaslighter is not a child, it's important to give him the same message: Some things are not open for debate.

Always Tell Yourself the Truth About Yourself

This one can be difficult, because a gaslighter is always giving you negative reports on who you are, and these criticisms may have a fair amount of truth. Your job is to resist the criticism used as a weapon and maintain a true, balanced, and compassionate view of yourself. This is no easy task when you're faced with gaslighting, but it's absolutely necessary to preserving your sense of self.

So if your gaslighter says something like "You're so forgetful," your inner dialogue might follow one of these three patterns:

1. "Is he right? Am I really so forgetful? When was the last time I forgot something? You know, I can't think of a time. I think he's really over the top on this one!"

2. "Is he right? Am I really so forgetful? When was the last time I forgot something? Well, I did forget to buy milk last week; maybe he's thinking of that. And I forgot to pick up the dry cleaning the week before. You know, two minor incidents don't add up to 'forgetful,' so I'm not going to worry about this."

3. "Is he right? Well, of course he's right! I've been a forgetful person since I was five years old. I'm the original 'absentminded professor.' But so what? It's not okay for him to use my faults against me, and it's not okay for him to try to make me feel bad. I'm not going to focus on this one fault, and I don't want him to focus on it, either, because it's just not that big a deal, since I'm really good in so many other ways."

Practice Opting Out of Arguments
with Your Gaslighter

Again, don't get caught in worrying about who's right and who's wrong. The important thing is not who can win the argument but how you want to be treated. At the end of this paragraph is a list of several tactics you might use to avoid the right-wrong debate. Edit them to fit your personality and that of your gaslighter. Some men, for example, will hear you better if you start a sentence with "I love you," as in "I love you, but I don't want to talk about this right now. We can talk later." Other men won't hear anything if you include an emotional hook and will listen only to a clear command: "Please stop talking about this now." You may need to experiment with the following options to find how they can work best for you.

Things You Can Say to Avoid the Right-Wrong Debate

- "You're right, but I don't want to keep arguing about this."
- "You're right, but I don't want to be talked to that way."
- "I'm happy to continue this conversation without name-calling."
- "I'm not comfortable with where this conversation is going. Let's revisit it later."
- "I think this conversation has gone as far as it can go."
- "I don't think I can be constructive right now. Let's talk about this at another time."
- "I think we have to agree to disagree."
- "I don't want to continue this argument."
- "I don't want to continue this conversation right now."
- "I hear you, and I'm going to think about that. But I don't want to keep talking about it right now."
- "I'd really like to continue this conversation, but I'm not willing to do so unless we can do it in a more pleasant tone."
- "I don't like the way I'm feeling right now, and I'm not willing to continue this conversation."
- "You may not be aware of it, but you're telling me that I don't know what reality is. And respectfully, I don't agree. I love you, but I won't talk to you about this."
- "I love having intimate conversations with you, but not when you're putting me down."

- "It may not be your intention to put me down, but I feel put down, and I'm not going to continue the conversation."
- "This is not a good time for me to talk about this. Let's agree on another time that works for both of us."

Allow Yourself to Be Angry, but Don't Get Drawn into an Argument about Your Feelings or Your Right to Be Heard

Anger can be a terrific way of making your feelings clear, whereas arguing only enmeshes you further. You may find it effective to choose one sentence that sums up what you want to say, and then simply keep repeating that sentence. Again, choose the style that works best for you and your situation. And, if necessary, experiment until you find the right choice.

Things You Can Say to Express Anger While Avoiding an Argument

- "Please stop talking to me in that tone; I don't like it."
- "I can't hear what you're really saying as long as you're yelling."
- "I can't hear what you're really saying as long you're speaking to me with contempt."
- "I don't want to talk while you're yelling at me."
- "I don't walk to talk while you're speaking to me with contempt."
- "I am not going to continue this argument right now."
- "From my point of view, you're distorting reality, and I really don't like it. I'll talk to you later, when I'm feeling calmer."
- "Perhaps you didn't intend to hurt my feelings, but I'm too upset to talk right now. We can talk about it later."

It can be challenging to stop the Gaslight Tango, especially if you've been doing the dance for a while, either with this partner or with several others. Sometimes you may find yourself struggling, or maybe you'll go through healthy periods interspersed with occasional relapses. Don't worry, that's how most change happens—in fits and starts, a little at a time. As long as you stick with it, you'll make progress. And if you're not making the kind of progress you'd like, consider finding a therapist, a support group, or some other type of help to give your efforts a boost.

If you can stop the dance in Stage 1, however, while you're still relatively comfortable with your own view of things, you're way ahead of the game, because you've avoided entering Stage 2 or even Stage 3. As we'll see in the next chapter, stepping out of the tango becomes far more challenging once you're more deeply entrenched in trying to win your gaslighter's approval. So the earlier you can opt out of this pattern, the better.

chapter 4

Stage 2: "Maybe You Have a Point"

Katie had been dating Brian for several months, and the gaslighting was starting to get to her. When they'd first started going out and Brian accused her of flirting with other guys, she felt bad for Brian and tried to reassure him. But she *knew* she wasn't doing anything wrong, and she tried hard to get Brian to see that, too. At that point, Katie was still in Stage 1.

Now, though, she was starting to worry that maybe she *was* flirting. "I don't *think* I'm flirting, but maybe I'm doing it unconsciously," she told me in one therapy session. "That's what Brian says—that I can't help myself. He says it's still flirting, though, that all the guys can see it, even if I don't notice. He says it's my sneaky way to punish him—but I don't *think* I want to punish him. Why would I? I love him." She paused for a minute and shook her head. "Maybe I want to punish him *because* I love him. Or maybe I just like making him mad. Brian says I do. He says I like to get him upset, but I don't see how I could, because I *hate* it when he yells. And he's yelling more and more lately, and the yelling is getting louder. I really can't stand it." She shook her head again. "But maybe I do like making him mad and I don't *know* I like it? It's all very confusing . . ."

Clearly, Katie had left Stage 1 gaslighting and moved into Stage 2. What's the difference? In Stage 1 gaslighting, you look at your gaslighter with disbelief. When he says something critical, intimidating, or manipulative, you think, "Oh, come on" or "That's just not true." Maybe you start to wonder, but you're still pretty firmly grounded in your own perspective.

In Stage 2, though, you're far more invested in winning your gaslighter's approval for being a good, capable, and lovable person—and he's even more invested in proving he's right. If you don't agree with him, he might step up his version of the Emotional Apocalypse: yelling more loudly, finding more pointed insults, giving you bigger doses of the silent treatment. You feel that you'll do anything to avoid this treatment, so you try even harder to please him. And, like Katie, you may tie yourself in knots trying to find a way to agree with him. Now, instead of starting with your own perspective, you start with his. It may even feel normal to be constantly on the defensive. When your gaslighter overreacts, you no longer wonder, "What's wrong with him?" Instead, you jump either to placate him or to defend yourself.

Have You Entered Stage 2? Are you . . .

- not feeling quite as strong as you usually do?
- seeing less of friends and loved ones?
- agreeing less with people whose opinions you used to trust?
- defending your gaslighter more and more often?
- leaving out a lot when you describe the relationship?
- making excuses for him to yourself and others?
- thinking about him constantly?
- having more trouble thinking through past interactions in which the two of you disagreed?
- obsessing—to yourself or others—about how you might have contributed to his anger, insecurity, withdrawal, or other unpleasant behavior?

(continued)

> - wondering frequently whether you should have done something differently?
> - crying more?
> - plagued more often and/or more intensely by the vague feeling that something is wrong?

Let's look again at that example from Chapter 3 of keeping your date waiting in the movie theater while you go get a drink. Here's how you might handle the situation differently in Stage 1 and Stage 2:

From Stage 1 to Stage 2

In Stage 1

- You'd like to win his approval and have him affirm what a good, capable, and lovable person you are, but you can live with the idea of not being able to do this. So you begin with your own point of view, and when he says something that seems incorrect, you might argue with him: "I did not leave you alone for twenty minutes! I checked my watch—it was only five minutes! And anyway, what's the big deal!"

- You consider your own point of view normal and his—when he's gaslighting you—as mistaken, distorted, or outrageous.

- When he behaves in a hurtful or bewildering manner, you wonder, "What's wrong with him?"

- You make judgments about what's going on: "He says I was gone for twenty minutes, but I know that's not right, or the movie would have started. And even if the movie *had* started, what's the big deal? I'm not sure I like a guy who gets so upset about such a little thing."

In Stage 2

- You *really* want to win his approval—it's become the only way you can prove to yourself that you're really a good, capable, and lovable person—so you begin with his point of view. You may argue—aloud or in your head—but you think of *his* point of view first: "He says I left him alone too long. Well, I know how awful it feels to be left alone, especially on a date. I guess I can't blame him for being upset. Hey, wait a minute. It couldn't have been *that* long! Yes, but I guess when you're on a date, even five minutes apart would seem like a big deal, so I can see why he'd be annoyed."

- When he behaves in a hurtful or bewildering manner, you wonder, "What's wrong with me?"

- You consider his point of view normal and fight desperately to get a hearing for your own perspective, because you can't bear the idea that his criticisms of you may be true: "Please, honey, think about it for a minute. I know you hated being left alone, but I really wasn't gone *that* long. Was I?" You hope that by winning the argument, you'll prove the one thing that really matters to you: You *are* a good, capable, lovable person, because this man agrees that you are.

- You lose your ability to make judgments or to see the big picture, focusing instead on the details of his accusations: "I *know* I wasn't gone *that* long.

But maybe I was, because it's true, I really don't keep track of time very well. I can't blame him for being upset about that, I guess. Hey, wait a minute, the movie hadn't started yet, so it *couldn't* have been twenty minutes. Aha! I'll tell him that. But maybe I was insensitive in some other way?"

Still not sure whether you've entered Stage 2? Take the following quiz for some more perspective.

"Always on the Defensive": Are you stuck in Stage 2?

1. Your boyfriend takes you out to an elegant meal to celebrate your promotion, and you're thrilled. Then he says, "It's good to see you so relaxed and happy. For the past several weeks, you've just kept snapping at me." Trying to stay calm, you ask him what he means. "You know," he says, "the other day when I told you that dress made you look fat, you got so angry you wouldn't speak to me for half an hour. You're just way too sensitive, aren't you?"
   You say:
   a. "Are you *insane*? Has no one *ever* told you how to talk to a woman?"
   b. "It's so hard to hear this. I just wanted to have a good time tonight. I'm willing to work on this issue, but can't I have one night off from what's wrong with me?"
   c. "I'm sorry. I guess I should be more self-confident."
   d. "Whether you're right or not, I don't want to be criticized right now."

2. You're on your way home, and you know your husband is waiting for you there.

   You feel:

   a. pleased to see him, though part of you wishes you could have dinner with friends.

   b. pleased to see him but a bit nervous. He's been so touchy lately!

   c. overcome with dread.

   d. excited about seeing him, with no reservations.

3. You're about to hand in an assignment late, and you know your boss will be mad. You had an excellent work record before he took over the department, but it's true: Your work has been slipping ever since he came onboard. Lately, he's been accusing you of trying to sabotage his leadership, and you're pretty sure he'll bring that up again.

   You think:

   a. "I wonder if he's right. Maybe I *am* trying to sabotage him."

   b. "I don't *think* I'm trying to sabotage him—I've never done that to anyone before—but I have to admit, it does look pretty strange—but I *really* don't think I have any hidden motive—but maybe there's something I'm not seeing . . ."

   c. "I can't face him again without a Valium."

   d. "My work is definitely not what it used to be. I just don't do well with this guy's management style."

4. You've been trying to diet, and everyone in the office knows it. Your colleague stops by your desk with some of her famous homemade muffins. You say politely, "Please, Anne. You know I'm dieting." Anne says sweetly, "These are low-fat. And besides, a pretty woman like you doesn't need to diet." You say, "Anne, I'm serious. If I start eating muffins, my whole eating plan will be thrown off." She says sweetly, "I've never seen anyone who had such a hard time accepting a little kindness! Maybe if you fed your emotions more, you'd have an easier

time staying on your diet." Then she puts a muffin on your desk and walks away.

You think:

a. "I never thought of it that way. Do I really have a problem accepting kindness?"

b. "That woman drives me up the wall! Who does she think she is? I could kill her and her stupid muffins! I feel like screaming!"

c. "Oh, what's the point? I'm so fat and ugly and hard to be with, it doesn't make any difference what I eat."

d. "God, what a control freak she is! I'm going right now to put this muffin in the break room. I won't see it—and she won't see it—and then I'm going to forget about it."

5. Your sister calls with a last-minute request for you to babysit. With her unerring instincts, she's picked the one night you happen to be free—a night you've been longing to spend at home, resting. Somehow, you let it slip that you theoretically *could* accommodate her. "The kids will be so disappointed not to see you," she says. "And you did say I could call any time. I guess you like the idea of being an aunt more than the actual responsibilities involved. I guess that's why you don't have any children of your own. Well, if that's how you feel, you made the right decision."

You say:

a. "Oh, no, you've misunderstood. I love your kids. And I'm responsible! Please, take that back!"

b. "How can you bring that up? You know how awful I feel about not having kids! What are you trying to do to me? How can you torture me like this?"

c. "You're right. I did say you could call any time. I can't believe I was so irresponsible. Please forgive me. And make sure the kids know how much I love them."

d. "I said you could call any time. I didn't promise to say yes any time. Sorry, that's just not a good night for me. What about next week?"

Are You Stuck in Stage 2?

If you answered (A): You're responding at a Stage 1 level: seeking your gaslighter's approval but still maintaining your own perspective. Be careful, though. Stage 1 gaslighting often leads to Stage 2.

If you answered (B): You seem to have entered Stage 2. You want so desperately to win your gaslighter's approval for what a good, capable, or lovable person you are, that you start by looking at things from his perspective. You may be trying to defend yourself, but look how much energy you've put into arguing with him, hoping to prove to yourself that his dire criticisms really aren't true. In a way, you've already let him win—simply by letting him into your head.

If you answered (C): Sounds like you're not even defending yourself anymore but just trying to endure defeat. Although you'd like to win your gaslighter's approval, you've almost given up hope that you ever will. If this is really how you feel, you've moved past Stage 2 and into Stage 3. You might want to skip ahead to the next chapter.

If you answered (D): Congratulations! You're keeping a firm grip on reality, resisting the Urge to Merge, and opting out of arguments rather than trying to prove you're right. You may care about your gaslighter, but you can live without his approval, because *you* know how good, capable, and lovable you are, no matter what he or anyone else thinks. Just being able to imagine this type of response is a big step forward.

The Three Types of Gaslighters in Stage 2

Any type of gaslighting relationship can move into Stage 2, but each gaslighter tends to escalate his gaslighting in a different way. The Intimida-

tor, the Glamour Gaslighter, and the Good-Guy Gaslighter are all likely to
have their own version of Stage 2 gaslighting.

Intimidator Gaslighters

If your gaslighter's mode is intimidation, he's likely to bring out the heavy artillery in Stage 2. He may employ one or more of the following tactics as his
Emotional Apocalypse to make you think you're about to lose the relationship: yelling, guilt tripping, belittling you, giving you the silent treatment,
threatening to leave you, making dire predictions ("You're too stupid to pass
the bar exam. I don't know why you're even trying"), or playing on your worst
fears ("You're just like your mother!").

Some Intimidators save their worst treatment for group situations, so
that you find yourself being mocked in front of other people ("It's lucky for
the lingerie industry that not everyone's breasts are as small as my wife's!")
and then told not to be "so sensitive" when you object. ("Oh, honey, I was
just teasing. Why can't you take a joke!") Other Intimidators are kind and attentive in public but bring out the insults in private. ("I bet you don't even
realize how badly you embarrassed me tonight. When you mispronounced
that French phrase, I wanted to go through the floor! Look, if you don't know
what you're talking about, why don't you just keep your mouth shut!")

Of course, not all intimidation is related to gaslighting. But if your
gaslighter is also an Intimidator, you're likely to get a double whammy. Suppose he's driving to Sunday dinner at his mother's house and you're in the
passenger seat. You object to how fast he's going, and the Intimidator
gaslighting begins:

YOU: Honey, please don't go so fast. It makes me nervous.

HIM: Don't talk to me when I'm driving! Do you want to make me have
an accident?

You don't want him to keep yelling, so you don't say anything.

HIM: Hey, I asked you a question! *Do* you want me to have an accident?
Answer me! Why don't you ever answer me!

YOU: I'm sorry. Of course I don't want you to have an accident. I'm so sorry I upset you. I promise not to do it again.

HIM: You didn't *upset* me. You did something *really stupid.* Don't you know any better? You *know* how hard it is for me to see my mother. Why would you bother me *now*?

YOU: I really didn't want to bother you, honestly, I didn't. And you're the one who insists on spending every Sunday with your mother.

HIM: *I* didn't pick this day to go. *You* were the one who said it should be Sunday. You said you were busy every other day this week. You're so selfish!

YOU: I'm not selfish! How can you say such terrible things about me?

HIM: Why are you still *arguing* with me? You're getting me even more upset. You obviously don't care about me at all.

YOU: Honey, I do care— *Please* believe me—

HIM: No, you don't! Are you going to argue with me about that, too?

Here are all the gaslighting dynamics in full bloom:

- A gaslighter who urgently needs to be right—no matter what the topic.
- A gaslightee who desperately wants to win her gaslighter's approval for what a good, capable, or lovable person she is. Otherwise, she'd tell him to stop yelling and interrupting; she might even insist he stop the car so she could get out.
- An Emotional Apocalypse—in this case, a terrifying combination of yelling, insults, *and* reckless driving that leaves the gaslightee scared, confused, and ever more desperate.
- The Urge to Merge, because the gaslightee is still hoping for a way that she and her gaslighter can be in complete agreement.
- A Gaslight Tango, because the gaslightee is still trying to show her gaslighter that he's misunderstood her and should think about her differently. She thinks that if her gaslighter sees her as good, capable, and lovable, it will prove she *is* that way—and that if he sees her as in-

sensitive, incompetent, or unlovable, it will prove she is *that* way. So winning the argument is of supreme importance to the way she feels about herself.

As you can see, it's possible to fight back with an Intimidator. But that doesn't stop the gaslighting, or prevent the Emotional Apocalypse—the yelling, the criticism, the threat to totally withdraw his love. He's still invested in being right, and you're still invested in winning his approval. Arguments don't change that. And even if you win, you've still given him power over your self-image—you've still agreed that how *he* sees you is the way you really are. So you argue desperately, every time, always needing him to affirm how good, capable, and lovable you are.

What *might* work—though there are no guarantees—is the strategy we've talked about in the previous two chapters: Resist the Urge to Merge and opt out of the fight. Let's see what happens if the gaslightee is no longer so concerned with winning the gaslighter's approval.

YOU: Honey, please don't go so fast. It makes me nervous.

HIM: Don't talk to me when I'm driving! Do you want to make me have an accident?

YOU: I'd really like you to slow down.

HIM: Hey, I asked you a question! *Do* you want me to have an accident? Answer me! Why don't you ever answer me!

YOU: I really need you to slow down.

HIM: Don't you know any better than to talk to me right now? You *know* how hard it is for me to see my mother. Why would you bother me *now*?

YOU: Right now I'm talking about slowing down. If you don't slow down, next time, we'll take separate cars.

HIM: You're unbelievable, you know that? You are the most selfish woman I've ever met in my life.

YOU: (*silence*)

HIM: You're not only selfish, you're stupid! And you obviously don't care
   about me at all!

YOU: (*silence*)

As you can see, opting out of the fight doesn't necessarily get your
gaslighter to behave any better. But at least you're holding on to your sense
of self and aren't getting drawn into an argument that you can never win.
You're not focusing on what your gaslighter thinks of you, or even on what
you think of yourself; you're simply focused on what you want: having a safe
and comfortable ride. The argument is no longer about whether or not you're
a good person but about whether your husband will drive at a speed you feel
comfortable with. Maybe this time he'll slow down, maybe he won't. Maybe
he'll keep trying to provoke you, maybe he won't. But if you stay committed
to opting out, and stick to what you've said about refusing to ride with him
the next time he acts like this, he may reconsider his behavior.

Glamour Gaslighters

An Intimidator is relatively easy to spot, because his behavior is so clearly unpleasant. Even if you blame yourself for it, you know you don't like it. But
Glamour Gaslighters may be harder to identify. These are the guys who look
so good "on paper," the guys who seem to be so perfect you can't believe
you're having such a hard time. In fact, they may seem so terrific that they
fool your friends and family, too. Your Glamour Gaslighter may have all of
you convinced that the problem isn't him; it's *your* inability to accept happiness, be more flexible, or tolerate ordinary imperfections.

Can you recognize this type of gaslighter? Do any of the following scenarios sound familiar?

The Glamour Gaslighter: Stage 2

- He sweeps you off your feet with a dozen roses but often shows up three hours late or refuses to be pinned down to any arrival time whatsoever. When you complain, he accuses you of being controlling, paranoid, or unspontaneous.
- He's constantly surprising you with romantic gestures—though they often don't key in to what you're actually feeling. But he seems so pleased with his efforts that you keep wondering what's wrong with you for not having a better time.
- He alternates between the most remarkable responsiveness—mental, emotional, sexual—and the most blatant insensitivity. When he's being responsive, you're ecstatic; when he's not, you blame yourself.
- He's generous and giving—but periodically he explodes into a temper, withdraws into an icy silence, or collapses into a childish misery. Although he refuses to blame you directly, you're sure it's your fault, though you can never quite figure out what you did.
- When you're together, life is wonderful, but then there are those little details that don't quite add up. For some Glamour Gaslighters, the problem is money: Your checkbook doesn't balance, unexplained charges appear on your credit cards, you can't figure out why sometimes he's flush and other times he's broke. For other Glamour guys, it's a sexual issue: When he's distant and evasive, you're sure he's cheating on you. Then he sweeps you back into a romantic embrace and you wonder why you're being so paranoid.

If you're involved with a Glamour Gaslighter, you may be nodding in recognition—yet still feeling confused. You can see the behavior, but you're still not quite sure why it's such a problem.

Well, I can tell you why: At least some—and maybe all—of the time, your gaslighter is completely involved in proving to *himself* what a romantic guy he is. That's his version of the gaslighter's need to be right. He *looks* like he's relating to you, but he's really only involved with himself. The actions he chooses to fulfill his needs may *seem* loving, attentive, and satisfying, but his lack of genuine connection with you leaves you feeling lonely. For example, suppose he brings you a huge, gorgeous bouquet of lilies to commemorate the anniversary of your first kiss. How romantic! You thank him for the thought, but then you remind him that you're allergic to lilies and he pouts for hours, conveying the silent but oh-so-clear message that you've been selfish and inconsiderate in rejecting his gift. Finally, he loses his temper over something apparently irrelevant, such as why you turned the air-conditioning up so high. He's managed to punish you for not going along with his romantic gesture, even though it was a gesture that literally made you sick. But if you're still invested in the relationship and still needing him to validate your sense of self, you may start asking yourself why you were so inconsiderate instead of wondering why your romantic, perfect boyfriend insists on giving you an inappropriate present.

Here's another way that a typical scene might go with one of these guys. Notice how behavior that might seem good in another context becomes manipulative and insensitive in this one as the Glamour Gaslighter keeps insisting that he's right—even while offering compliments and gifts.

YOU: Where were you? Did something happen? I've been holding dinner for three hours. You never even called.

HIM: I was out buying you this gorgeous negligee. I had to go to three stores to get the one that would be perfect with your eyes.

YOU: Well, it *is* beautiful, but three hours?

HIM: I don't know why you're so hung up on time! Life is about more than watching a clock, you know.

YOU: But I was worried.

HIM: You're so uptight! Why do you always have to keep to a schedule?

YOU: I don't have to keep to a schedule! Anyone would be upset after being kept waiting for three hours—

HIM: But we're not "anyone." Why should we judge ourselves by other people? Do you really want to be that conventional? It's so boring!

YOU: Are you saying I'm boring?

HIM: Of course not! Look, I can see that I've upset you, and I'm sorry. Let me take you out to dinner. Then afterward, I'll give you one of my special two-hour massages. And then we can try out that negligee!

YOU: Well, that does sound pretty nice . . .

Who could fault a guy who brings lovely presents, takes you out to dinner, gives you a two-hour massage, and then follows it all up with great sex? The flood of presents and apparent consideration *should* feel good. But after the third or fourth or twentieth time your guy has kept you waiting, you may not feel much like enjoying his romantic treats; you may feel too frustrated over the way your concerns keep getting brushed aside. As long as you're locked into Stage 2 gaslighting, though, you're going to blame yourself, not your guy, for the annoyance and confusion you feel. Because you still need his approval so that you can feel good, capable, and lovable, and because you want to hold on to the relationship, you're likely to adopt his perspective, not your own. You may even convince yourself that you *are* uptight, conventional, demanding, just as he says; and you might wonder what's wrong with you for not appreciating his romantic gestures. To opt out of this Glamour Gaslighting Tango, you'll have to be willing to give up some goodies.

YOU: Where were you? Did something happen? I've been holding dinner for three hours. You never even called.

HIM: I was out buying you this gorgeous negligee. I had to go to three stores to get the one that would be perfect with your eyes.

YOU: I can't look at presents when I'm so angry.

HIM: I don't know why you're so hung up on time! Life is about more than watching a clock, you know.

YOU: I've told you so many times that I don't like being kept waiting. Next time, I'm not going to wait more than twenty minutes. I'll put the food away and go on to something else.

HIM: You're so uptight! Why do you always have to keep to a schedule?

YOU: I've told you clearly what I'm going to do next time, so there's nothing more to talk about.

HIM: Sure there is. You're a wonderful, glamorous woman. Why should you keep to a schedule like other women? Do you really want to be that conventional? It's so boring!

YOU: You're not listening to me, so I guess I'll go to bed now.

HIM: Look, I see I've upset you, and I'm sorry. Let me take you out to dinner. Then afterward, I'll give you one of my special two-hour massages. And then we can try out that negligee!

YOU: Maybe another time. I don't feel like being close to you when you're not listening to my concerns.

As you can see, the problem with this type of gaslighter is that he's not *really* responding to you and your concerns—he's just as concerned as the Intimidator with being right—but meanwhile he's putting up a very attractive smokescreen. With an Intimidator, you can object to the yelling, insults, or freeze-outs without needing to analyze what's behind them. But with a Glamour Gaslighter, much of the behavior would, in another context, be highly desirable. What woman *doesn't* want romantic dinners, long massages, and beautiful presents? But if you want the behavior to change, you've got to have the faith in yourself to stick with your own feelings of discomfort and frustration rather than focusing on his glamorous or generous promises, even if you both end up going to bed mad.

Good-Guy Gaslighters

Like the Glamour Gaslighter, the Good-Guy Gaslighter also presents a confusing picture. It looks like he's being cooperative, pleasant, and helpful, but you still end up feeling confused and frustrated. See if any of these scenarios sound familiar.

The Good-Guy Gaslighter: Stage 2

- One minute, he's giving you the perfect advice about how to handle your mother; the next, he's looking blank when you want to continue the conversation. When you ask what caused the freeze-out, he either won't tell you or assures you there isn't a problem.

- You argue for hours over a specific concern—who's going to pick up the kids or where to go on your next vacation. Then suddenly he'll end the argument by giving in and doing exactly as you've asked. Perhaps he doesn't seem really satisfied, but you've gotten your own way, so how can you complain? Or perhaps he ends the discussion on a generous note: "Okay, we'll do the vacation your way. You always have such wonderful ideas, I'm sure it will be great. Remember that time we went to Maine and stayed at that cute little bed-and-breakfast you found?" But, despite this apparent generosity, you feel tricked. Although he's given in so gracefully, you know—consciously or not—that he's going to argue just as hard the next time something comes up. And when he gives in, you feel that it's not so much because he cares about your feelings as because he wants to prove what a good guy he is. You end up thinking you must be crazy, ungrateful, or incapable of being satisfied, because after all, he's such a great guy.

- He'll do his share—and more—of the household and relationship work. Yet you never quite feel as though he's fully participating. And when you ask for emotional reassurance or try to connect with him more deeply, he'll look at you blankly. Why, you wonder, are you so selfish and demanding?

Here's how a Stage 2 conversation might go with a Good-Guy Gaslighter. As you read it, ask yourself why the woman involved is so frustrated and confused.

HIM: This Sunday I was thinking we could go for a drive in the country.

YOU: Oh, that sounds so nice, but we're supposed to go to my family's for dinner.

HIM: Oh. (*long silence*)

YOU: What's wrong?

HIM: Nothing.

YOU: No, I can tell you're upset. What's wrong?

HIM: Really, it's nothing.

YOU: *Please* tell me what's wrong.

HIM: Well, it's just that we've been to your family's quite a bit this month, haven't we? And to be honest, you're always so cranky after you get back from visiting them. I'm not so sure it's good for you to spend so much time with them.

YOU: They're my family. And I don't think I'm *that* cranky after we visit them. Do *you* have a problem with them?

HIM: Oh, no! I love your family, you know that. I was only concerned about you. If you want to go there on Sunday, of course we'll go.

So you go to your family's, and your husband barely says a word to anyone. Now, let's see what happens on the drive home.

YOU: I guess you didn't have a very good time today, did you?

HIM: What are you talking about? I had a wonderful time! I love visiting your family—you know that.

YOU: But you didn't talk to anybody. And you looked miserable the whole day.

HIM: I honestly don't know what you're talking about. Don't you remember? I spent two hours talking with your dad about gardening. And when your mother told that joke about her trip to Bermuda, I almost died laughing.

YOU: That's not how I remember it.

HIM: Well, that's how it happened.

YOU: Okay. What did you think of my sister's new baby? Wasn't she the most gorgeous kid you've ever seen? And so alert! I can't believe she's only three months old.

HIM: I guess . . . (*long silence*)

YOU: What's wrong now?

HIM: Why do you think something's wrong?

YOU: You haven't said a word to me for fifteen minutes. And you look so angry. You must be upset about something.

HIM: Honey, absolutely nothing is wrong. But maybe now you see what I meant when I said that visiting your family makes you cranky.

As you can see, the Good-Guy Gaslighter finds a way to make it look like he's doing everything you want—without ever *really* giving you what you want. And he's invested in making sure that his version of events is the version you accept. Instead of either refusing to spend another Sunday with your family or being a genuine good sport and making it a nice day, he engages in "disrespectful compliance," going through the motions of agreeing while finding all sorts of little ways to show how unhappy and resentful he feels. This guy's Emotional Apocalypse is the pout, looking unhappy or angry without admitting that there's a problem. Other Good-Guy Gaslighters might invoke their own Apocalypses; they might explode in rage about a seemingly little thing, try to make you feel guilty about another issue, or "accidentally" make a hurtful remark and then apologize profusely.

Now what's your role in all of this? Well, if you're very invested in maintaining the relationship, winning his approval, and continuing to think well of your gaslighter, you won't admit the obvious. You won't say, "My husband is being dishonest about his feelings and pouting (or having a tantrum or guilt-tripping me or insulting me) when he doesn't get his way—and I don't like that!" Instead, you'll say to yourself, "He's such a good guy—so cooperative, always does what I ask—what's *wrong* with me that I don't appreciate him more?" You'll worry that *you're* crazy for thinking something is wrong. After all, he's told you it isn't, and you know how important it is to him to always be right. He may even be able to convince you that it's you, not him, who doesn't like spending time with your family. After all, look how cranky you are *now*!

Of course, the gaslighter in this situation is entitled to refuse to spend yet another day with your family. But he's *not* refusing, he's engaging in gaslighting, trying to make himself look like a good guy instead of being clear about what he wants. If you're involved with a guy like this, you can easily become confused.

I once heard a friend describe how she feels when she hasn't gotten enough sleep. "I think I'm fine," she told me. "Then I do something really stupid, like leave my keys in the mailbox, or try to pour extra milk back in the orange juice carton, or stare at the phone for five minutes without being able to remember who I started to call. I realize from my actions that I must not be functioning at top speed. But honestly, even then, I may not feel sleepy, confused, or inefficient. I *feel* just fine, but I'm acting like someone who's wandering around in a fog!"

I think this is a perfect description of what can happen to women involved with Good-Guy Gaslighters. We *think* everything is fine. We look at our guy and see a romantic, loving, devoted spouse who seems to do everything we ask. Yet we find ourselves crying, lonely, stressed out, confused, or numb. That isn't the response of a woman involved in a genuinely satisfying relationship—and yet, like my sleep-deprived friend, we may not be conscious of being deprived. We're just acting it out.

So what's the solution if you're with a Good-Guy Gaslighter? Let's see what happens when you stop worrying about his approval, refuse to idealize your guy, and hold on to your own reality, even in the face of his need always to be right.

HIM: This Sunday I was thinking we could go for a drive in the country.

YOU: Oh, that sounds so nice, but we're supposed to go to my family's for dinner.

HIM: Oh. (*long silence*)

YOU: What's wrong?

HIM: Nothing.

YOU: You know, honey, I'm tired of asking you what's wrong and having you refuse to tell me. And now that I think of it, the last time you went to my family's, you never said a word to anyone and seemed to have a miserable day. So I'll go see them by myself and we can go for a drive another time.

HIM: I don't know why you're saying any of this. I love your family. And nothing is wrong now.

YOU: I don't want to argue about this.

HIM: But I really want you to see how much I love you, and how much I love your family. I don't see why you're making such a big deal about this. If you want to go see your family, we'll go. When have I ever objected to doing that?

YOU: You don't object in words, but your actions speak for you. So the choice is yours: you can come with me and make a genuine effort to have a good time, or you can stay home. I don't want to argue about it anymore.

In real life, that conversation might take a little longer, but you can see the difference in approach. Now you're opting out of the argument. You're refusing to debate what you know to be true. You *know* how your husband has behaved, and you're relying on your own sense of truth, not on what he *says* is true. Your husband may well start to pout, but you're refusing to be scared of his Emotional Apocalypse and his veiled threat of withdrawing his love.

At the same time, you're resisting the Urge to Merge. You're not trying to convince your husband to agree with you or putting out any effort to win his approval. You're simply making your own decision and sticking with your own reality. And when you do that, nobody can gaslight you.

The Explanation Trap: Stage 2

My patient Nella was a dreamy, romantic woman in her early forties who felt she'd finally found the great love of her life. Nella was a museum curator who often traveled to Europe and Latin America on business. She had a satisfying professional life but had never settled into a lasting romantic relationship. Now she thought that Frederick, charming and devoted, was finally "the One."

But Nella soon realized that life with Frederick had its difficulties. He disliked all of her friends and relatives, and made a huge fuss whenever she spent any time with them, so she found herself progressively more isolated. He began to complain about her out-of-town trips, even though he was retired and she often invited him to accompany her. But Frederick refused, so Nella started turning down the top assignments she had once enjoyed so much. Nella had been planning to get training in her field, but Frederick's possessiveness about her time put an end to that, too. As if all those problems weren't bad enough, Frederick turned out to be an Intimidator Gaslighter, who was continually finding new ways of belittling Nella. When things got really bad, he simply stopped talking to her—his Emotional Apocalypse— and she always ended up begging him for attention so that she could feel she was loved again.

Although Nella had talked about these issues with me, it had taken her several months to identify the toll that her gaslighting relationship had taken on her life. Now she was at the point where she could list the problems: her diminished contact with friends and loved ones, her lowered sense of self-esteem, her loss of work opportunities, the continual postponement of her professional plans. But when I asked her how she felt about continuing the relationship, she smiled.

"Oh, Frederick is such an *interesting* man!" she said enthusiastically. "There's just so much going on with him: You never know what's going to happen next, and he's so complex. I've never been involved with someone who was such a mystery."

As we talked further, I began to see that instead of responding emotionally to the way Frederick treated her—the put-downs, the freeze-outs, the insistence that she turn down trips or avoid her friends—Nella was responding intellectually to "the problem of Frederick." *Why* did he behave in such a difficult, demanding way? What was behind his need to insult her or stop speaking to her? Was there a way to tell when the insults would stop and the freeze-outs begin, so that she could avoid them? And what about those special times when Frederick suddenly opened up to her, confessing his deepest fears and weaknesses? How could he be so trusting one minute, so suspicious the next? Maybe his mother had something to do with it. Or perhaps it was his older sister. Nella could spend hours happily analyzing her difficult boyfriend.

If Nella were to respond emotionally to her experience, she might quickly tire of being treated with such little regard. But she kept herself interested in the relationship by thinking about it. Nella had developed a Stage 2 version of the Explanation Trap. Instead of finding the abusive aspects of Frederick frustrating, painful, or off-putting, she found them interesting, because they offered her so many opportunities to come up with explanations. In fact, before going out with Frederick, Nella had been involved with a man who sounded to me like a much steadier, nicer guy. When I asked about him, Nella readily agreed that her previous boyfriend had treated her very well indeed. But, she told me, that man simply wasn't as interesting as Frederick.

Nella's frank description of her interest in Frederick's abusiveness made me aware of a contrast I'd noticed in many women, myself included. When we're involved with people who don't treat us so well, our relationships preoccupy us a great deal. There's always a lot to think about, talk about, analyze. With a nicer, more reliable person, the relationship doesn't offer as much food for thought. We enjoy it, sure, but it doesn't take up nearly so much of our time or focus. When our romantic partner (or friend, or boss) is taking care of himself—coming forward with attention and affection; managing his own feelings; expressing his dissatisfactions in polite, appropriate ways—there simply isn't as much for us to do.

So, like many women involved in Stage 2 gaslighting, Nella seemed to be more interested in the drama and analysis involved in a bad relationship than in the relatively mundane experience of a good one. Instead of seeing her relationship as a bulwark of support or a steady source of love, it was as though Nella were viewing it as a particularly challenging math problem, whose very difficulty was a major source of interest.

Why do some of us become so excited about analyzing our gaslighters? I've come to believe there are two reasons.

Dealing with an Unpredictable Person Makes Us Feel More Alive

I once had a patient describe her childhood experience with her father. "Every night when he came home, I never knew which man would walk in the door," she told me. "Maybe he'd have his arms full of toys and be ready to play with us for a few hours before dinner, or maybe he'd lash out with specific insults for each one of us, or maybe he'd just want to be left alone. So every afternoon, my brothers and I would say to each other, 'What kind of mood do you think Daddy will be in tonight?' Honestly, it was high drama every day."

On some level, my patient might have preferred a more reliable father, one whom she knew she could count on to present the same steady, loving face every night. But she learned to enjoy mobilizing her resources every day to encounter the new challenges that her father continually provided. Just as wilderness enthusiasts describe with pleasure the unexpected incidents that might greet them on a hike or a skiing trip, my patient saw her relationship with her father as a constant adventure that brought out her best and made her feel fully alive. And when she grew up, she looked for romantic partners who offered her similar opportunities for "adventure."

Trying to Understand Our Gaslighter
Makes Us Feel More in Control

If we've grown up with parents who failed to provide us with a steady, predictable kind of love, we learned at a very early age that life is unpredictable. One response to this unpredictability is the attempt to expand our own control. The more we can control, the more we can be sure of—and the less we can be hurt by an unreliable parent, friend, or lover who fails or disappoints us.

Unfortunately, the very nature of relationships involves a loss of control. The other party in the relationship is free to love us or not love us, to come through for us or fail us, to treat us well or badly. In the end, it's his decision, not ours, how he behaves toward us; all we can do is respond. Focusing on the Explanation Trap gives us the illusion of having more control than we do. It suggests that, if we only understood our gaslighter, we could take the necessary steps to change his behavior. So the worse he treats us, the more interested we become, because he seems to offer so many opportunities for intervention.

WHAT'S THE SOLUTION, then? How do we free ourselves from the Explanation Trap? Once again, we have to look to ourselves and our Flight Attendants. We have to look clearly at our behavior and ask ourselves whether we're happy with our actions: For example, are we happy with the fact that when he yells at us, we beg him for forgiveness instead of asking him to stop yelling. We have to focus on our emotional responses and allow ourselves to feel whatever we're feeling. We have to see that the frequent letdowns, frustrations, and crying jags that provoke our attempts to explain are inextricably bound up with the romance, adventure, and "aliveness" we cherish, just as a hangover is an inevitable aspect of a night of heavy drinking.

Some Flight Attendants Who Might Signal Danger

- Frequent feelings of being bewildered or confused
- Bad or restless dreams
- A troubling inability to remember details of what happened with your gaslighter
- Physical indicators: sinking stomach, tight chest, sore throat, intestinal difficulties
- A sense of dread or hyperalertness when he calls or comes home
- An extra effort to convince yourself or your friends of how good the relationship with your gaslighter really is
- The feeling you're tolerating treatment that compromises your integrity
- Trusted friends or relatives who frequently express concern
- Avoidance of your friends, or refusal to talk with them about your relationship
- A loss of joy in your life

Often, my patients will ask me how to preserve the highs of their gaslighting relationships while freeing themselves from the lows. Alas, that can't be done. While other—perhaps deeper—satisfactions can be found in a steadier, more reliable relationship, it's true that such a connection may not seem as romantic or adventurous as one with an abusive, complex person whose next move is always unexpected. Even if you and your gaslighter are able to turn over a new leaf, refashioning your relationship into something healthier and more satisfying, you won't preserve the unexpectedness that causes you to go through life with that thrilling sense of hyperalertness. By definition, your new, healthier relationship will be less challenging and more predictable, requiring you not to defend yourself but simply to open yourself to giving and receiving. And you will need to accept that your partner's behavior is still completely beyond your control; all you can do is decide your own response to whatever he chooses to give you.

So if your relationship is bringing you hours of frustration (along with occasional bursts of joy), or if, like Nella, you're making decisions that don't fit with your larger vision of what you want out of life, consider the possibility that you're caught in the Explanation Trap. Allow yourself to experience the totality of your relationship, and then turn to the exercise "Finding Your Inner Truth" (page 107) to figure out what you'd like to do next.

The Negotiation Trap

Another version of the Explanation Trap—especially common among women involved with Good Guy Gaslighters—is the Negotiation Trap. Like women caught in the Explanation Trap, those of us caught in the Negotiation Trap tend to focus not on the overall satisfaction that a relationship brings us but on our success—or lack of success—in negotiating with our partner.

For example, Laura was an emergency-room nurse in her early sixties involved with Ron, a cabinetmaker who displayed many of the characteristics of the Good-Guy Gaslighter. It wasn't uncommon for the two of them to spend hours negotiating the minutest aspect of their relationship. When they were dating, they'd figured out an elaborate system of who paid for what and under what circumstances. They negotiated their sexual pleasure, figuring out how each of them could get what he or she wanted in bed without either of them feeling exploited or frustrated. They worked out schedules that would accommodate their demanding work lives, their wish for time alone and with other friends, and their need for "couple time." The negotiations continued as they moved in together, got married, and had four children. It seemed that no detail of their lives together was too large or too small to be worked out.

But when Laura came to see me, she'd been unhappy for quite a while. The negotiations that had once made her feel energized and strong now left her feeling weak and exhausted. Now, every time she raised an issue that con-

cerned her, she felt she was in for hours of argument in the guise of negotiation. For example, suppose she expressed frustration that Ron was rarely
home because he had recently joined a Masters softball team for senior citi-
zens. Instead of responding to her loneliness and frustration, Ron would begin to negotiate with her—how much time he was "allowed" to spend away
from home, how his involvement with softball compared with her member-
ship in a weekly book club, what he might do to make up for this time once
the softball season was over. It *looked* as though he was being cooperative and
responsive, but in fact, the negotiations had become Ron's way of ignoring
Laura's concerns while trying to convince her that he was really paying attention to them. And because Laura was so committed to the idea of negotiation, she didn't feel able to express the anger or sadness she felt about Ron's
absences or about his ignoring her, she felt that she, too, had to keep the performance going, pretending to negotiate when what she really wanted was to
weep in frustration.

As we talked, it became clear that both Laura and Ron were using the negotiating process to avoid connecting on a deeper, more emotional level. Ron
wasn't being honest about what he really wanted (time to play softball) or
how he really felt (it meant more to him to play softball than to spend time
with Laura). But since he could always point to his Good-Guy behavior and
his willingness to negotiate, Laura had come to believe she had no grounds
for complaint. Instead, she felt lonely, bewildered, and numb.

Laura's frustrations grew when she and Ron visited a couples counselor.
Because so much of couples counseling focuses on helping the partners negotiate, their therapist had a hard time understanding where the problem lay.
To all three of them, it seemed as though Laura and Ron had excellent communications skills—leaving Laura even more bewildered about her persistent unhappiness.

As we worked together, Laura came to see that she had been involving herself in these negotiations as a way of avoiding her true feelings about Ron
and her relationship, a way of not having to face how frustrated, lonely, and
ignored she felt. Whenever she expressed dissatisfaction about the relation-

ship, Ron could always prove that there was no problem—or at least, none that he was responsible for. Wasn't he always willing to negotiate with her? Didn't he often agree to her requests? Then how could there be a problem? This left Laura feeling crazy. Because she also believed in the negotiation process, Ron could always prove to her that she had no reason to be unhappy.

And yet she was. Laura wasn't willing to face the truth: that her negotiations with Ron had become an elaborate performance. Ron tried to prove that he was right, and Laura tried to prove to herself that he was right, too, so she wouldn't have to face how dissatisfying her marriage had become.

Certainly, negotiations can be enormously productive. Be careful, though, not to let the negotiation process blind you to your own emotional reality. If you're not feeling satisfied by the end result, it doesn't matter how you got there, what he says about it, or whether your victory looks good "on paper." All that matters is your own deepest, most authentic sense of your inner truth.

Finding Your Inner Truth:
Clarifying Techniques for Stage 2 Gaslighting

1. **Write down a verbatim dialogue with your gaslighter and look at it.** Now that you're not actually talking to your gaslighter, how does he sound to you? Reasonable? Helpful? Or absolutely out of left field?

2. **Talk to a trusted friend or mentor.** Trust me, the people who know you best know all your faults! If you share them with your gaslighter's criticisms, they should be able to help you get some perspective, especially if those criticisms contain a grain of truth. Your gaslighter may be very skilled at turning a genuine issue into a completely distorted portrait. For example, you might indeed have a chronic—and annoying—problem with lateness. But that doesn't mean your difficulties with being on time are a deliberate attempt to

(continued)

humiliate your gaslighter. He may have the right to be annoyed with you. But that doesn't entitle him to make wild accusations ("You're only late to make me crazy." "You deliberately keep me waiting to torture me!" "Believe me, all of our friends are talking about it; they can't believe how badly you treat me."). A friend or mentor can help you regain your sense of proportion. ("Well, you *are* often late, and it *is* annoying. But I don't think you're doing it to get back at Joe; it's the way you are with everybody!")

3. **Pay rigorous attention to your feelings.** Often, when you're with a gaslighter, you can't cut through the fog of verbiage and emotional abuse. So you may not be able to think your way to clarity while you're talking. But you can always say, "I don't like the way I feel. Let's continue at another time," and cut the interaction short. Talk to your gaslighter on your own terms and your own timetable, and let your feelings tell you when you've had enough.

4. **Go away for a weekend—or just out for a cup of coffee.** Sometimes, you just need some time away from your gaslighter to realize how crazy the situation has become. If you can spend some time with a friend or someone who makes you feel good about yourself, so much the better. The contrast between how well things work in that relationship and how confused, hurt, and frustrated you feel with your gaslighter should help you see your gaslighting relationship more clearly.

5. **Insist on your own perceptions.** I recommend having a sentence that says—to both you and your gaslighter—that you own your own perceptions and express them with authority. Here are a few suggestions.
   - "I know you feel that way, but I don't agree with you."
   - "I see things differently."
   - "That is your perception, but mine is different."

Freeing Yourself from Stage 2

As we've seen, the difference between Stage 1 and Stage 2 is the difference between isolated incidents and consistent behavior. In Stage 1, occasional gaslighting moments occur; these are moments that you can often identify and remember. In Stage 2, gaslighting has become your whole reality, the defining character of your relationship. Just as a fish doesn't know it's in water, you no longer see yourself in an unusual situation. The constant mobilization for defense—against the insults, the put-downs, the confusing romantic gestures, the unsatisfying Good-Guy negotiations—that's just the way your life is. As long as there is any part of yourself that believes you need your gaslighter to feel better about yourself, to boost your confidence, or to bolster your sense of who you are in the world, you leave yourself open for gaslighting.

Now, though, you've begun to regain your awareness, and you sense that the way things are is not how they always were or how they must always be. You've started to look at your gaslighter with new eyes and to wonder how your relationship might be different. Whether you're dealing with a partner, relative, friend, colleague, or boss, you're ready to make some changes.

So how do you begin? Here are some suggestions for breaking free from Stage 2 gaslighting.

Take It Slow

How long has it taken you to realize that there's a problem in your relationship? How long has it taken you to act? Don't expect your gaslighter to go any more quickly than you have. In fact, he may need more even time than you did to come to terms with your new challenges and demands. Remember, for as long as he's been gaslighting you, you've been dancing the Gaslight Tango with him. Now you're changing the rules—and that's terrific. But it won't happen overnight.

I suggest finding one small, specific step to begin with. For example, Katie decided that when Brian began accusing her of flirting with other men, she would stop trying to defend herself and simply withdraw from the argument. She wouldn't ask Brian to stop yelling at her or tell him how upset she was or threaten to leave him if the accusations continued. She would just opt out, using silence and short, simple statements that don't invite a response, and see what happened next. You'll find examples of simple statements in the list on page 76 that you can keep repeating. Here's a pair of before and after snapshots of how this process worked.

Before Katie's Decision

BRIAN: Did you see that guy looking at you tonight? Who does he think he is?

KATIE: Brian, I'm sure he didn't mean anything by it. He was just being friendly.

BRIAN: Wow, you are so naïve! I would think after all this time you'd get it. He wasn't just "being friendly," Katie. He was making a move.

KATIE: He really wasn't. He was wearing a wedding ring.

BRIAN: Oh, like that would stop any guy. And what were you doing checking him out, anyway? Why did you even notice whether he had a ring or not? You must have been pretty interested yourself.

KATIE: Of course I wasn't interested. I'm with you.

BRIAN: Bad enough the guy flirts with you right in front of me, now you have to start checking out other guys. Can't you even wait till I'm not around before you start trying to replace me?

KATIE: Brian, I'm not trying to replace you. I want to be with you. I chose you. Please, please, believe me. *You* are the one I want. I would *never* cheat on you.

BRIAN: The least you could do is be honest with me.

KATIE: But I *am* being honest with you. Can't you see how much I care about you?

BRIAN: If you care so much, then admit you were checking out that guy.

Do me the courtesy of being honest and admit you were checking out
that guy.

KATIE: But I wasn't! How can you say such terrible things about me? I
love you so much. *Please* believe me! Please, Brian—

BRIAN: Don't lie to me, Katie. That's the one thing I can't stand.

*The fight continues for more than an hour, with Brian becoming angrier and more in-
tense about proving he's right, and Katie becoming more and more desperate about
trying to win Brian over.*

After Katie's Decision

BRIAN: Did you see that guy looking at you tonight? Who does he think
he is?

KATIE *takes a deep breath and says nothing.*

BRIAN: Wow, you are so naïve! I would think after all this time you'd get
it. He wasn't just "being friendly," Katie. He was making a move.

*Katie thinks, "But he was wearing a wedding ring"—and she almost says it. But she
doesn't. Instead, she says,* "We're going to have to agree to disagree."

BRIAN: And what were you doing checking him out, anyway? You must
have been pretty interested yourself.

Katie wants to say, "I wasn't checking him out!" But she says, "We're going to have
to agree to disagree. I really don't want to continue this conversation."

BRIAN: Oh, so now you won't even talk to me? Now you're freezing me
out? What are you doing, planning how you're going to leave me for
that guy?

*Katie wants desperately to tell Brian she isn't going to leave him. If she could only
reassure him, maybe he would calm down! But she remembers her plan not to
say anything. She reminds herself that when she responds to Brian in this mood, he
twists her words or refuses to believe her, so she fights back the tears and just doesn't
answer.*

BRIAN: Bad enough the guy flirts with you right in front of me, now you're
actually interested in him. You never really cared about me, did you?

And now you won't even give me the courtesy of a reply. When are you planning to leave, Katie? Have you been planning it all along?

Katie rode out the argument, and eventually Brian stalked out of the house. Katie felt terrible—she wanted Brian's approval so much, and she needed to feel that he still loved her and believed in her. She couldn't bear hearing him accuse her of lying and infidelity; she worried that if he thought these things about her, maybe she really *was* like that; and because she was so invested in seeing herself as a loving person, she hated even more the way he cast doubt on her love for him. The more he insulted her, the more she wanted to beg for his assurance that he didn't *really* think so badly of her. She didn't want to be a bad person in anyone's eyes, especially not Brian's, to whom she had given the power to judge who she really was. But she also knew that the more she begged, the angrier and more insulting he got. So she opted out.

This approach can feel counterintuitive to many of us who have been in gaslighting relationships. When someone we care about and may even have idealized starts telling us how awful we are, our natural impulse is to deny it and to beg for reassurance. So we have to learn to go against that impulse and train our behavior in another direction. Instead of begging for our gaslighter's approval—which may make him even more anxious or more angry—we have to find ways of opting out of the argument.

Katie wasn't yet ready to walk away from Brian when he was behaving this way. She was still invested in believing that his judgments about her were true, and she still hoped to "win" good judgments from him. But she was beginning to see that trying to get Brian to approve of her only led to terrible arguments that made them both unhappy, whereas keeping quiet and using short statements had at least cut the argument short. Later she would practice more assertive things to say in response to Brian, perhaps from the list on page 76 or page 77—one sentence that she could repeat without entering into an argument. At this point, all she could manage was not to argue—so that's all she did. She was surprised to find that even taking that small step made her feel a little bit stronger. Not engaging in the gaslighting process had helped her to see that maybe she didn't need Brian's approval to feel good about herself, that maybe her world wouldn't fall apart if he accused her of bad behavior and withheld his love. She didn't *like* Brian being mad at her, or thinking badly of her, but it hadn't killed her or left her in a puddle on the floor. Knowing she could survive his criticism and maybe even live without his love gave her courage.

Find a Good Time to Raise the Issue

Often, when we're anxious about raising a touchy issue, we pick the worst possible time to do so—when our partner is running out of the house on the way to work, for example, or when we're driving to visit the in-laws and are already tense. Then, when our partner justifiably points out that he's late or snaps at us because he's anxious, we tell ourselves he'll never change. Well, maybe not, but until we bring up the issue at a good time, we'll never really know. Try to find a good time to talk, free from situations or people that might trigger his anxieties. If you can wait and plan to raise your concerns, rather than simply blurting them out, you may be surprised at how much better the conversation goes. And even if it doesn't, you'll have the satisfaction of knowing you gave it your best effort.

Feisty Trish, the litigator whose husband, Aaron, was always accusing her of being irresponsible about money, really had to struggle over this one, but eventually she learned to approach Aaron at better times. Here is a pair of before and after snapshots of Trish, so you can see how it worked for her.

Before Trish Learned to Wait and Plan

AARON: Okay, I'm off to work. By the way, your credit-card bill arrived again. I hate to think of what's inside it. Why you can't learn to manage your money is beyond me.

TRISH: I manage my money! I'm never late with a bill. I pay every single one.

AARON: What about last December? And the October before that? I seem to remember quite a few late fees piling up. Where's my briefcase?

TRISH: That's not fair! You know I was in the middle of a big case. And I can afford to pay a few late fees.

AARON: *You* can afford it? I thought it was *our* money. But that's what I love about my fluffy-headed little wife, she's just got to make sure the poor, deprived credit-card companies don't go bankrupt. What *would* they do without her? Okay, gotta go.

Trish remembers her new plan of opting out of the argument and telling Aaron how she feels about his put-downs.

TRISH: Look, Aaron, when you tell me I don't know what I'm doing, I feel—

AARON: Trish, I'm late. I don't have time to hear about your feelings.

TRISH: But I wanted to tell you—

AARON: Not only do you have no sense of money, you don't have any sense of time, either. Let me explain it to you. If I'm there to meet with my client, I *earn* money. If I'm late, I *lose* money. See how simple it is?

Aaron dashes out the door, leaving Trish frustrated and upset.

After Trish Learned to Wait and Plan

AARON: Okay, I'm off to work. By the way, your credit-card bill arrived again. I hate to think of what's inside it. Why you can't learn to manage your money is beyond me.

Trish wants to say something, then remembers that she's decided to wait and plan rather than blurt things out. She takes a deep breath.

TRISH: Bye, Aaron. I'll see you tonight.

That night, Trish waits until after dinner; she knows they both get cranky until they've had a chance to eat, rest, and unwind. Aaron also likes to watch the evening stock-market report, so Trish decides to wait until that's over. She knows he'll want to watch the game after that, but she thinks that if she waits too long, it will be late, and Aaron will be frustrated that she's keeping him up when he needs his rest. So after the stock-market report is over, Trish comes into the TV room.

TRISH: Aaron, I'd like to talk to you about something. Is now a good time?

AARON: Well, I kind of wanted to watch the game . . .

TRISH: When would be a good time?

AARON: Is it important?

TRISH: It's important to me.

Aaron turns off the TV and indicates that Trish should go ahead.

TRISH: This morning, when you were leaving for work, you made that remark about how I can't manage my money.

AARON: Well, you can't.

TRISH: Whether I can or not, it really hurts my feelings when you talk about me like that. Can we make a deal? If you have a serious concern about me and money, we can find a time when you talk to me and tell me what's bothering you. Otherwise, can we agree not to talk about it? I seem to get upset pretty much every time we do, and I don't like being so upset with you.

AARON: Oh, come on. Why are you making such a big deal about this?

TRISH: Because it's a big deal to me. I feel really strongly about this.

AARON: Well, you know what? I feel really strongly about not wasting our money on the credit-card companies! Do you know what their profit margins were last year? It's outrageous! And it's all because of people like you, people who don't understand the way debt corrodes their financial status. It's such a spoiled-little-rich-girl way of behaving—and I feel strongly about *that.*

Boy, does Trish ever want to answer that *remark! But she remembers her plan to opt out of arguments rather than try to win them. So instead she finds a way to end the conversation.*

TRISH: Okay, I'm not going to talk about this any more right now. If you want to finish watching the game, you can.

Trish walks out of the room.

Trish could have stayed in the room and tried some other strategies for dealing with Aaron—strategies I'll share with you in Chapter 6. But for this first effort, Trish didn't trust herself not to get caught up in their old pattern, and she knew that if she and Aaron kept arguing, he would simply wear her out with his logic, put-downs, and dismissiveness. Like Katie, Trish was taking it slow. Although she hadn't gotten the results she wanted, she did feel she could raise the issue again. And she was pleased that they had had their first-ever conversation about money that hadn't ended in a fight. She also felt stronger and more empowered for having told Aaron straight out that his remarks hurt her feelings.

Notice, by the way, that Trish let Aaron tell her when would be a good time to talk. That way, he wouldn't feel ambushed. And maybe feeling in control of the time would help him feel less threatened during what was sure to be a challenging conversation. Remember, gaslighters are driven by their own need to be right. When they feel threatened and anxious, they need to be right even more intensely, and they often step up the gaslighting. So if you allow your gaslighter some control over a difficult situation, you may be giving him the breathing room he needs to calm down and hear your concerns.

Raise the Issue in a Nonblaming Way

Nothing is guaranteed to provoke a fight faster than telling someone "You *always* do such-and-such," or "You're attacking me," or "You're behaving badly." Instead of telling your gaslighter what he's doing wrong, try describing the problem and including your own participation.

Here's another set of before and after snapshots of Trish. Previously, she'd gone for the heavy artillery during their arguments. Then she found a nonblaming way to bring up her concerns.

How the "old" Trish raised the issue in a blaming way

TRISH: I can't *stand* the way you talk to me! You're always putting me down and accusing me of being stupid. You sound like such a jerk when you talk to me like that! And it really makes me crazy, so please don't do it!

AARON: I wouldn't *have* to say all those things if you would *finally* learn to manage your money! You seem to think you're allowed to do anything you want, and I have to just sit here and take it! Well, let me set you straight—that's not how marriage works. If you're acting like an idiot, I have the right to say something about it.

TRISH: See, you just called me an idiot again! I don't want you to do that anymore!

AARON: I'll stop calling you an idiot when you stop acting like an idiot. Don't *my* feelings count at *all* around here?

The argument then continues for an hour or more, until Aaron either wins or becomes too tired to continue.

How the "new" Trish raises the issue in a nonblaming way

TRISH: Aaron, there's this thing that happens between us that I'm really not happy with. You tell me I don't know how to manage my money, and I know I get very upset and defensive. And I know I do things with my money that you really don't like. But it's still hard for me to hear you put me down. I really care about what you think, and when you call me an idiot or say I can't understand something, it hurts my feelings. I know you don't mean to do that. But that's how I feel.

AARON: Oh, so now I'm not allowed to say anything to you? I'm supposed to just watch you wasting all our money and not say anything?

Trish wants to respond to his accusation. She wants to say, "I don't waste our money, and besides, some of the money I spend is mine!" She really wants Aaron's approval. She wants to feel smart, competent, and not spoiled, and she can't stand hearing him speak so badly of her, because she's afraid that what he thinks is true, and if she can win the argument with him, that will make it not true. But she puts all those feelings aside and focuses on her plan to opt out of the argument.

TRISH: Can we make a deal? If you have a serious concern about me and money, we can find a time to talk about it. I promise I'll listen. Otherwise, can we agree not to talk about it? I seem to get upset pretty much every time we do, and I don't like being so upset with you.

AARON: Well, too bad. I'm not going to watch every word I say around here. This is my home, too.

TRISH: I really feel strongly about this. I wish you'd think about it. Would you at least think about it, and we could talk again later?

AARON: I really don't see what there is to think about.

TRISH: Okay, well, now you know how I feel. I'm going to go make myself a cup of tea. (*She leaves the room.*)

As you can see, Trish is going to have to raise this issue more than once. But at least she hasn't provoked a fight. And she's left the door open for future conversations. She also knows that while Aaron hates to admit he's wrong on the spot, he might go away and think about what she's said, so she's giving him time to process her request in his own way. She's trying to set up a situation that doesn't trigger their gaslighting tendencies—his need to be right and her need for his approval. She's giving them both the space to act differently, so that he can think about her words, and she can tolerate his bad opinion of her without begging for reassurance.

Say What You Will and Won't Do

When you get further along in this process and feel a little braver, you may be willing to take this step. Let's go back to the conversation we just witnessed and see how Trish might have gone a little further.

AARON: Well, too bad. I'm not going to watch every word I say around here. This is my home, too.

TRISH: I really feel strongly about this. I wish you'd think about it. Would you at least think about it, and we could talk again later?

AARON: I really don't see what there is to think about.

TRISH: Okay, well, now you know how I feel. And from now on, whenever

I feel you're putting me down, I'm going to say, "There's that thing you do, that thing we talked about." If the conversation doesn't change course, I'm going to say it again. And then I'll give it a third try. And then I'll walk out of the room. From now on, I will not stay in the room when I feel I'm being put down.

AARON: Where did you learn to say that, in therapy?

TRISH: Yeah, maybe. I'm going to go make myself a cup of tea. We can talk about this another time. (*She leaves the room.*)

Once again, Trish is giving Aaron time to process what she's said without expecting an immediate response; it could take hours, or it could take days. That way, even if he still needs to be right, he may be able to make room for her new behavior while saving face.

Of course, if you say you're going to behave this way, it's important that you be committed and consistent. Don't make empty threats or back down when your gaslighter steps up the intimidation, manipulation, or romantic gestures. And since our tendency is to seek our partner's approval and beg him for reassurance, it feels completely counterintuitive to walk away rather than to argue, plead, or cry. But believe me, opting out of the argument is the only way. Engaging in the fight will only prolong the gaslighting. You may have to do this many times, but in the end, it will be worth it, even if you need to sacrifice a few happy bedtimes in the process.

Stand Your Ground

If your gaslighter responds to your concerns with an attack—"You're too sensitive!" "That's so unreasonable!" "Who handles a conversation that way?"—simply repeat your intention: "I don't want to be talked to that way anymore, and I won't stay in the room if it happens." If necessary, end the conversation yourself: "I've said what I have to say, and I don't want to argue about it. I know you've heard me, and now you know what to expect."

Let's see how this strategy worked for Katie and Brian. By this point, Katie is feeling a little stronger, so she's not merely staying silent during their arguments; she's taking a more assertive path. But she still has to fight her tendency to seek Brian's approval and beg for his reassurance that she's a good and loyal girlfriend who loves him wholeheartedly and sincerely. It's not easy, but she's committed to this new way.

BRIAN: Did you see that guy looking at you tonight? Who does he think he is?

Since Brian hasn't said anything about her yet, Katie doesn't respond. Since she's not going to argue with him, there's nothing for her to say.

BRIAN: Wow, Katie, you are so naïve! Didn't you see how that guy was making a move on you?

KATIE: (*taking a deep breath*): You know, Brian, there's this thing that happens between us that I'm not so comfortable with. I know you don't mean to make me feel bad, but when you call me names like "naïve," my feelings are hurt.

BRIAN: But you *are* naïve! What am I supposed to do, let you go through life letting any guy who wants to come on to you? How do you think that makes me feel?

KATIE: I really wish you wouldn't yell at me.

BRIAN: Oh, so now you're telling me how I am and am not allowed to talk to you! Don't I have any rights at all around here? And why are you so sensitive, anyway? What's the big deal?

KATIE: Brian, I really don't want to be called names, and I don't want to be yelled at. From now on, when you do either of those things, I'm going to say, "There's that thing you do." I'll say it three times. And if you still don't hear me, I'll walk out of the room.

Katie has to stop herself from adding, "okay?" at the end of that last sentence. She wants so much to reassure Brian that she loves him and to beg him not to be so mean. She still feels worried that if Brian thinks badly of her, maybe she really is a bad person, so she really wants Brian's approval. But she's committed to trying this new way, so she stops there.

BRIAN: You are so unreasonable! You're getting more like your mother every day! Where in the world did you ever get the idea that you could talk to me that way?

KATIE: There's that thing you do.

BRIAN: You can't talk to me like a child! I'm a grown man! How dare you talk to me that way?

KATIE: There's that thing you do.

BRIAN: You're being ridiculous. If you have something to say to me, say it! Don't keep repeating that stupid phrase.

KATIE: There's that thing you do.

BRIAN: What about *my* feelings? Don't you think it hurts *my* feelings to have you ignore me like this? No matter what I say to you, it doesn't seem to make any difference!

Katie has a really hard time with that one, because it's true. She is so empathic, she can feel Brian's frustration, and she knows how much he hates being ignored. He has often told her that his mother used to ignore him whenever he was most upset, and now here she is, doing the same thing. She feels terrible about doing something that she know must be so painful for the man she loves. But she reminds herself that if she changes course and tells Brian how much she loves him, he'll go right back to accusing her of flirting with that other guy. The gaslighting will continue, and she really wants it to stop. So she takes a deep breath and walks out of the room.

Katie doesn't yet know what impact her new behavior will have on Brian. And at first, frankly, she feels worse about what she's done than she ever did about staying in the argument. She feels guilty for hurting Brian, worried about what he'll do, sorry for his pain, and desperate to rush back to him and get him to tell her that he still loves her and will forgive her for being so hard on him.

A few hours later, though, Katie starts to feel something different. Now that the smoke has cleared, she begins to feel a little stronger and a little more sure of herself. She isn't looking forward to repeating the scene she's just played. But she knows that if Brian keeps insulting her and accusing her of flirting, she'll have to go through this new approach several more times at least. She's not happy about that, but she does feel more self-confident. The insults didn't go in so deeply this time. They didn't totally destroy her sense of herself as a good person. She could begin to see that Brian's unreasonable response didn't mean she was bad. It just meant Brian was unreasonable. She's also curious: *Will* this make a difference in her relationship?

How Your Gaslighter Sees It

It's easy to imagine that our gaslighter is acting out of the very worst motives—that he is expressing a negative opinion of us that mirrors our own worst fears about ourselves. But he may honestly not realize how hurtful his words have been. If your gaslighter grew up in a household where people spoke disrespectfully, he may think this is how people always talk to each other, or he may feel that any less exaggerated language simply won't be heard. So stand your ground, but don't insult him. Keep it simple and focused. If he complains about how you're always late to his family gatherings, don't start pointing out that he's never been very nice to *your* mother, either. Simply say what you want and what you intend to do, and then try to listen—openly and lovingly—to your partner's response. For more suggestions on how to continue opting out and really turning off the gas, go on to Chapter 6. I'll talk you through the whole process in detail.

It's a real challenge breaking free from Stage 2, because the relationship has now become defined according to the gaslighting pattern. Sometimes, too, efforts to opt out of Stage 2 can bring you not to a genuinely healthy relationship but rather to a new version of Stage 1, in which your partner periodically tries to gaslight you and you occasionally go along with it. So ending the gaslighting once it's gotten to this point is definitely challenging, but definitely worth it. Painful as Stage 2 gaslighting can be, it's much easier to deal with than the total, overwhelming gaslighting dynamic that characterizes Stage 3.

chapter 5

Stage 3: "It's All My Fault!"

It was a rainy day in April when Gail, a fashionable, dynamic woman in her forties who ran a successful catering service in Los Angeles, stood staring at the shelf in her local pharmacy. She found herself thinking about ipecac, a liquid given to children to induce vomiting when they swallow something poisonous. She knew her boyfriend, Stuart, wanted Chinese food for dinner; maybe he wouldn't notice the taste if she mixed it into his pork fried rice. She imagined the peace and quiet she could enjoy with him throwing up in the bathroom all night. She looked over at the pharmacist's counter. She couldn't believe what she was thinking.

Stuart yelled at her nightly and questioned her judgment about *everything*. She knew that tonight would be really bad; she wanted to go to an upcoming food convention, but she also knew Stuart would tell her that there was no point to her going because she had no idea how to run a business, and that she was just trying to get away from him. What about their time together? Didn't she have any consideration for him? She couldn't stand the way her head would ache and her heart would pound when he yelled. But she was always abandoning the people she loved; that's what Stuart said, and maybe he was right. And for so many reasons, she couldn't imagine breaking up with him. He said they were soul mates; her family loved him; the sex was great;

they owned an apartment together; and more than anything, she knew that if she could make him feel more secure, he would be kinder and gentler to her.

She took a deep breath and left the pharmacy. She could never do that to him. He was right about her anyway. She kept hearing his voice over and over in her head. It was ridiculous to go to the food convention when all he wanted was to be with her. Gail was in Stage 3.

JILL WAS AN intense young woman in her early twenties, with a café-au-lait complexion and dark, wavy hair. The first time she came to see me, she could barely finish a sentence. Agitated and tense, she'd urgently spit out a few words. Then, as though she'd suddenly run out of energy, she'd let her voice trail off and her gaze wander. Throughout the confused maze of incidents, details, and attempts to sum things up, I was able to pick up one recurring theme: *I don't recognize myself anymore.*

Jill had been a budding journalist who produced nightly news reports for a major TV station. But when a reorganization hit her company, she'd been transferred to a team that was responsible for producing longer features and in-depth series. Whereas her first supervisor had admired Jill and appreciated her talents, her new boss seemed threatened by her. As the story emerged, I saw that he had effectively gaslighted Jill. From a confident, ambitious, and talented young woman, she had become a virtual basket case: nervous, uncertain, and profoundly bitter.

"I thought I was such hot stuff, but it looks like I'm *nothing*," she said to me. "Why did everybody make such a big deal about me those first few years out of college? Why did they lead me down the garden path if I'm such a . . ." Her voice trailed off again.

Jill was mired deep in gaslighting's Stage 3, the phase in which you have assimilated your gaslighter's perspective and use it as your own. In Stage 1, as we've seen, you marshal evidence against your gaslighter, trying to show him that he's wrong. You may or may not fear his Emotional Apocalypse, but you definitely feel the Urge to Merge and look for ways the two of you might agree. In Stage 2, you argue with him and with yourself more desperately. Feeling a greater fear of his Emotional Apocalypse and a more urgent sense of the Urge to Merge, you try even harder to make your two points of view align. By Stage 3, you've adopted your gaslighter's point of view and are marshaling evidence on *his* behalf, not your own. That's because you still believe that you need your gaslighter to feel better about yourself, to boost your confidence, or to bolster your sense of who you are in the world. And in Stage 3, you're not only willing to consider your gaslighter's perspective, you're actively taking it on.

Thus, when I mildly questioned Jill's assessment of her own abilities, reminding her of the awards she'd won and the promotions she'd received during her first few years in her field, she angrily told me I didn't know what I was talking about and proceeded to lecture me—clearly, in her boss's terms—about her terrible failings.

Jill had become so invested in her boss's ability to see her clearly and judge her accurately that she was embracing his perspective—even at her own expense. She needed to believe her boss had this magical power because she still hoped that, one day, she'd get him to see how good she really was. Feeling terrible about how little he thought of her now and abdicating her own judgment about her abilities was worth it to her so that she could hold on to the hope that someday he'd think she was a good journalist. Then she could finally relax, secure in the knowledge that she *was* a good journalist.

Much of my work with my patients in gaslighting relationships centers on keeping them from moving into Stage 3, because this is a phase in which gaslightees are often also getting many other kinds of abuse. Besides being asked to agree to perceptions that don't ring true, they're frequently being yelled at, taken advantage of, and otherwise exploited. This is possible—even for women who were once strong and independent—because the Stage 3 gaslightee has simply given up. She's accepted, usually without realizing it, that she lives in a world in which the gaslighter gets to make all the rules and those rules can change at a moment's notice. She becomes nervous about making *any* move because she can never be certain what to expect.

Have You Entered Stage 3? Do you . . .

- frequently feel listless, apathetic, lackluster?
- find it virtually impossible to spend time with friends and loved ones?
- avoid meaningful conversations with people whose opinions you used to trust?
- continually defend your gaslighter to others and yourself?
- avoid all mention of the relationship so you don't have to try to make others understand?
- often find yourself crying for no reason?
- experience stress-related symptoms, such as migraine, upset stomach, constipation or diarrhea, hemorrhoids, hives, acne or rashes, backache, or other disorders?
- suffer several times a month or more from minor or major illnesses, such as colds, flu, colitis, digestive problems, heart palpitations, shortness of breath, asthma attacks, or other disorders?
- find yourself unable to remember clearly an interaction in which you and your gaslighter disagreed?
- obsess—to yourself or others—about how you might have contributed to his anger, insecurity, withdrawal, or other unpleasant behavior?
- feel plagued more often or more intensely by the vague sense that something is wrong?

Let's look yet again at that example of keeping your date waiting in the movie theater while you go to get a drink of water. Here's how you might handle such an incident in Stage 2, and how it might go in Stage 3.

From Stage 2 to Stage 3

In Stage 2

- You *really* want to win his approval—it's become the only way you can prove to yourself that you're really a good, capable, and lovable person—so you begin with his point of view. You may argue—aloud or in your head—but you think of *his* point of view first: "He says I left him alone too long. Well, I know how awful it feels to be left alone, especially on a date. I guess I can't blame him for being upset. Hey, wait a minute. It couldn't have been *that* long! Yes, but I guess when you're on a date, even five minutes apart would seem like a big deal, so I can see why he'd be annoyed."

- When he behaves in a hurtful or bewildering manner, you wonder, "What's wrong with me?"

- You consider his point of view normal and fight desperately to get a hearing for your own perspective, because you can't bear the idea that his criticisms of you may be true: "Please, honey, think about it for a minute. I know you hated being left alone, but I really wasn't gone *that* long. Was I?" You hope that by winning the argument, you'll prove the one thing that really matters to you: You *are* a good, capable, lovable person, because this man agrees that you are.

- You lose your ability to make judgments or to see the big picture, focusing instead on the details of his accusations: "I *know* I wasn't gone *that* long. But maybe I was, because it's true, I really don't keep track of time very well. I can't blame him for being upset about that, I guess.

Hey, wait a minute, the movie hadn't started yet, so it *couldn't* have been twenty minutes. Aha! I'll tell him that. But maybe I was insensitive in some other way?"

In Stage 3

- You still want to win his approval, but by now you feel hopeless about ever being able to do it, at least on a permanent basis. But you can't disengage because you feel completely submerged in his point of view, or else you feel apathetic, so it's a struggle to have a point of view at all. You no longer feel moved to defend yourself—what's the point? "He says I left him alone too long. I guess I did. I'm always doing inconsiderate things like that. I don't know why I can't be a better person. But I guess I can't." You may still hope that someday he'll validate you by thinking you are good, capable, and lovable.

- When he behaves in a hurtful or bewildering manner, you know it's your fault—or else you feel numb, disconnected, or simply hopeless. You wish you could please him, but you're pretty sure you can't.

- You consider his point of view normal, and you can barely remember a time when you thought any other way. Or you may be trying to silence or defeat your own perspective, in order to better align with his. "I *thought* I wasn't gone all that long—but see, that's just the kind of inconsiderate thing I'm always doing. What's *wrong* with me? Why can't I think before I make such stupid, hurtful mistakes?"

- You aren't challenging his perceptions in any way, neither in the big picture nor in the details: "He says I was gone for twenty minutes. It's so weird that I thought it was five. I guess I really don't have any sense of

time at all. To me, it didn't seem
like that much time had
passed—but I guess that's why
I'm always screwing up."

Stage 3: When Defeat Feels Normal

As with your entry into Stage 2, your transition into Stage 3 may pass imperceptibly. Indeed, one of the greatest dangers of Stage 3 is your increased loss of perspective. Feeling defeated, hopeless, and joyless may now come to seem so normal that you can't quite remember your life ever was any other way. Even if you have some distant notion that things have changed, you may want to resist memories of another, better time, which only make you feel worse about how things are now. Likewise, you may want to avoid the people and relationships that could "bring you back to life." It may seem too painful to open up, even temporarily, when staying in your gaslighting relationship demands that you remain shut down.

Stage 3 gaslighting is truly soul-destroying. Some of my patients describe a listlessness that spreads through almost every area of their lives—food no longer tastes good, they no longer enjoy time with their friends, a lovely walk in the countryside leaves them unaffected—until finally, all of life has lost its savor. Other patients talk about a growing inability to make even the smallest decisions: where they'd like to eat lunch, what movie they'd prefer, which clothes they want to wear that morning. Still others describe a lack of connectedness; they feel as though some other person were living their lives, going through the motions while they are hiding deep within themselves, trying not to be found.

To me, the worst aspect of Stage 3 is the hopelessness. Like all gaslightees, you have idealized your gaslighter and wish desperately for his approval. But by Stage 3, you've pretty much given up on believing that you'll ever get it. As a result, you think the worst of yourself.

Melanie, for example, the Stage 3 gaslightee whose husband, Jordan, berated her so angrily over not getting the right salmon for his dinner party, spent the worst part of her marriage feeling confused, overwhelmed, preoccupied, and numb. As we explored these feelings together, she came to see that, to a large extent, they were the result of emotional and physical exhaustion.

"Every time I even *think* about disagreeing with Jordan, I stop myself," she told me. "I know he'll just hit me with all those questions—battering me with his words and his insults and his reasons and his logic—and I just don't have the energy to keep fighting any more. I know he's going to win—he always does—so what's the point? It's easier to give in, and it's easier still to try to keep the fight from ever happening by trying to figure out what he wants and then just doing it."

I asked Melanie how she felt about being in a relationship where she saw herself as so unable to affect the other person.

"I don't know," she said listlessly. "What difference does it make *how* I feel? This is just the way it is."

A few weeks later, the question came up again. This time, Melanie fought back the tears. "I just hate it, all right?" she said to me. "I hate feeling that no matter what I do, no matter how nice I am, no matter how hard I try, it won't make any difference. Jordan is going to think the way he wants to think, and I just can't get through to him. I wish he would love me the way he used to; he used to be really nice, and I miss those days. And I thought if I just tried harder, we could get back there. But now I'm just exhausted. I *would* try again, I guess, if I thought it would do any good. But clearly, I'm not good enough for him. I don't know why he's stayed with me this long."

Melanie had completely bought into Jordan's opinion of her as incompetent and careless, and she was terrified of his Emotional Apocalypse—belittling. As you'll recall from Chapter 1, Jordan frequently told his wife how stupid and inconsiderate she was. From Melanie's point of view, she had two choices: either disagree with Jordan and start a battle she knew she could never win, or simply give in and agree with his bad opinion of her.

If Melanie had not so desperately wanted Jordan's approval of her as a capable wife worthy of his love, she might have seen a third choice. She might have been able to step back and be critical of him rather than of herself. Perhaps she could have said to herself, "I don't see why nothing I do is good enough for this man. Maybe he's just unreasonable and hard to please." She might have questioned whether she really wanted to be married to such a difficult, demanding partner. And she might have been able to opt out of the endless conversations in which she was continually criticized. (I'll give you a step-by-step plan for doing this in Chapter 6.)

But Melanie, like all gaslightees, had idealized her gaslighter. She had been deeply in love with Jordan when they married, and she'd seen their relationship as her haven, her place to feel safe and protected. In that way, Melanie was prone to the Urge to Merge. She wanted to be married to a strong man with whom she'd never *have* to disagree because they would always see things the same way.

The possibility that she might have been wrong about this—that her judgments about Jordan were simply not correct and her idea of marriage might not be so healthy— felt too threatening even to consider. "If he's not the man I thought he was, well, then the whole thing was just a lie," she told me once, roused to unusual anger. "I'll never believe that—never! It's not his fault. It's mine!" Because Melanie needed to believe that Jordan was a wonderful, loving husband whom she could always trust implicitly, and because she really *couldn't* please him, she had fallen into Stage 3 gaslighting. Indeed, she had come to therapy hoping I could "fix" her so that she'd be a better wife for Jordan. "If I just get better," she kept saying, "then maybe we could go back to the way things used to be."

The Three Types of Gaslighters in Stage 3

Just as each type of gaslighter has his own version of Stage 2, so is he likely to have his own version of Stage 3. You may experience different types of Stage 3 gaslighting depending on whether you're involved with an Intimidator, a Glamour Gaslighter, or a Good-Guy Gaslighter.

Intimidator Gaslighters

Just as Melanie sought to please Jordan, Jill longed for the approval of her new boss. When she'd started working for him, she'd hoped to impress him with her talent and skill. After all, hadn't she graduated at the top of her class from a prestigious journalism school? Hadn't she already won several awards for her work? And hadn't her previous boss praised her and written her a glowing recommendation? Jill had every reason to expect that her new boss would be thrilled with her hardworking, ambitious approach to the job.

Unfortunately for Jill, her new boss seemed threatened by her. When Jill told me he was a quiet, reserved man who rarely spoke, I wondered if he had trouble with her direct, intense, no-nonsense approach. Or perhaps racial and/or gender attitudes were involved. Whatever the reason, it was clear from day one that this new executive producer did not enjoy working with Jill and was not going to give her the kinds of top assignments she'd come to expect.

At first, Jill took her new boss's attitude as a challenge. She worked harder than ever to impress him, wanting desperately to win his approval, as she had been able to do with her last boss. Jill's version of the Urge to Merge was imagining a boss who would basically be in tune with her own values and judgments: If she really was doing a good job, he would recognize that and express his approval. She refused to accept that her boss might be too unreasonable to appreciate her good work, or that his idea of "good work" might be very different from her own.

So Jill prepared long memos explaining her ideas and sought one-on-one meetings with her boss to make a case for her projects. When he avoided answering her requests, she persisted, insisting on a clear yes or no. To Jill, these were the attributes of a successful journalist. To her boss, they simply seemed like the rude behavior of a pushy woman. The more Jill tried to impress him, the more he backed off.

But Jill's boss didn't simply turn down her requests; he found a hundred little ways to convey to her that she wasn't doing a good job. If Jill submitted a two-page memo explaining her latest idea, her boss sent it back with a brief e-mail saying, "Not enough information." If Jill's follow-up memo was three pages long, he'd write back, "Too long. Boil it down for me." If Jill insisted on a meeting with him, he'd refuse to see her, saying that he considered her too dependent on his opinion and expected her to figure out this job on her own—unless, of course, she wasn't up to it? But if Jill went out and took the initiative, he'd chastise her for being disrespectful and a "loose cannon," then criticize her at staff meetings for not being a team player. The more Jill tried to win her boss's good opinion, the less he seemed to think of her.

If Jill had not wanted this man's approval so desperately, she might have been able to see that, indeed, nothing she did was ever going to please him. She might have been able to say, "Clearly, I can't win with this guy, so I guess I have three choices: I can stick it out until something better comes along; I can quit right away; or I can file an EEOC complaint against him and try to get him punished for his outrageous behavior." None of those choices was especially appealing to Jill, and she would certainly have been justified in calling her circumstances "unfair." But at least she would have been facing things with open eyes and making the best choices available in a bad situation.

Instead, Jill chose to blame herself. Although she would have been the first to admit that she didn't like her new boss very much, she related to him as a man whose opinion meant the world to her—as indeed, it did. The worse he treated her, the harder she worked to impress him. Then, when all her efforts inevitably failed, she blamed herself. A *good* journalist would have pleased this man. A *good* journalist would have found some way to get around whatever personality or other issues were involved. A *good* journalist would have made this job work out. Jill hadn't done those things, so she must not be a good journalist.

I wanted Jill to see that her situation would look very different to her once she recognized how dependent she had become on her boss's opinion. If she could find a way to let his approval matter less—to judge herself rather than let him judge her—she could free herself from the gaslighting. But for a long time, Jill wasn't ready to give up her hope that *somehow* she could please this man. And when she finally admitted defeat, she still didn't blame him. She blamed herself.

"I can't stand not being able to get through to him," she'd tell me in session after session. "It makes me crazy knowing that, no matter what I say or do, he just won't listen. No matter how good I am, he won't see it. No matter how hard I work, he doesn't care. He just doesn't care what I do. And that makes me feel like . . ."

"Like what?" I said when she faltered.

"Like I'm worthless," Jill finally said in a very small voice. "Like I managed to fool every other person I ever worked with. But *this* guy has really got my number."

Because Jill depended on her boss for her sense of herself as a competent, intelligent person, she was vulnerable to his opinions. And, like Liz, the woman who had so much evidence that her outwardly charming boss was secretly sabotaging her, Jill was having trouble viewing her situation accurately. Instead of being realistic about what they could accomplish, given their unreasonable, gaslighting bosses, both women kept trying to "make it work" and then blamed themselves for "not being good enough." Although Liz had gone only as far as Stage 2 gaslighting—consistently preoccupied with her relationship with her boss—and Jill had descended to Stage 3—hopeless, joyless, and in despair—the pattern was essentially the same: a gaslighting boss who needed to be "right" and a gaslightee who needed his approval. To free themselves from gaslighting, Liz and Jill both needed to have a sense of their own worth and be *willing* to walk away from their jobs—even if they didn't actually go. Only then could they resist the gaslighting, because only then could they resist the Urge to Merge, accept that they and their bosses might have different thoughts and feelings, and give up their desperate attempts to win their bosses' approval at any price.

Glamour and Good-Guy Gaslighters

So far, we've looked at the Stage 3 women Melanie and Jill, who were both involved with Intimidator Gaslighters, men who insult and belittle. But what about the women involved with Glamour and Good-Guy Gaslighters? What does Stage 3 look like for them?

Remember Sondra, the social worker who seemed to have the perfect marriage with her understanding husband, Peter, the one who described her life as joyless and numb? By the time she came to me for coaching, she was in the midst of Stage 3 gaslighting. She couldn't even imagine what would make her happy at this point. "I just feel flat," she kept saying. "Flat and numb."

Sondra kept insisting that she had a terrific marriage and that she and her husband shared everything, so I asked her what they enjoyed doing together. Sondra said they were too busy to do much besides take care of the house and kids. Earlier in their marriage, Sondra had tried to make more "couple time." But somehow it never happened. "He really wanted to, and so did I," she told me. "But then, I don't know. We just didn't."

I suggested that Sondra ask Peter for a night out together and see what happened. At our next meeting, she told me, "Well, he said he'd be happy to. He thought it was a great idea. But when we got out our calendars, he showed me how there really wasn't time. So we're going to try for next week."

The following week, Sondra reported, Peter seemed to be enthusiastic about their "big date." He had brought the subject up himself, somehow gotten reservations at the most exclusive restaurant in town, and even offered to get the sitter.

Sondra was excited, and her view of Peter as a genuinely "good guy" was confirmed. But when their night out actually came, she was disappointed. Peter had put in an unusually long day at work, she reported, and he hadn't had much energy. They went to the restaurant that he'd gone to so much trouble to arrange for, but he was too tired to eat much and seemed preoccupied through dinner. And when they went to see the movie that Sondra had chosen, Peter fell asleep halfway through. Although everything had gone "according to plan," their night out had not been a success.

To me, Sondra's experience was a perfect example of Good-Guy Gaslighting. While it *looked* as if Peter was being a good guy, he wasn't really connecting with Sondra or giving her the intimacy and companionship she wanted. He'd put on a big show of going out with her. But his actual behavior left Sondra unsatisfied—and unable to complain. "He *gave* me everything I wanted," she kept saying. "I guess it's my fault that I'm still not happy."

"But, Sondra," I said. "He *didn't* give you what you wanted. You wanted a nice evening out with your husband, and he wasn't really present. He was just going through the motions. That's very different from what you wanted."

"Maybe," she said listlessly. "But I don't see how I can complain."

Of course, if Sondra and Peter's unsatisfying night out had been an isolated incident, it wouldn't have mattered very much. But Sondra often felt that Peter did what she wanted in a way that left her dissatisfied. In my opinion, he was more interested in living up to his Good-Guy image than in really connecting with Sondra. And she was completely submerged in his point of view, needing to see Peter as a good guy, just the way he needed to see himself.

My coaching client Olivia faced a similar problem with her Glamour Gaslighter, Martin. A somber, dark-skinned woman with dramatic high cheekbones and a tall, slender body, Olivia had once been a model and currently worked as a buyer in a local department store. Now in her early forties, she'd been married to Martin, a real-estate agent, for more than fifteen years. At first she'd loved his romantic nature and his extravagant, glamorous gestures. Now, though, she felt the glamour was wearing thin.

"Last night, for example," Olivia told me, "I came home from work really tired. Martin said, 'Oh, baby, don't worry. I'll give you the best massage of your life.' But what I really wanted was to soak in a hot tub by myself and then to have a quiet dinner and just talk. Or maybe curl up on the couch and watch TV—just something dumb and quiet. Instead, Martin had to make this whole big production with the massage oils and the scented candles and the mood music. And he kept talking at me, telling me how beautiful I was and how good he was going to make me feel. It was like he was describing me to someone else. It didn't feel like he was talking to *me*."

I asked Olivia whether she had told Martin how she felt, and she just shrugged. "He hasn't heard a word I've said for the past ten years," she said sadly. "I don't know why he'd start now."

Just as Sondra felt that Peter's "good deeds" weren't really responsive to her, Olivia often had the sense that Martin's gestures were more about his own romantic fantasies than about her preferences or needs. Like all Stage 3 gaslightees, Olivia had come to feel that nothing she did made difference anymore. "What I do, what I say—it just doesn't make a dent," she told me. "And if I do manage to get through, that's even worse; then he'll just pout for a week. I can't stand that—it makes me feel so guilty. All he's trying to do is be a good husband—why can't I enjoy it more?"

Despite their unhappiness, neither Sondra nor Olivia was ready to leave her Stage 3 gaslighting relationship. Like the other gaslightees we've seen, they both felt as though the problem must somehow be their fault. Sondra blamed herself for being too demanding. Another woman, she felt, would appreciate Peter's efforts instead of always feeling dissatisfied. She wanted me to help her learn to be happier with Peter rather than try to change him.

Olivia also felt the problem lay with her. She thought if she were more spontaneous, romantic, and energetic, she'd be able to keep up with Martin. Olivia's two sisters and her mother had all been in bad marriages—all three husbands had either walked out or cheated—so Olivia felt all the more guilty for not being able to appreciate devoted, romantic Martin.

Both women also feared the Emotional Apocalypse that is almost always a part of gaslighting. In Sondra's case, the Emotional Apocalypse was rage. While Peter tried to be a good guy most of the time, he would sometimes explode in anger, and Sondra was never quite sure when he'd reach the end of his fuse. After the tantrum was over, he'd act as though it hadn't happened. If Sondra brought it up, Peter would apologize briefly and then change the subject. Sondra felt that he never seemed to grasp how upsetting she found his flare-ups. "But he's *said* he's sorry," she told me when I pressed her on this issue. "How can I ask him to keep talking about it?" Once again, Peter had "done everything right." And once again, he hadn't really satisfied Sondra.

For Olivia, the Emotional Apocalypse was Martin's pouting and all the guilt she felt as a result. She already felt guilty for not appreciating him enough, so having him "drag himself around the house with that hangdog look," as she put it, was just too much, especially since he'd always get her a big present afterward—making her feel more guilty than ever.

Women involved with Glamour or Good-Guy Gaslighters may have a difficult time explaining—to others or to themselves—what the problem is. Cooperation and romantic gestures seem like good things. What could possibly be wrong with them?

What's wrong is the gaslighting.

A Glamour Gaslighter is putting on a big show for his own benefit while trying to convince his gaslighter that it's all for *her* benefit. He tells his partner she *should* enjoy his romantic gestures, but he's not really checking in with her to see if she does. He's just putting on a show and insisting that she enjoy it.

A Good-Guy Gaslighter is getting his own way while trying to convince his wife that *she's* getting *her* way. Or he's withholding a part of himself while trying to convince his wife that he's giving his all and encouraging her to think she's crazy for wanting more.

As a result, the gaslighted woman feels lonely, confused, and frustrated, but she can't say why. If she objects, her gaslighter will invoke his Emotional Apocalypse: he might yell, threaten to leave her, or barrage her with criticism. And if he follows the Emotional Apocalypse with an apology, as Peter does, or with a big present, as Martin does, she feels even worse. At no point have her feelings really been considered, but at every point she's being asked to believe that they have. That's lonely and frustrating, and if it goes on long enough, it leads to depression.

Take Care of Yourself: Mind-Body Work

One of the hardest aspects of Stage 3 gaslighting is the way it makes you feel disconnected from your emotions and the best self you used to be. An excellent way to reconnect is through some kind of mind-body

(continued)

activity: yoga, tai chi, martial arts, and other forms of moving meditation. All these practices are based on a system of quieting your mind and opening to your deepest self—not through discussion, analysis, and imaging but through vigorous movement that integrates body, mind, and spirit. Find a class at your local gym, yoga center, or martial arts center, or ask at your health-food store or alternative bookstore for recommended teachers.

You may prefer simply to meditate, which you can learn from a book or from a class. (See what your local yoga teachers or martial arts instructors recommend.) In meditation, you sit for fifteen to thirty minutes focusing on your breathing and allowing your thoughts simply to dissolve. People who meditate report feeling calmer, more connected, and more able to handle stress. Meditation is also an excellent way to give your deepest self the time and space to make itself heard.

Why Do We Stay?

What keeps otherwise strong women like Melanie, Jill, Sondra, and Olivia in their Stage 3 relationships? As we've seen, the major dynamic in a gaslighting relationship involves a gaslighter who needs to be right in order to maintain his power and his sense of self, and a gaslightee who idealizes the gaslighter and desperately seeks his approval. As long as any part of you believes you need your gaslighter to feel better about yourself, to boost your confidence, or to bolster your sense of who you are in the world, you leave yourself open for gaslighting.

Beyond that basic dynamic, though, I've identified four major reasons that people stay in gaslighting relationships, even when those relationships have become draining, joyless, and debilitating.

The Threat of Violence

In addition to the other reasons I've identified, women who reach Stage 3 sometimes fear—or may even have experienced—physical violence or the threat of physical violence from their gaslighter.

If you or your children have been physically assaulted, or if you believe you might be, leave your home and go somewhere safe—the home of a loved one, a shelter, even a restaurant—where you can make phone calls and decide on your next step. Your first concern needs to be protecting your physical safety and your children's. The emotional dynamics can be worked out only when you know you and your children are safe and will remain so.

Material Concerns

Quite honestly, many women don't want to give up the economic security or standard of living that their gaslighting partner (or perhaps boss) can provide. Although they know they're not happy, they believe—rightly or wrongly—that a lower standard of living would make them even less happy. Many women also feel that their children would suffer in the event of a divorce (or job change), for financial and/or emotional reasons. Some women see their Stage 3 gaslighters as good fathers even if they're difficult husbands, or they see that their children are devoted to their fathers, even if some aspects of that relationship are also cause for concern. Women working for Stage 3 gaslighters may have jobs that offer unique opportunities for creativity, professional advancement, or financial gain.

Of course, sometimes we perceive these potential benefits and obstacles incorrectly. We exaggerate the gains of staying in a gaslighting relationship, and we minimize the opportunities we'd find outside it. Jill, for example, was sure she'd never get another job as good as the one she had. That was part of the power her boss had over her—her sense that he controlled her entire professional life. As she began to emerge from her gaslighting, though, she came to realize that she was young and talented, and had a good work record. Even if this boss wouldn't write her a glowing recommendation, her former boss and her journalism-school professors certainly would. She still had plenty of time to make her mark in her chosen field—with or without her boss's help.

Likewise, when Melanie thought about leaving Jordan, the first fear she had concerned money. Melanie had been raised by a single mother, and all her childhood memories revolved around her mother's fear of not being able to pay the bills. It took Melanie quite a while to realize that her own position as a marketing analyst was far better paid than her mom's string of waitressing jobs. Although she might not be able to live in such a nice apartment or go on the luxurious vacations that Jordan provided, she did not need to worry about basic survival.

Sometimes, of course, our material concerns are absolutely justified. When I once asked Sondra whether she could ever consider leaving Peter, she blanched in horror. "How could I do that to my kids?" she asked me. "They adore him." As a divorced mother myself, I knew what she meant. It's hard to separate children from their father, and any mother who does so will want to take her children's needs into account. Divorce may be the right decision, but there will be real losses, too.

Likewise, had Jill's situation been different, she might have been right to fear for her professional future. If she'd been in her fifties, for example, she might have correctly assumed that it would be harder for her to find a new job, especially at an advanced level. Or she might have been working at a unique company that specialized in a particular type of journalism, so that leaving would mean switching to another type of journalism, working with lower budgets, or facing some other unwanted change. Choosing to leave her gaslighting boss might have meant facing a real professional setback.

For good or ill, we don't always know what the future holds. We don't really know how a divorce will affect our children, or how staying in a bad relationship will affect them. We don't really know how we'll feel about living on less money, or what kind of job we'll be able to get. All we can do is make our best educated guess, and then weigh the possible loss against the price for remaining in a gaslighting relationship, especially one that leaves us depressed and joyless. When you're in Stage 3, you often feel as though you're not entitled to much of anything, including joy. But joy is out there. You can find it, and you're as entitled to it and as deserving of it as anyone else.

Fear of Abandonment and Being Alone

Many of us can't bear the idea of being outside a relationship, so ending a romantic partnership may feel to us like the end of the world. We simply can't imagine life alone.

Many of us, too, have a general fear of abandonment that affects every one of our relationships, including those with friends, colleagues, and bosses. In all these cases, the idea of leaving or diminishing a relationship may trigger profound feelings of aloneness that seem far more painful and terrifying than even the worst gaslighting. So we idealize our gaslighter and try desperately to make it work rather than face how unpleasant and unsatisfying the relationship has become.

For some of us, our very sense of identity is organized around being in a relationship, or having a particular job. When I explored with Melanie, for example, how she might feel about not being married to Jordan, she said bleakly, "I'll just be nothing. I'm *nothing* without him."

Jill said something very similar. "If I can't succeed at this job," she told me, "then I'm just a *nothing.*"

Once again, we need to remember that we don't know what the future holds. Despite our terror, we may feel a huge relief when we free ourselves from a gaslighting relationship. We may discover that we don't feel alone at all but rather empowered and content. Or perhaps we continue to miss our gaslighter but are still happy to have left. And yes, sometimes leaving or limiting a gaslighting relationship does indeed trigger all the loneliness and anxiety that we feared, but despite our pain, we know we've made the right decision.

Often in our culture, there's a message that if you do the healthy thing, you'll find happiness, pure and simple. I think that the truth is more complicated and that even the healthiest decision may bring sorrow, grief, and fear. But if we face our fears and choose wisely, we may be grateful for the decision that preserved our integrity.

Fear of Humiliation

Let's face it, once you've reached Stage 3 gaslighting, you're in a relationship that isn't working very well. For many of us, it feels like a profound humiliation to admit that things have turned out so badly. Leaving the relationship seems like an admission of failure, whereas staying seems to offer us the chance to recoup our losses.

Certainly that's how Melanie felt about her marriage, and how Jill felt about her job. Both women found it humiliating to admit that they didn't have the power to fix their situations. Melanie thought that a healthy person could make things work with Jordan, while Jill believed that being on outstanding journalist could win over her unreasonable boss. Rather than look realistically at their gaslighters, they just wanted to put their heads down and keep trying. Even the most monumental effort seemed preferable to admitting their "failure."

Unfortunately, we can't get very far by avoiding the truth. Whether or not you decide to end your Stage 3 gaslighting relationship, you'll never find a way to become happier—either outside it or within it—by ignoring your situation. You have to admit that something isn't working and to look rationally and rigorously at whether improvement is possible.

Melanie needed to be ruthlessly honest with herself about the kind of man Jordan was. She needed to see how unfair and unreasonable his criticisms were, and how deeply they wounded her. She needed to look at how unhappy she had become, and how distraught, confused, and frustrated she felt. She needed to admit that *this* was her marriage—not some idealized haven she hoped to regain if she did enough therapy but this actual, depressing, Stage 3 gaslighting relationship. Maybe things could get better with Jordan and maybe they couldn't, but nothing could improve until Melanie faced the truth.

Likewise, Jill needed to see how unreasonable her boss's actions were.

She had to face the possibility that he might prefer to lose her—a good journalist—because of irrational prejudices or preferences of his own. She needed to accept that she might not be able to win him over and to ask herself what she wanted to do if that were the case. Working harder and hoping for the best weren't going to help. But looking at things truthfully would.

If you struggle with feelings of humiliation, you may need to show yourself a great deal of compassion and accept the idea that there's no shame in having made a mistake, or even several mistakes. You may even decide that the pain of humiliation is a small price to pay for freeing yourself from misery.

You should also remember that time heels many wounds. A situation that seemed totally humiliating as you were leaving it may become only a distant, wry memory when you've moved on to a better job or a more satisfying relationship.

The Power of Fantasy

Many of us remain in difficult relationships because of the fantasies we have about our gaslighters and about ourselves. We see a gaslighter as our soul mate, the man we can't live without, the great love of our life. Or we have a romantic notion of "friends forever" and precious memories of a long-standing friendship. Maybe we have fantasies of climbing the career ladder and feel that if we leave an employer gaslighter, we're selling out our own hopes for professional advancement and growth. And when it comes to families, our fantasies are especially powerful. Many of us have intense feelings about the parents or siblings who have known us from early days, seeing them as people we owe everything to, should be able to depend on, or can be especially close to. Even after we grow up and move out, we may feel lost because we've left them but not the fantasy that we should have an all-powerful person in our lives who can take care of us and love us unconditionally.

For all of us, fantasy plays a powerful role in gaslighting relationships, though we may not recognize it as such. When my patients, friends, and acquaintances make passionate statements about their gaslighters, they believe they're only stating facts. Here are some examples.

- "It started so well. I can't believe we can't get back there."
- "He's my soul mate. No one has ever made me feel the way he does."
- "I think about him all the time. I love him so much. I can't imagine life without him."
- "She's my best friend. She's always been my best friend. She's always been there."
- "She knows me so well. Nobody knows me the way she does."
- "She can see right through me. I need someone like that in my life."
- "I have so many wonderful memories of her. We've been through so much together."
- "This is the best job I ever had. I owe this man everything. I can't let him down."
- "I'll never get another job like this one."
- "No one will ever take a chance on me the way he did."
- "He's so talented, and he's really going places. I don't want to lose my chance to benefit."
- "She's my mother. She'd do anything for me. How can I let her down?"
- "I've always been able to depend on my father. Even if he does yell at me, he always comes through for me in the end."
- "My sister is like my best friend. Even if we fight all the time, I know I can count on her."
- "I've always looked up to my big brother. Even when he seems to belittle me, I know he's really on my side."

I believe that my patients and friends are sincere when they make these statements. But I also believe—whether they're aware of it or not—that they're not quite telling the whole truth.

What is really going on when we cling so hard to relationships that leave us exhausted, miserable, and confused? And why do we give up so much to remain in them?

Those of us who stay in gaslighting relationships have decided—usually unconsiciously—that we need to be able to tolerate *anything*, and that we have the power to fix anything. Melanie, for example, needed to believe that she was a kind, nurturing person whose all-encompassing love would create—single-handedly if necessary—a happy marriage. No matter how badly Jordan behaved, she should, she could, and she would be loving enough to make things work. Facing how unhappy she was with Jordan meant giving up this idealized version of herself and accepting that she couldn't overcome her husband's difficult ways solely through the power of her love.

Likewise, Jill needed to see herself as so strong and so talented that no boss could ever bring her down. She wanted to believe that she could do good work in even the most difficult situation and that, by the sheer force of her abilities, she could transform a bad job into a good one. Acknowledging that her boss didn't *care* how good she was felt like giving up her very self.

As you can see, these are fantasies of power. We've made up a vision of ourselves as able to transform any situation if only *we* do things right. Instead of giving up on our gaslighter and moving on, we try desperately to prove that we can change him. Failing that, we try to convince ourselves that his bad behavior doesn't really matter because *we* are so strong.

The roots of this effort reach back to childhood. Parents who are disappointing and unreliable put their children in an emotional corner. To face the truth about them—that they sometimes behaved like self-absorbed children—would be overwhelming. What two-year-old, four-year-old, or even twelve-year-old can bear to realize that her mommy can't protect her, that her daddy may not come through? How terrifying to be a child with unreliable, unloving parents! We know we're not old enough or strong enough to take care of ourselves, so if *they* won't do it, who will? And if even Mommy or Daddy won't love us, we must be so unworthy and unlovable that no one else will.

So instead of seeing things with such terrible clarity—instead of realizing that our parents *can't* take care of us or love us the way we'd like because of their own limits—we begin to blame ourselves ("It must be my fault"), just as we'll later do with our gaslighter. But we don't stop there. We make up fantasies to compensate for the reality of neglect and disappointment, fantasies that seem to give us more control. If we are strong enough and powerful enough, maybe it won't matter that our parents can't come through for us—

we can take care of them, instead! "No matter what Mommy does, I'll be okay," the little girl might say to herself. Or "No matter how much Daddy disappoints me, it doesn't matter." We try to see ourselves as strong, tolerant, understanding, forgiving—anything to make our parents' failings irrelevant.

Unfortunately, beneath these hopeful ideas about ourselves lies a pool of sorrow, anger, and fear—the feelings of a child who can't depend upon having a loving, powerful adult to take care of her. We all need recognition, admiration, and love from others, and when someone comes along who promises these things, we are drawn to him. But those who are prone to gaslighting are more than drawn; we are compelled by three fantasies:

1. Just as during our childhood our parents were our sole source of nurturing, now our gaslighter will be our sole source of nurturing. He and he alone will give us the reliable love that our parents didn't. He is our soul mate, our perfect mentor, our best friend. And the proof of his love is the approval we seek.

2. If he isn't the provider we need, we believe we can change him. By sheer force of our tolerance, love, and example, we will transform him into the parents we deserved and wanted.

3. No matter how badly he behaves, it doesn't matter, because *we* are strong enough (or forgiving enough, or nurturing enough) to transcend it. If we are not larger than life in our capacity to change him, then we are larger than life in our capacity to put up with him.

So instead of our gaslighter's bad behavior making us like him less, it actually makes us love him more, because it offers yet another chance to prove how strong we are. If only we'd been that strong as infants, as children! Alas, we were not—but we can make up for it now! *Now* we'll transform this into a good relationship by sheer force of will. And if that means putting up with someone who insults us, or ignores us, or seems more preoccupied with his own needs than with ours—if that means tolerating a difficult lover, boss, or friend—then so be it. At least *now* we're getting something good in return for all our misery—this wonderful soul mate, this fabulous mentor, this terrific best friend. We cling to that fantasy of the relationship because it seems like the chance to avoid our deepest fear: that no one will ever love us the way we want to be loved and, just like when we were children, we'll be disappointed and alone. And all the while, his bad behavior makes us like ourselves less as we continually fail at winning his approval and proving how good, capable, and lovable we are.

Well, if that's how things are working for you, there's bad news and then there's good news. The bad news is that we may indeed have to give up our fantasies of what this gaslighting relationship might mean. When a patient says, her voice breaking in sorrow, "I'll never find another man like that," I have to say, as calmly as I can, "No, you might not. But would you really want to? You tell me all the time how miserable you are. Is it really worth it for you to stay in this situation?"

Or a patient might say, in anger or in panic, "What will I do without this job? What if I never find another position as good as this one? What if I can't work in my profession again, or not at this level? What if I never find a mentor who understands me like this man does?" And I have to answer, "You might not find a situation as good as this. But staying surely prevents you from even imagining a better one."

And if a patient says, "I've known this friend since I was fourteen years old. No one I meet now will ever know me as a teenager; she's the only one I still know who did," I have to agree. "You are losing something important if you lose this friendship," I have to say. "But think how often you tell me you're unhappy about the way she treats you. Bearing that in mind, do you still think the friendship is worth so much unhappiness?"

So the bad news is that we may really be giving up something special if we choose to leave our gaslighting relationships. We may *not* find another man we love so passionately, find so exciting, or consider a twin soul. We may *not* find another mentor or career opportunity to match the one we're letting go. We may never find a friend we care for as deeply, or one who knows us as well as that gaslighting best friend who's driving us crazy.

The good news is that if we have the courage to leave these gaslighting relationships and look honestly at what they've cost us, we can begin to see an end to the terrible fear that's been haunting us our entire lives—the fear of being unloved and alone. We can see that now we *are* old enough to "become our own parents," to take care of ourselves in a way we couldn't when we were little. We can see how full of love the world is—how many loving friends and supportive colleagues and potential life partners might enter our lives to replace that single "soul mate" on whom we've depended so heavily.

If we can see that our true selves don't really depend on another person's maintenance, that we are no longer the helpless infants or young children who needed so desperately to turn our parents into heroes, then we can finally begin to enjoy the people in our lives for who they are, rather than needing them to be the good parents we never had. We can become our own parents, caring for ourselves, so that our romantic partnerships and work relationships and friendships are based on love and desire, not on need and desperation. And we can be sure that, if we're being treated badly, we'll have the courage to say no and leave if we have to, which multiplies exponentially the chances of being treated well.

In my experience, people who leave gaslighting relationships may not go on to duplicate that sense of magic, that sense of a relationship that rescues them from everything they most feared. Freed from the need to heal past griefs, relationships become both more ordinary and more satisfying. Perhaps the adrenaline will be gone. But is that so bad? What if seeing your new guy's name on your caller ID made you smile deep in your heart instead of making your heart turn somersaults? What if being together brought you a sense of ease and peace instead of making you so nervous you couldn't eat? What if your love no longer felt like a thrilling, dangerous adventure or a challenging, bewildering math problem but instead brought simply a comforting, secure, and enjoyable companionship?

If you give up the fantasies that have driven your gaslighting, you can still have compelling conversations, satisfying sex, deep friendships, significant work relationships, but they may not have the intensity of the connections you formed when you needed the relationship so deeply. Your new connections may not feel as though they're saving your life or turning your world upside down, but they also won't leave you on pins and needles. You won't get that knot in your stomach whenever the phone rings (or doesn't ring!) or lose sleep wondering how you could have behaved differently to make him happy. You can go on as an adult, knowing that sometimes you may be lonely, and often you may feel loved—and either way, you won't ever again subject yourself to another person's bad treatment.

Take Care of Yourself: Getting Therapy and Other Kinds of Help

If you're feeling ready to consider a change—or at least to learn more about your options—you may decide that you'd like some help. As a therapist myself, I recommend therapy as a mode of supporting the growth you seek. Therapy can be frustrating and painful at times, but it can also be wonderfully nurturing and supportive. There is nothing like the relief of knowing that someone else believes in you, understands your concerns, and is committed to helping you reach your goals.

If therapy itself isn't for you, consider enlisting another type of helper or supporter. Life coaches, while usually not trained as therapists, can be good at helping you define your goals and take specific steps to reach them. Religious leaders and pastoral counselors can offer support and spiritual insight (and some of them are also trained as therapists). You might join a support group at a local community center or at your religious institution. If you or someone close to you struggles with substance abuse or some other form of addiction, a 12-step program might be right for you.

Of course, no matter what other steps you are taking, I would always urge you to reach out to your friends and loved ones, at least to all those people whom you trust to have your best interests at heart and a

(continued)

clear view of your situation. (It can be hard, sometimes, finding people who meet both those qualifications!) But sometimes even the best of friends are not enough. Sometimes you need someone who stands a little bit outside your life to help you figure out the next stage of your journey. A therapist or another type of helper can be that "outsider" who helps you find the road back in.

Creating Your New World

I'd like to leave you with a very special visualization exercise that my wonderful colleague and mentor the psychoanalyst Frank Lachmann once shared with me. Whenever I've felt myself giving in to others more than I'd like, or losing my sense of clarity about who I am and what I want, I return to this exercise. Although it could have many applications in your life, as it has in mine, it may be especially useful in helping you to cope with the exhaustion and confusion that so often accompany Stage 3 gaslighting.

Whom Do You Allow into Your World?

1. Imagine that you live in a beautiful house, with a beautiful fence around it. Take a moment to picture this house—its setting, its rooms, its furnishings. Take a moment to visualize the fence as well. What is it made of? How high is it? I want you to imagine this fence as very powerful, so powerful that no one can breach it.

2. Now, find the opening in that fence, the doorway or gate through which welcome guests may enter. Realize that you are the sole gatekeeper here; you have complete power over who enters and who does not. You may invite in anyone you choose, and you may keep anyone out, too, without even giving a reason. Take a moment to feel what that power would be like. You might want to allow the faces of those you'd

let in float into your mind, as well as picture the people you'd want to keep out. Experience your power as gatekeeper of your house.

3. Now imagine you've decided that only people who speak to you with kindness and consider your feelings with regard can come in. And if anyone enters and then abuses you or challenges your reality in any way, he must leave and can't come back until he's prepared to treat you nicely. (You may also get tired of the people who alternate between dismissing you and treating you with regard, so perhaps you will decide not to let them in no matter how nice they're being!)

4. Continue to visualize your house, your walls, and your gate for at least fifteen minutes. Allow yourself to see who wants to come in and whom you want to let in. Picture what happens as you decide yes or no. See the responses of the people you've rejected or accepted, and experience your response to their responses.

5. Afterward, if you like, write for a few minutes about what you learned from this experience, or talk about it with a friend. Remember, you can use your walled house as a sanctuary that will be there for you any time you want it.

So now you understand what entraps you in the Gaslight Tango, and you've seen how difficult the three stages of gaslighting can be. It's time to turn off the gas! And in the next chapter, I'll show you how.

chapter 6

Turning Off the Gas

A s Katie and I worked together, she began to explore ways to Turn Off the Gas. At first she was optimistic about making her relationship with Brian better. But she discovered that her efforts to convince him she was a good and loyal girlfriend and not a flirt often led Brian to step up the gaslighting and escalate his Emotional Apocalypse, yelling and insulting her. She found this response frightening and upsetting, and was often tempted to give up.

Katie needed to understand that you can't Turn Off the Gas until you've fully mobilized yourself to take action, so you'll be prepared for any resistance you may encounter, both from your gaslighter and from yourself. You can change a gaslighting relationship only when you are willing to leave it, even if you never actually have to leave. But you need to become comfortable with the idea that you and your gaslighter are each allowed to have your own thoughts, so that you neither have to give in to his negative view of you nor have to convince him to validate you as good. And you need to be willing to leave if your gaslighter continually punishes you for having your own thoughts. Until he knows you're willing to walk away, he may not be motivated to change his behavior.

So in this chapter, I'm going to share with you a six-point plan for mobilizing yourself, getting yourself to the place where you're ready to take action. Then I'll show you five ways to Turn Off the Gas.

> ### Mobilizing Yourself to Turn Off the Gas:
> ### A Six-Point Plan
>
> 1. Identify the Problem.
> 2. Have Compassion for Yourself.
> 3. Give Yourself Permission to Make a Sacrifice.
> 4. Get in Touch with Your Feelings.
> 5. Empower Yourself.
> 6. Take Just One Step to Improve Your Life. Then Take Another.

Making the Decision to Turn Off the Gas

Let's look a bit more closely at what I said earlier: You will only ever be able to change your gaslighting relationship if you are willing to leave. That's so important, I'm going to say it again: *You have to be willing to leave.*

Now there may be many situations in which you find you don't *have* to leave. Sometimes gaslighting creeps into a relationship gradually and can be rooted out again. Sometimes a person resorts to gaslighting only when he's feeling especially insecure, and you can solve the problem by simply refusing to engage and by avoiding key Gaslight Triggers—phrases, actions, or situations that can incite you or your gaslighter to engage in the Gaslight Tango. If your guy is willing to admit that there's a problem, a good couples counselor might be able to help, or your own new awareness may be enough to shift the dynamic. With some gaslighters, you may simply be able to reduce your involvement without cutting off all contact. In Chapter 7, I'll help you figure out whether leaving is right for you. But if you're not *willing* to leave, the process won't work.

Why not? Because, like Katie, you'll almost certainly come to a point—even if things have been going well—when your gaslighter slips back into his old ways. That's just human nature; people don't change all at once. Your gaslighter may even step up the gaslighting, perhaps invoking a more severe version of his Emotional Apocalypse, from yelling to screaming, from occasional criticism to constant criticism, from periodic freeze-outs to days of silence. At some point in the process, he may do everything in his power to get you to go back to your old, gaslighted self.

It may not be only him who has trouble changing. You may have your own doubts about this new path. You may be overcome by the Urge to Merge or overwhelmed with longing for your gaslighter's approval. You might be tempted to forget all the bad times and remember only the good ones. That's human nature, too. Most of us find it very difficult to change, and we rarely change quickly or all at once.

So what's going to help you resist those powerful forces that try to keep everything just as it was? What will enable you to act differently, even though both you and your gaslighter feel so intensely that everything "should" remain the same?

The only thing that will help your relationship change is your deep commitment to having the life you want—a life that is gaslight-free. To maintain that commitment, you need to be willing to do *anything*—even leave the love of your life, or your best friend, or your perfect job. You have to be willing to let your gaslighter have his own thoughts while you have yours, neither giving in to his view nor committed to winning him over to yours. Both you and your gaslighter need to know that you will not stay in a relationship where you're not being treated with respect and where you're punished for having your own point of view.

Again, you may not actually have to go. But if you're not yet *willing* to go, you may not be able to stick out the challenging path ahead.

Turning Off the Gas: Are You Willing to Let the Relationship End?

IF YOU'RE HAVING TROUBLE DECIDING

- *Visualize yourself in the relationship next week.* See yourself in as much detail as possible. What are you wearing? What's the expression on your face? What's the expression on your gaslighter's face? What's he saying? How do you feel when you hear him speak?
- *Now visualize yourself in the relationship next year.* Again, see yourself in as much detail as possible. What is your life like? Where are you working? What makes you happy? See yourself with your gaslighter. What are you each saying? How do you each look? How do you feel as you imagine the two of you?
- *Go on to visualize yourself in the relationship three years from now.* Once again, see yourself in as much detail as possible. What is your relationship like? What is your life like now? Is it the life you want?
- *Now, ask yourself how likely it is that the relationship you are in will bring you the future you want.* Ask yourself what your future will be like if you continue on as you have. Ask yourself what you are willing to sacrifice to stay in your relationship. Ask yourself what you are willing to sacrifice to get the life you want.

There are a few other things I'd like you to keep in mind. First, as you read through the six suggestions for mobilizing yourself, remember, this is a journey that may involve many roads. Feel free to try these ideas in any order that feels right to you. I think it may be useful to follow the progression I've outlined here, but if skipping ahead to a later step gets you moving, then that's the path that is right for you. You may even find yourself doing more than one step at the same time.

You should also know that you may not feel good about this process right away. Like Katie, you may find yourself panicked, lonely, or sad. As Katie began to resist Brian's gaslighting, she would wake up in the middle of the night, heart racing, stomach clenched, thinking only of how lonely she'd be if she had to break up with him. While she was at work, she'd suddenly feel like bursting into tears as she thought about how lonely she'd been before she met Brian, and how happy she'd been in those first wonderful weeks of their relationship. She'd think of the way his face had lit up when he'd seen her, or that time he gave her the foot rub, and she'd wonder how she could ever go back to life without him. Or maybe she'd remember one of the times he accused her of being too flirtatious, and her jaw would clench in an anger more powerful than she ever remembered feeling before.

Then Katie would think about how much she hated the way Brian was always accusing her of things. She would remember how much she didn't like fighting with him, and how awful she felt when he yelled at her. She would recall how good it had felt to stand up to him, to make it clear to both him and herself that she wanted to be treated with respect and that she didn't want to be punished for having her own point of view. She still felt anxious, sad, and lonely, but she felt determined, too.

As you start to see how things could be different, you too may get in touch with levels of anger and despair that you didn't even know you were feeling. You may feel moody and unpredictable—excited one minute and exhausted or depressed the next. All of this is also normal when people are making changes, so try not to take any of these feelings too seriously. Just experience them and let them pass. And if you have moments of exhilaration, euphoria, and being on top of the world, enjoy those feelings while you can, knowing that they, too, will probably pass! It's going to take a while before all your emotions even out, so be patient and persistent.

I also want you to remember that changing your own behavior is an extraordinary achievement and one that will repay you handsomely for the rest of your life. Whether you're able to save this relationship or not, the changes you make in yourself will stand you in good stead for a healthy, happy, and satisfying relationship in the future, either with your current gaslighter or with someone else. You may also be amazed at how all sorts of things in your life begin changing—how your relationships to work, friends, partner, family, and the world at large are all improved by your efforts to turn off the gas in any other part of your life. So even while you're mourning the loss of what you may be giving up, remember to celebrate or at least appreciate the things you're gaining.

Finally, I'd like you to be aware that the process of turning off the gas—and of mobilizing yourself, to do so—may take a long time. You may be able to accomplish wonders in a few days, or you may see no results at all for weeks. You may see some progress and then feel that you and your relationship are in trouble again. You will almost certainly have bad days as well as good days—times when you feel sure you're slipping backward as well as times when you know you've almost arrived. Either way, try to keep breathing, be compassionate toward yourself, and stay close to the people you love and trust. As long as you're committed, you'll get there in the end.

Things You Can Do to Bolster Your Resolve

- Commit to talking with trusted friends or loved ones once a day, or a therapist at least once a week, to keep your perspective.
- Write down your last three conversations with your gaslighter and edit them, reminding yourself how you'd like to handle situations such as these in the future.
- Remember the last time you felt joyful. Write a description, or create or find a picture that evokes that time. Post it where you can see it every day, to remind yourself of what you want your new life to be like.

> **Six Ways to Mobilize Yourself to Turn Off the Gas**
>
> 1 Identify the problem.
> 2. Have compassion for yourself.
> 3. Give yourself permission to make a sacrifice.
> 4. Get in touch with your feelings.
> 5. Empower yourself.
> 6. Take just one step to improve your life. Then take another.

Mobilizing Yourself to Turn Off the Gas: A Six-Point Plan

Here are six ways to mobilize yourself to turn off the gas. You can do them in the order I offer here, or in some other order that makes more sense to you. The important thing is just to get started.

1. Identify the Problem.

As we've seen, it can be difficult to explain—even to ourselves—what the problem is, especially when we're involved with Good-Guy or Glamour Gaslighters. My coaching client Olivia, the department-store buyer with the Glamour Gaslighter husband, told me about a frustrating conversation with a puzzled friend. "He gives you presents you don't really like?" the friend had said in disbelief. "He wants to give you massages when you'd rather take a bath? And *that's* what you're upset about? Girl, what is *wrong* with you?"

Olivia sputtered and stammered as she tried to articulate the problem. Martin's gifts—a frilly blouse, a fluffy nightgown, a sexy piece of lingerie—seemed to Olivia to be intended for his "fantasy woman," not for Olivia herself, who wore tailored suits and simple underthings, and liked to sleep in the nude. And her husband's famous massages always felt like such big productions that Olivia never really found them relaxing.

As we've seen, Olivia felt guilty about not appreciating her husband's romantic gestures. A great deal of our early work together was spent in figuring out why her husband's presents left her feeling worn out and frustrated rather than loved and cherished. "I mean, some people just aren't all that good at giving presents," Olivia would say.

"Have you told him how you feel about his gifts and his romantic gestures?" I'd ask.

"Well, yes. Sort of. I told him I didn't really feel like a massage. I just wanted to snuggle with him on the couch and watch TV. But he kind of glazed over, and then he looked so hurt . . . I felt like I'd really let him down."

"So you let him down by not appreciating what he wanted to do for you."

"Well, yes."

"Olivia," I asked her. "Was the massage to make *him* feel good or to make *you* feel good?"

She looked at me in disbelief. Clearly, she had never thought of thing in quite that way before. But eventually, Olivia was able to identify her problem: *My husband does many nice things for me, but they don't seem to relate to the person I actually am. I often feel that his good deeds and presents are more about making him feel good than about making me feel good. And what's worse, I end up feeling like there's something wrong me with because I don't like his presents.*

Identifying her problem gave Olivia a sense of relief she'd never expected. Finally, she understood why she'd felt so disconnected and dissatisfied. She'd found a way to describe her situation that went beyond simply calling her husband "bad" or "good" and focused on her sense of what wasn't working for her.

When you identify your problem, I suggest identifying *what he does* and *what you do* as well. For Olivia, that part of the process looked like this:

What he does to gaslight me: Gives me gifts that don't fit who I am and then expects me to be grateful.

What I do as a gaslightee: Feel like there's something wrong with me for not liking the gifts, feel lonely and misunderstood.

More Examples of How You Might Identify Your Problem

- My husband is often telling me things that are wrong with me, and I end up feeling bad about myself. I used to argue with him, but now I don't think it's worth it. I don't like hearing all those bad things, and I don't like being so depressed all the time.

What he does to gaslight me: Insult me

What I do as a gaslightee: Argue with him (before). Accept it and feel bad (now).

- I keep getting involved in long, repetitive arguments with this friend, and nothing ever really gets resolved. I always end up wondering why I can't be a better friend. I'm tired of feeling so bad about myself. None of my other friends make me feel that way!

What she does to gaslight me: Accuse me of being a bad friend

What I do as a gaslightee: Argue with her, beg her to change her mind so it doesn't turn out to be true that I'm a bad friend

- My boss seems to like me, but I know there's something fishy going on at work. She's not inviting me to the top-level meetings I used to go to, and she's cut back my contact with the firm's most important clients. She insists there's no problem, so I know she's lying to me. I don't like not knowing what's going on.

What she does to gaslight me: Cuts me out of the loop and lies to me about it

What I do as a gaslightee: Act like I believe her (try to believe her)

- My mother is so good at making me feel guilty. I just *wish* I could get her to say I'd done something right. I hate wishing for that, though.

(continued)

It makes me feel so small and stupid, as if I'd crawl on the ground to get her to say "Good girl."

What she does to gaslight me: *Act like I've done something wrong*

What I do as a gaslightee: *Try even harder to get her to praise me so it doesn't turn out to be true I'm doing something wrong*

2. Have Compassion for Yourself.

One of the most soul-destroying aspects of being treated badly is the message we give ourselves that we deserve it. And as we seek to become more responsible and understand how we, too, participate in the destructive dynamics we're trying to escape, we can come to feel that we really *do* deserve to be treated badly. After all, we participated. We argued with our gaslighter, or submitted to him, or gave him the message that we didn't mind. We tried to control the situation or sought to make ourselves feel secure. Therefore, we're just as guilty as he is, and we deserve whatever happens to us, right?

Wrong. The goal of this process is not to berate yourself, burden yourself with guilt, or apportion blame. Your only goal is to change your situation for the better. In order to do that, you need to know how you, too, are contributing to the problem and what you might do to alter it. But that's very different from deciding that you "deserve" what's happening or that you are somehow "to blame" for it.

How would you react if you saw a little girl who kept trying to interest an angry, withdrawn, or deceptive adult in playing with her? What would you think if she kept going back to the same unreceptive person again and again, trying new ways each time to get him to engage with her? What if she followed her first few attempts with tantrums, or hitting, or angry words? What advice would you give her? What spirit would you give it in? What else would you tell her about herself?

I would like to believe that you'd view that little girl with compassion, even if you also advised her to stop returning to the adult who is treating her so dismissively. You might try to get her to behave differently, but you would also understand that she's doing her best in a bad situation, even if her best isn't so good for her right now.

Let me invite you to treat yourself with the same compassion you'd show that child—or any of your friends or loved ones—to feel love and appreciation for yourself even as you seeking to understand more about who you are and what you've done. Sometimes being compassionate toward ourselves is the hardest task of all. But in my experience, that is often when change truly begins.

3. Give Yourself Permission to Make a Sacrifice.

There's no way around it: Leaving your gaslighting relationship may well cost you something. And so, being *willing* to leave (even if you don't actually end up leaving) often means facing the prospect of tremendous loss.

"I'll never meet a man like that again," my patients tell me. "I'll never again be with someone so exciting, so attuned to me, so sexy, such a perfect soul mate."

Or "I'll never have a job this good again. I'll never again find a position that so perfectly fits my talents and abilities, my goals and dreams."

Or "I'll never have a friend like that again—someone who knows me so well, who's been through so much with me."

Or "I can't imagine what our family life is going to be like if I stop speaking to my mother/father/sister/brother/aunt/uncle/cousin. What will Thanksgiving dinners be like? Who'll come to—or stay away from—my birthday parties? How can I deprive my children of a relative?"

As we saw in the previous chapter, you may be exaggerating how much you'll lose. It may well be that you'll meet another man, find another job, make another friend who brings you just as much pleasure as the gaslighter, maybe even more. There may be solutions to your family situation that you can't imagine right now, solutions that will be far more satisfying than your current setup. You may find that you value different things the next time around, or that you're finally able to get what you've always wanted but in a better form.

Or you may be absolutely right. By risking your gaslighting relationship, you may indeed be losing something you'll never have again.

The point is, you don't know. What you *do* know is that you're involved in a relationship that is undermining your spirit and sapping joy from your life. You may already have made serious compromises with regard to work, friends, partners, family, simply to maintain the gaslighting relationship. You may already have given up on some hopes and dreams for yourself. Almost certainly, your gaslighting relationship is unlikely to get better if you do nothing. The only hope for change is if you act differently. And yes, you may be risking something of great value if you do that.

So, is making a change worth it to you? You won't be able to know ahead of time how it's all going to come out, what risks you're really taking, what gains you'll really get. So are you willing to take a leap of faith?

The only person who can answer that question, of course, is you. Are you willing to act, knowing that you may be taking a great risk, simply because you are unwilling to continue as you are?

I'll never forget what a patient said to me once about why she finally left her gaslighting relationship. "I didn't know what would come next," she told me. "I just wasn't willing to keep feeling this bad." Sometimes that's all you need to know.

Questions to Help You Take That Leap of Faith

- Did I make a decision today that made me feel good about myself? What was it?
- Did I make a decision today that made me feel bad about myself? What was it?

(continued)

> - Am I living a life of integrity in accordance with my values?
> - If not, what must I do to bring my life into alignment with my values?
> - What's my vision of the best life I'm capable of?
> - What must I do to achieve that life?

4. Get In Touch with Your Feelings.

Often, we disconnect from our feelings so that we can remain in our gaslighting relationships. In order to turn off the gas, we have to turn on our feelings.

To reconnect to your feelings, try the following exercise.

Awakening Your Feelings: *Have a pen and paper handy. Jot down the answers to these questions in any form you like: sentences, brief notes, anything that works for you. You can also draw or diagram your answers.*

1. Recall the last event that made an emotional impact on you. It could be as major as a loved one's illness or as minor as a disagreement with a bank teller. Describe the incident.
2. What did you feel?
3. What did you think?
4. What did you do?

Here's how Katie completed this exercise the first time she tried it.

1. *When I went to buy coffee at the corner grocery and I couldn't find the right change, the clerk kept looking at me like he was really mad, and finally he said, "Just get out of the way so you're not holding up the line."*
2. *I felt bad. I felt stupid. I felt like I should have been able to find the change.*
3. *I thought I was too slow.*
4. *I smiled at him and told him I was sorry.*

When Katie brought her exercise in to show me, I helped her see that she hadn't used feeling words to describe her emotions. "I felt stupid" wasn't really a feeling but a thought. Katie thought not being able to find the change quickly enough meant she was a stupid person. "I felt like I should have been able to find the change" was also a thought, an idea about what she *should* have done. I asked Katie to try that part of the exercise again, using feeling words, such as *sad, angry, frustrated, distraught, worried, anxious, scared, ashamed, proud, excited, happy,* and so on, words that really described her *feelings* and not her *thoughts.*

"I guess I felt ashamed," Katie told me. Then she shook her head. "Isn't that silly?" she said. "Why should I be ashamed of something like that?" Getting in touch with her feelings had allowed Katie to feel the feeling, and then let it go. If Katie hadn't become aware of being ashamed, she might have unknowingly carried that shame with her for a long time.

I asked Katie to try the whole exercise again. Here's what she came up with the second time.

1. *Brian was mad at me because another guy smiled at me on our way home from the store. He yelled at me. I said, "There's that thing you do." He yelled louder. I walked into my bedroom and shut the door.*
2. *I felt scared when he was yelling. I felt proud when I walked away. I guess I was also ashamed.*
3. *I thought he shouldn't have yelled at me. I thought I should have stayed. I also thought I had to go.*
4. *I stayed in the bedroom and waited until he was done yelling. Then I came out and made dinner.*

Katie was fascinated by the exercise because she saw how many different feelings she had about the same incident, and how many different thoughts. "I didn't realize I *was* proud," she admitted. "It's a good feeling."

Clues That You May Be Burying Your Feelings

- You feel "numb," flat, apathetic, or bored.
- You don't enjoy the things that used to give you pleasure.
- You feel sexually "dead." You don't enjoy sex, and attractive people don't turn you on, not even a little.
- Several times a month, or more, you experience physical symptoms such as migraine, stomach or intenstinal ailments, backache, bouts of cold and flu, or accidents.
- You have disturbing dreams.
- You find yourself reacting emotionally to things that you know don't mean much to you—crying at a TV commercial, for example, or losing your temper with a clerk.
- Your eating patterns change. Either you eat compulsively or food doesn't interest you.
- Your sleeping patterns change. Either you're sleeping longer hours or you're having difficulty falling asleep, or sometimes both.
- You feel tense and jumpy for no apparent reason.
- You feel exhausted for no apparent reason.

5. Empower Yourself.

Often, a gaslighting relationship leaves us feeling helpless and incompetent, as though we can't do anything right. Beginning to see and own your strengths can be a critical part of making changes.

Jill—the ambitious journalist who'd moved into a debilitating Stage 3 gaslighting relationship with her new boss—found this step especially helpful. As you'll remember from the previous chapter, Jill felt humiliated that she hadn't been able to win her boss's respect through her hard work and talent. "I thought I was such hot stuff, but it looks like I'm *nothing*," she would frequently repeat. Or "If I can't succeed at this job, then I'm just a *nothing*."

Wanting desperately to win her boss's approval, she had given him complete power over her self-concept. If he said she was doing a good job, then she was. If he said she was incompetent, then that, too, must be true. How could Jill challenge a relationship where so much was at stake?

Jill and I worked at reminding her of other competencies and strengths, abilities that had nothing to do with her job per se. I asked Jill to list her strengths, and when she insisted that she had none—or none that mattered—I asked her to interview at least three friends, each of whom was to help her identify at least five strengths.

When Jill came in for her next session and got out her list of strengths, she began to cry. Suddenly, all the sorrow she'd felt about her boss's long, slow erosion of her self-image came rushing to the surface, and she grieved over the way she'd let him tell her who she was. Remembering that other people saw different things in her helped Jill connect to what she saw in herself.

Knowing she had strengths that were so visible to others also gave Jill the courage to accept her shortcomings. "Before, it was like I was such a terrible journalist, I *needed* that man, I needed him to be anything at all," Jill said later. "It was like I was *nothing,* and only he had the power to make me *something.* But when I realized that I already was *something,* then I didn't need him quite so much. And then I could finally think about what was wrong with our relationship. Before that, I couldn't afford to."

Empower Yourself By . . .

- listing your strengths.
- challenging self-critical or negative thoughts, such as "I'm no good," or "I'll never be happy."
- doing things that make you feel competent.
- avoiding people who have negative opinions of you and who sap your energy.

(continued)

> - surrounding yourself with people who see and support your strengths.
> - relying on your strengths and letting them help you cope with your challenge areas.

6. Take Just One Step to Improve Your Life. Then Take Another.

It's amazing how powerful it is to take action—any action, even the smallest, that will make your life better. Even if your action seems to have nothing to do with your relationship, taking it will make help you mobilize to turn off the gas.

For example, one of my patients realized one day that she frequently got invitations from clients to social events related to the public relations firm where she worked—gallery openings, theater events, cocktail parties, the occasional screening of a new film. Her husband was always invited, too, but he never wanted either of them to go. In his mind, evenings were a time when a married couple should stay home together.

So for my patient, accepting one of these invitations was a small but significant step toward taking action to improve her life. She enjoyed herself, and realized that, for her, the pleasure was well worth facing her husband's accusations that she was selfish and too involved in her career. She hadn't directly confronted him about gaslighting or about changing their relationship. But she herself had begun a change.

Another patient of mine enrolled in a life drawing class. She'd always been nervous about the idea of drawing nude bodies, but she loved to draw, and this seemed like a good opportunity to develop a talent she enjoyed. She never mentioned the class to her husband, and when he found out about it, a few weeks later, he didn't particularly care. But the sense of empowerment she got from taking this action for herself helped move her to challenge her husband later.

Part of why it's so hard to turn off the gas is that after weeks or months or years of being gaslighted, you're often not the same strong self you were when you entered your gaslighting relationship. So restoring that self—giving that self the chance to take action—is a powerful tool in your mobilization for turning off the gas.

Turning Off the Gas

Okay, are you all mobilized now? Then it's time to start turning off the gas! Here's a basic prescription, five little shifts in perspective that may help you alter the dynamic between you and your gaslighter. You don't have to do them all at once. You don't have to do them in any particular order. You may not even have to do them all. Just start with the one that makes the most sense to you and see what happens.

Five Ways to Turn Off the Gas

1. Sort out truth from distortion.
2. Decide whether the conversation is really a power struggle. And if it is, opt out.
3. Identify your gaslight triggers, and his.
4. Focus on feelings instead of "right" and "wrong."
5. Remember that you can't control anyone's opinion—even if you're right!

---

1. Sort Out Truth from Distortion.

Often, our gaslighters tell us their version of events and we get completely thrown. There's just enough truth in them to make us think that the whole package is true. So sorting out the truth from the distortion can be a helpful first step in turning off the gas.

This approach was especially helpful to Liz, the woman with the lying boss who was trying to sabotage her. Her boss always had a plausible explanation for whatever she objected to. If she asked him about a client getting a memo saying that Liz didn't want to work with him, her boss would insist that the client was lying. If Liz produced a copy of the memo and asked who had sent it, her boss would go into a complicated explanation of office reorganization; or he'd blame the memo on someone in Liz's division; or he might just shrug and look confused. Because he always seemed so warm, friendly, and unruffled, there were no obvious cues that anything was wrong—no yelling, no insults, no overt unpleasantness, except maybe from Liz herself as she became increasingly frustrated. And because everyone else in the company seemed charmed by him, Liz emerged from each encounter with her boss feeling more and more crazy, a feeling intensified by the fact that he was always so calm and Liz herself was becoming frantic.

Things started to turn around for Liz when she challenged herself to sort out truth from distortion. She found that forcing herself to look calmly and honestly at the truth—rather than at her boss's accusations or her own defenses—clarified her thinking to an extraordinary extent. "It was as though I was hanging upside down from the ceiling," she told me once. "And then I said, 'Liz! What do you think?' and I could almost literally feel myself and my world turning right-side up again."

What Liz's Boss Said	What Liz Used to Think	Sorting Out Truth from Distortion
"There's no problem here."	"Oh God, why do I think there's a problem, then?"	"Okay, I know there's a problem. Way too many things just don't add up. So for some reason, he's not telling me the truth."
"I wish you felt you could trust me."	"I don't trust him, but I wish I could. It would be so	"I don't trust people who distort the truth."

nice to make this
all work out . . ."

| "Maybe if you were more flexible, we'd get along better." | "Why is he criticizing me? Why can't he see how hard I work? Why can't he see how hard I'm trying?" | "The problem isn't my not being flexible, it's that he's trying to sabotage me, and then he lies about it." |

Of course, if Liz's boss had been a trustworthy, helpful person, he might have said the exact same words to her, and in that case, they would have been both true and sincere. But in this situation, they were manipulations. Sometimes you can't go by just the words—or even by a person's tone of voice, body language, and general affect. Sometimes, you have to ask yourself what you *really* think, and go with that deep perception. If you find out you're wrong, admit it and correct your error. If you find out you were right, congratulate yourself and move on. Either way, your starting point needs to be *your* sense of what's true, not your gaslighter's. If you've idealized your gaslighter and want to think well of him, you may be tempted to substitute his version of events for yours. But don't. That's how you start dancing the Gaslight Tango.

2. Decide Whether the Conversation Is Really a Power Struggle. And if It Is, Opt Out.

Part of why gaslighting is so insidious is that you don't always realize what the conversation is *really* about. Let's look again at the way Katie and Brian argued over whether Katie was flirting. What's really going on here?

BRIAN: Did you see that guy looking at you tonight? Who does he think he is?

KATIE: Brian, I'm sure he didn't mean anything by it. He was just being friendly.

BRIAN: Wow, you are so naïve! I would think after all this time you'd get it. He wasn't just "being friendly," Katie. He was making a move.

KATIE: He really wasn't. He was wearing a wedding ring.

BRIAN: Oh, like that would stop any guy. And what were you doing checking him out, anyway? Why did you even notice whether he had a ring or not? You must have been pretty interested yourself.

KATIE: Of course I wasn't interested. I'm with you.

BRIAN: Bad enough the guy flirts with you right in front of me, now you have to start checking out other guys. Can't you even wait till I'm not around before you start trying to replace me?

KATIE: Brian, I'm not trying to replace you. I want to be with you. I chose you. Please, please, believe me. *You* are the one I want. I would *never* cheat on you.

BRIAN: The least you could do is be honest with me.

KATIE: But I *am* being honest with you. Can't you see how much I care about you?

BRIAN: If you care so much, then admit you were checking out that guy. Do me the courtesy of being honest and admit you were checking out that guy.

KATIE: But I wasn't! How can you say such terrible things about me? I love you so much. *Please* believe me! Please, Brian—

BRIAN: Don't lie to me, Katie. That's the one thing I can't stand.

The fight continues for more than an hour, with Brian becoming angrier and more intense about proving he's right, and Katie becoming more and more desperate about trying to win Brian over. If she can't convince him, she feels he will have proven what a bad, disloyal girlfriend she is. And she needs to prove to both of them that she's a good, loyal girlfriend and a loving person.

Mired in gaslighting, neither Brian nor Katie was talking about the actual incident. For Brian, the encounter was actually a power struggle over whether he was right. And for Katie, the conversation was also a power struggle: She was trying to get Brian to approve of her so that she would not have to worry about whether his accusations were true.

So what's the difference between a power struggle and a genuine conversation? In a genuine conversation, both people are really listening and addressing each other's concerns, even if they get emotional sometimes. Here's another way a couple might have handled that situation:

> HIM: I can't believe you were flirting with that guy!
>
> HER: But it was just being friendly and talking! It didn't mean anything!
>
> HIM: It sure looked like it meant something. How am I supposed to tell?
>
> HER: You don't have to tell, honey. I promise you, you're the only guy for me. You're still the guy I'm going home with. You're the only one I want.
>
> HIM: That sounds good when you say it. But when I see you making eyes at those other men, it makes me crazy.
>
> HER: I didn't realize it bothered you so much. I'm sorry. But I have to tell you, if I'm not free to talk to other people because you'll think I'm flirting all the time, it's going to make *me* crazy.
>
> HIM: That's terrible! You don't care about how I feel at all!
>
> HER: I do. I really want to work this out. Let's think some more about how we can make this work for both of us.

As you can see, a lot of heated emotions are coming up in that conversation, but no gaslighting. Two people have very different opinions, but no one is pulling power plays; they're just saying how they feel and what they want. He is saying how he feels if he sees her flirting. She is saying how she feels if she's not allowed to talk freely to other people. He's not trying to prove that he's right, and neither is she; they're just trying to solve a difficult problem: how they can both be happy when, at the moment, they want opposite things.

So if you and your gaslighter are genuinely working something out, by all means, engage. Talk for hours, or schedule several conversations. If the issue is important enough to both of you, you may find yourself talking about it for years to come. Being in a couple doesn't mean you always have to agree; on some things you may never agree. As long as you are talking and listening respectfully—however emotional you may become—there's no problem (though it may feel painful or scary sometimes).

But if you decide that a power struggle is going on, your first step in turning off the gas is to identify it as such and disengage. Otherwise, you're still dancing the Gaslight Tango.

Here's an example of a power struggle between my patient Mariana and her friend Sue. The issue seemed simple: Mariana wanted the two women to meet in her neighborhood, while Sue preferred to meet closer to her own home. But look at the way the real issue gets lost and the Gaslight Tango begins.

MARIANA: So maybe you can come down here next week.

SUE: I'd rather meet uptown.

MARIANA: That's really not convenient for me. Can't you come down?

SUE: We *always* meet in your neighborhood. I don't know if you realize that, but it's true.

MARIANA: No, we don't.

SUE: Out of the last seven times we've met, five of them have been in your neighborhood, and frankly, I'm sick of it. It makes me feel completely disregarded by you, Mariana. I really think you believe you're the center of the universe. It's very hurtful.

MARIANA: I'm not trying to hurt you! How can you say that about me?

SUE: I don't know what else I'm supposed to believe. You seem to think that just because you work long hours at that job of yours, you can make everybody else accommodate you. But I have a life, too, you know. Or don't you think that's important?

MARIANA: Of course I think it's important. You're a wonderful friend. Please don't be mad at me. I'll meet you uptown if you want.

SUE: But I hate that I had to force you into it. Now I feel like you're being selfish *and* manipulative. You're going to give me what I want, but you're going to make me pay. I feel like there's no way for me to win. Whatever happens, you're on top.

MARIANA: Please don't think that. Our friendship means so much to me. I can't stand hearing you say these things.

SUE: Well, what do you expect when you behave in such a selfish way? I feel like nothing I care about matters to you. Maybe we shouldn't see each other for a while.

MARIANA: *Please* don't say that. What can I do to make this better?

You Know It's a Power Struggle If . . .

- it includes a lot of insults.
- you keep covering the same ground.
- one or both of you bring in points that are way off topic.
- you've had the same argument several times before and never really gotten anywhere.
- no matter what you say, the other person keeps having the same response.
- you feel as if the other person is simply in charge.

Clearly, neither Sue nor Mariana is really talking about where to meet. Maybe Mariana *does* choose the meeting place more often and should now offer to be more accommodating. Maybe Sue *does* have a legitimate grievance. But neither woman is concerned with figuring out what's really going on or with making actual plans. They just want to find out who has more power. If Sue has more power, she can get Mariana to change her mind and agree that Mariana has been a bad friend. If Mariana has more power, she can get Sue to change *her* mind and agree that Mariana is really a good friend.

Because Mariana had given up her sense of self and was allowing Sue to define her, Sue was always the judge and jury, while Mariana was the defendant, begging for a good verdict. As a result, these arguments—even the ones she won—made Mariana feel weak and exhausted. She never got what she was *really* after, an inner sense that she was a good person and a good friend.

She got only Sue's temporary "not guilty," which Sue might rescind as soon as the next "trial" began. Mariana might well win some temporary victories— she might occasionally get Sue to take back her most negative statements— but she never won a permanent victory, in which Sue agreed once and for all that Mariana was a good friend. No matter what Mariana did, Sue always kept the power to judge. Indeed, Mariana kept giving Sue that power, hoping that Sue would use it to judge Mariana "good" and thereby validate her sense of self. That's why, in the end, whatever the verdict, Mariana would always come around to agreeing with Sue; she wanted Sue, not herself, to be the one to decide her worth.

Gradually, Mariana came to realize that when one of these power struggles started, she had to commit not to winning but to opting out. Trying to win the argument would only keep her in the courtroom, begging for mercy from a powerful judge. Opting out would mean Mariana had turned off the gas and would perhaps become her own judge, making her own decisions about who she was, how she should behave, and whether she was "good."

Mariana began to use a few phrases to help her disengage: "We'll have to agree to disagree." "I think we've gone as far as we can go." "I'm feeling browbeaten, and I don't want to continue." Sue's response was uneven. Sometimes she respected Mariana's efforts and the two women could shift the conversation to more pleasant topics; other times Sue would hang up the phone in a huff and then apologize later. But at least Mariana was reinforcing her own strength and her responsibility to judge herself, rather than giving Sue the power to judge her and engaging in a power struggle that she could never win.

Things You Can Say to Opt Out of a Power Struggle

- "You're right, but I don't want to keep arguing about this."
- "You're right, but I don't want to be talked to that way."
- "I'm happy to continue this conversation without name-calling."
- "I'm not comfortable with where this conversation is going. Let's revisit it later."
- "I think this conversation has gone as far as it can go."
- "I don't think I can be constructive right now. Let's talk about this at another time."
- "I think we have to agree to disagree."
- "I don't want to continue this argument."
- "I don't want to continue this conversation right now."
- "I hear you, and I'm going to think about that. But I don't want to keep talking about it right now."
- "I'd really like to continue this conversation, but I'm not willing to do so unless we can do it in a more pleasant tone."
- "I don't like the way I'm feeling right now, and I'm not willing to continue this conversation."
- "You may not be aware of it, but you're telling me that I don't know what reality is. And respectfully, I don't agree. I love you, but I won't talk to you about this."
- "I love having intimate conversations with you, but not when you're putting me down."
- "It may not be your intention to put me down, but I feel put down, and I'm not going to continue the conversation."
- "This is not a good time for me for me to talk about this. Let's agree on another time that works for both of us."

And if You Want to Opt Out While Still Expressing Anger

- "Please stop talking to me in that tone; I don't like it."
- "I can't hear what you're really saying as long as you're yelling."
- "I can't hear what you're really saying as long you're speaking to me with contempt."
- "I don't want to talk while you're yelling at me."
- "I don't walk to talk while you're speaking to me with contempt."
- "I am not going to continue this argument right now."
- "From my point of view, you're distorting reality, and I really don't like it. I'll talk to you later, when I'm feeling calmer."
- "Perhaps you didn't intend to hurt my feelings, but I'm too upset to talk right now. We can talk about it later."

3. Identify Your Gaslight Triggers, and His.

Remember, both you and your gaslighter are dancing the Gaslight Tango. In all likelihood, both of you have Gaslight Triggers, situations that start you dancing. If you can identify these triggers, you'll have a better chance of avoiding them.

Now let's be clear: I am *not* saying that you are responsible for his gaslighting. Nor is he responsible for your participation in the Gaslight Tango. I *am* saying that either of you might start the tango and that each of you might be more likely to start it in certain situations. So try to approach this topic without shame or blame. Focus instead on identifying those Gaslight Triggers so that you can start turning off the gas.

Identify topics and situations that may trigger gaslighting. Gaslighting is a response to stress; people become either gaslighters or gaslightees when they feel threatened. Here is a list of some stressful topics and situations that often trigger gaslighting. Ask yourself whether you and your gaslighter seem to have trouble when any of the following come up:

Money

Sex

Family

Holidays

Vacations

Life decisions: marriage, a move, job change

Children

A difference of opinion

"Rules," for example, "We have to bring something when we're invited for dinner" or
   "You can't show up to a formal event without a tie."

Trish and Aaron often engaged in the Gaslight Tango when money issues were on the table. Because Aaron was so money-conscious and so nervous about debt, he frequently swung into gaslighting when a bill arrived or an unexpected expense occurred. Knowing this, Trish decided to be extra careful to avoid her own part in the Gaslight Tango when money was a topic, to make sure she never got caught up in a pointless back-and-forth about her competence.

Olivia realized that Martin tended to swing into gaslighting whenever sex was a concern. If she seemed to be rejecting him sexually in any way, he might engage in his own version of Glamour Gaslighting, stepping up the romantic performance with his candles and mood music to prove that he really was a sexually attractive guy. Although Olivia wasn't going to have sex with him when she didn't feel like it, she could make sure to say no in the nicest way possible—and then be on guard for any gaslighting that might follow.

My coaching client Sondra—the one with the supposedly perfect marriage—felt that family issues really set her Good-Guy husband off. Peter tended to engage in gaslighting whenever his family or Sondra's was involved. Sondra, meanwhile, became especially critical of Peter when she was anxious about their children, and that reaction provoked Peter's gaslighting. So that was a trouble area, too.

Sondra thought long and hard about whether her marriage would be improved simply by seeing less of their families. She decided to give it a try. Although she wasn't willing to cut back on seeing her family, she was okay with visiting them alone.

Sondra also realized that her bouts of being anxious and critical made Peter feel insecure. If Peter saw that Sondra was upset or dissatisfied, he felt powerless and worthless because he truly believed that a good husband should be able to please his wife at all times. Feeling powerless provoked Peter to gaslight in order to regain his sense of power: If he could prove that he was right and Sondra was wrong, and that her dissatisfaction was *her* fault, not his, then he'd feel stronger and better about himself. Sondra understood that she wasn't responsible for this process, but her anxiety and criticism were setting it in motion.

So she spoke directly to Peter, saying, "I realize that whenever we're talking about our kids, I tend to get really anxious and I start acting like you can't do anything right. I know I can trust you to be a good father, and I'm sorry if I ever gave you any other impression. I'll try to catch myself, but if you see me getting overly anxious again, I'd really like you to remind me about it."

To Sondra's amazement, Peter took her up on her offer. The gaslighting didn't stop, but it declined considerably, although Sondra was then "stuck" with changing her own behavior! "Now I have to actually *be* less anxious about the kids," she said to me jokingly as she described the first time her husband called her on her worrying. "Thanks a lot!" But I could see that her main feeling was relief. Both she and Peter were happier with these arrangements, and while there was still more work to be done, Sondra felt this was a good start.

Can you identify topics or situations in which you and your gaslighter are especially prone to dancing the Gaslight Tango? Take a moment and jot them down.

Identify things you say or do that might trigger gaslighting. Again, I want to be very clear. If your words or actions are triggering your partner's gaslighting, that does *not* mean you're responsible for his bad behavior. Nor does it mean you have to bend yourself out of shape to avoid making him mad. But there may be relatively easy ways to choose new words or actions that work better for your relationship.

For example, some men feel manipulated and defensive when a woman begins to cry. While I certainly don't think there's anything wrong with crying per se, take a moment to think about whether crying has triggered gaslighting in your relationship. Does your gaslighter seem to feel threatened by your tears? Does he start trying to prove that he's right about something soon after he sees you cry? Does he step up the Intimidation, Good-Guy manipulation, or Glamour gestures to get you to stop crying? Do your tears bring on the Emotional Apocalypse? If you think your crying has become a Gaslight Trigger in your relationship, consider whether you can keep yourself from crying in front of your gaslighter, either by controlling your tears or by leaving the room.

Likewise, some men respond especially badly to particular phrases. Peter, for example, couldn't stand to hear Sondra say "You've hurt my feelings." Whenever she said this, he started in gaslighting, trying to cloud her sense of reality and prove how right he was. If instead of saying "You've hurt my feelings," Sondra simply said "I wish you'd find another way to say that," Peter was fine. But something about the statement, "You've hurt my feelings" really seemed to get to him. Sondra could still speak up for herself, but a little change in words made a big difference.

Martin, for his part, had a lot of trouble with the statement, "That makes me sad." Olivia realized that her husband really needed to feel that he could make his wife happy, and when he felt he couldn't, he'd start to gaslight her, trying to get her to admit everything was fine. Although Olivia wasn't willing to hide her sadness from Martin *all* the time, she understood that he took this feeling a lot more seriously than she did. She decided that if she felt really sad, she'd ask him to comfort her, because whenever he could do something for her, he was less likely to gaslight her. But if her sadness was less urgent, set off by a bittersweet movie or the story of a distant friend, she'd save her mournful response for her women friends.

Another Gaslight Trigger for many men is being asked to do something they can't. Early in their relationship, for example, Katie asked Brian to help her move. It happened that the only time she could make this move was a day Brian was supposed to be out of town on business. He couldn't change his work schedule, but he hated not being able to come through for her. Katie got her brother to help instead, but Brian's stress and frustration provoked an early bout of gaslighting, in which he accused Katie of using her brother to show him up and insisting that Katie's brother had never liked him.

If Katie had realized that this situation would be a Gaslight Trigger for Brian, she might have handled it better. Instead of mentioning casually that her brother was helping her and then falling into a long argument, she might have said, "Honey, I know how much you wish you could help me move, and believe me, I love you for it. And I know that if I really needed you to, you might even change your work schedule for me. But I honestly don't want you to. Just knowing you're willing to do that makes me feel so loved and protected, I can't tell you! Don't worry. I'll find another way to handle the situation." She might have given Brian time to absorb this message and then told him on another occasion that her brother was "taking his place."

Maybe that approach would have prevented Brian's gaslighting, maybe it wouldn't have. But at least Katie would have done her best, *and*, she would have geared herself up to avoid responding as a gaslightee.

Think about your gaslighter. Are there particular situations in which he's especially prone to gaslight you? Might there be any way to ease his stress and reduce his need to gaslight? When those situations arise, can you commit to be extra careful not to participate in his gaslighting?

Identify power plays or manipulative actions that may trigger gaslighting. Now we're getting into a more sensitive area. Think about the ways in which *you* aren't always being your best self. Do you set off your gaslighter by being overly critical or demanding? Do you belittle your gaslighter or play on his vulnerabilities? Do you say or do things that you *know* will make him crazy?

To be honest, I'd be shocked if you told me that you never indulged in these kinds of power plays. None of us are saints; we all do sneaky and manipulative things sometimes. But if you can identify a pattern that's helping to trigger your gaslighter, this might be a good time to try changing it.

For example, Trish—my patient who always fought with her husband about money—realized that she often brought up Aaron's working-class background when she wanted to get back at him. She'd make some casual but cutting remark about how it was a wonder he knew so much about fine wines given where he grew up, or she'd point to a poorly dressed woman and say, "Do you think your mother would like that hat?" For a while, Trish felt justified in these little power plays on the grounds that Aaron was so critical and belittling of her own wealthy background. But when she realized that her remarks tended to set off bouts of gaslighting, she found herself motivated to give them up.

Is there some power play of your own that sets your gaslighter off? Would it be something you could think about giving up?

Identify the ways you seek your gaslighter's approval and insist on his reassurance. Believe me, I know what it feels like to desperately need another person's reassurance. I know how it feels to imagine that only your gaslighter's approval will make you feel safe or prove that you're a good, capable, and lovable person. But I also know that seeking reassurance from your gaslighter, or trying to get him to alleviate your anxiety, often makes *him* anxious and so, ironically, triggers more gaslighting.

That's how it worked for Katie. The more desperate she felt for Brian to believe that she was a good and loyal girlfriend, and the more wounded she was by his insults, the more upset Brian became, and the more he stepped up the gaslighting. In Brian's mind, his job was to protect Katie and make her happy. If she felt anxious, scared, or miserable—and especially if he felt he was the reason—he became tremendously threatened. And when Brian felt threatened, he turned to gaslighting, which, of course, made Katie even more anxious, scared, and miserable. Talk about a vicious cycle!

The good news is that Katie had the power to help break the cycle. If she could interrupt her own feelings, she could help cool out a potential gaslighting situation. Let's take a look at the way this worked in yet another fight about whether Katie had been flirting:

BRIAN: Did you see that guy looking at you tonight? Who does he think he is?

Katie knows that telling Brian he's wrong will just make him want to prove he's right. So instead, she asks a question.

KATIE: Wow, you're obviously seeing something I'm missing in this situation. Huh. Can you tell me more?

BRIAN: The way his eyes lit up when he saw you, the way he leaned over to get close to you . . . There were just a million ways he came on to you. I can't believe you missed it. You're so naïve!

Katie is very upset to hear Brian call her naïve, but she realizes that showing she's upset will only cause him to step up the gaslighting. So instead, she makes a joke.

KATIE: Boy, if I didn't know I was the most sophisticated woman in the world, I might be worried!

BRIAN: What?

KATIE: You called me naïve. But you didn't mean it, right? I know my fabulous boyfriend would never say anything to me except the most wonderful compliments.

BRIAN: Oh, never mind.

Notice how different the dynamic is in this situation. Katie has found a way to defuse the power struggle. She didn't argue with Brian, and she didn't get upset by what he said, both of which tend to make him feel threatened and then step up the gaslighting. By choosing alternate responses to a trigger situation, Katie has interrupted the Gaslight Tango, and has begun to turn off the gas.

Some Alternate Responses to Trigger Behaviors

Make a joke: "Boy, if I didn't know I was the most beautiful woman in the world, I'd start to think I should worry."

Ask a question: "Oh, you think I'm stupid? Wow, you're obviously seeing something I'm missing in this situation. Can you tell me more about what you're seeing?" P.S. If you do this in a sarcastic tone, you are throwing fuel on the fire, but if you can ask sincerely, you may open up a response.

Identify the behavior: "Last time you said that to me [or said something in that tone], you were upset about having to go to your mother's for dinner. Is there something similar going on now?"

Express compassion: "I'm sorry you're having such a hard time right now. Is there anything I can do to help?"

4. Focus on Feelings Instead of "Right" and "Wrong."

Often, a gaslighter will make an accusation that rings true. Perhaps you *were* flirting a bit too heavily with that guy at the party and you owe your man an apology. Maybe when you stood your girlfriend up for a date with that hot new guy from the office you *were* being a bad friend. Your gaslighter zeros in on these failings and missteps, and you wince in recognition.

Then your gaslighter takes it a step further. Brian, for example, insisted that Katie was purposely trying to humiliate him. "You want to publicly demoralize me, don't you?" he'd keep repeating. "Why can't you just admit it?"

"But I *can't* admit it. It isn't true!" Katie would reply, bewildered. She'd search her soul and *know* she hadn't been malicious; maybe, at most, she'd been a bit insensitive. But after several hours of bitter accusations, she'd begin to wonder if Brian was right. After all, he seemed so sure . . . And he hadn't been convinced by any of her arguments . . . And she knew she'd done *something* wrong . . .

Likewise, Mariana's friend Sue was a master at finding Mariana's flaws and shortcomings. Whenever she did, Mariana felt completely disabled, as though Sue's accuracy in pinpointing her flaws gave Sue complete power in defining who Mariana was. Mariana became unable to stand up to Sue and all the more desperate to seek her approval.

The only way to free yourself from this trap is to stop worrying about which one of you is right and focus on your feelings. If you're feeling genuine remorse, then apologize and do your best to make it up. But if you're feeling bewildered, attacked, devastated, or terrified, then something fishy is going on. No matter what you did—even if you *also* feel regret for it—you are being gaslighted, and you should disengage from the conversation immediately.

For Mariana, a turning point came after she had canceled plans with Sue at the last minute in order to go out with a guy from work. Here's how Mariana opted out of the power struggle during their phone call the next day.

SUE: How could you do this to me? You *know* how much I count on seeing you! We had plans. And then you cancel at the last minute so you can go out with some guy?

MARIANA: I know. I'm sorry. You have every right to be angry. He's just so cute. And I haven't had a date in months. But you're right, it's no excuse. How can I make it up to you?

SUE: What do you mean, make it up to me? You were deliberately trying to show me how little I mean to you, how superior you are to me. You've always been jealous that I have a boyfriend and you don't. Is this your way of getting back at me?

MARIANA: Whoa, Sue, you're way off base. I *shouldn't* have canceled our plans, but I didn't do it because I wanted to be mean to you. I just *really* wanted to go out with Jared.

SUE: I don't believe you. And I think you know better. You were trying to get back at me. Admit it!

This is the point at which Mariana would usually try even harder to defend herself. But now she was trying to turn off the gas. So instead, she disengaged.

MARIANA: Look, I'm sorry I canceled our plans, and if you tell me how I can make it up to you, I'd really like to make this better. But other than that, there's nothing more to say.

SUE: What do you mean, nothing more to say? Not only are you insulting me but now you won't even *deal* with me!

MARIANA: I mean it. If this is how the conversation is going to go, I don't want to talk about it any more.

SUE: This is unbelievable! Is this another way you're trying to get back at me?

MARIANA: No, it's not, and I've apologized. Now I need to go on to something else. And if you're not willing to do that, I'm going to hang up.

Practice Opting Out

- **Check out the box on page 180.** Pick the statements that fit your personality best and that your gaslighter will be most likely to hear. Edit them if you have to, or make up your own.

- **Role-play with a friend.** Coach your friend on how to play your gaslighter, telling her what he is likely to say. Then play yourself and see what it feels like to use these new statements.

- **Write your own script.** Write out a conversation yourself. Imagine what your gaslighter might say and then come up with your own responses. You might even like to practice saying them aloud. "If he says, 'What a jerk,' I'll say, 'Look, honey, I don't want to be talked to that way.' If he says, 'I'll talk to you any way I want,' I'll say, 'Then I'm going home.'"

- **Focus on a few statements.** Remember, your goal is to opt out of the argument, not to expand it. Pick one or two helpful statements

(continued)

and then just keep repeating them, or stay silent. Your gaslighter is deeply committed to being right, so you aren't going to change his mind. But you may show him that his behavior has consequences he doesn't like. And over time, that might motivate him to change.

- **Choose your consequences.** Decide ahead of time what consequences, if any, you will announce. Here are two examples: "Next time you're more than twenty minutes late, I'm leaving the restaurant." "I'll remind you three times that you're yelling, and then, if you don't stop, I'll leave the room." Just make sure not to announce any consequence you aren't prepared to act upon. Your goal is not to threaten but simply to act in your own best interests.

- **Pick an exit strategy.** If your gaslighter refuses to end the argument, then you have to end the conversation—by hanging up, walking away, changing the subject, even offering to make him tea, as Trish did in Chapter 4. Knowing how you'll terminate the conversation—even if you don't have to use this plan—will make you feel more empowered from the start.

5. Remember That You Can't Control Anyone's Opinion—Even if You're Right!

I know one of my own biggest hooks in the gaslighting process was my desperate wish to get my ex-husband to agree that I was right. I simply couldn't stand that he thought it was okay to be three hours late, and that the problem was *my* oversensitivity, so I'd argue with him endlessly, trying to get him to change his mind. I now see that I was just as committed to controlling his thoughts as he was to controlling mine. For example, when he'd come home three hours late and I'd object, he'd go all-out to convince me I was being unreasonable, unspontaneous, overly controlling. But I was equally committed to convincing him that my frustration was justified.

Twenty years later, I still think I was right and he was wrong—of *course* my frustration was justified! But that's beside the point. What kept me locked into the Gaslight Tango was my inability to accept that my husband was going to see things his own way, regardless of what I did. If he wanted to think I was unreasonable, he would, no matter how hard I argued or how upset I got. As soon as I understood that he—and he alone—had power over his own thoughts, no matter how right I might be, and that he wasn't going to change, no matter what I said or did, I took a significant step toward freedom.

My patient Mitchell—the one whose mother was so dismissive and contemptuous of his new wardrobe—had a similar experience. A great deal of our work together revolved around his grasping the basic notion that his mother was free to see him any way she chose. His job was not to change her opinion but rather to stop caring so much about what she thought. If Mitchell could cease idealizing his mother and seeking her approval, her frequent insults and attempted guilt trips would no longer have any power over him.

For a long time, Mitchell was unwilling to accept that he couldn't control his mother's response. Although his mother sometimes showered him with approval and affection, at other times she seemed cold, withdrawn, almost cruel, and Mitchell found the contrast extremely frustrating. He wanted to believe that his mother's shifts in behavior toward him were somehow related to his own actions, that her coldness reflected his failings while her warmth was a response to his strengths. He hated the idea that his mother's behavior was regulated by her own internal dynamics and not by his shortcomings or successes.

Mitchell's struggle was especially poignant because children *should* be able to count on their parents for a steady stream of love and approval. Even when parents don't approve of a particular action, they can still convey a basic regard for their children, but that's just what Mitchell's mother withheld. Mitchell longed for that kind of motherly approval, and it was hard for him to accept that he was unlikely ever to get it.

So for Mitchell, the way to free himself from his mother's gaslighting was to accept that, finally, he couldn't control her opinion. "I can't control her opinion—even if I'm right" became Mitchell's new mantra. Although at first he found it terrifying to feel "right—and alone," he came to like the feeling of being separate and clear. Giving up his efforts to control his mother's responses gave Mitchell a new freedom to discover and act upon his own.

Choosing Your Next Step

So now you've started to turn off the gas, and you may be getting a wide range of responses. Maybe, as with Sondra and Peter, you and your gaslighter are beginning to find new ways of being together. Maybe, as happened for Melanie and Jordan, your gaslighter absolutely refuses to change. Or maybe, as for Katie and Brian, you're still trying to sort out how you feel about what's possible and what isn't.

You may already have decided on your next step. But if you haven't, turn to the next chapter. That's where I'll talk you through the decision of whether to stay or go.

chapter 7

Should I Stay or Should I Go?

Katie was confused. She had been wholeheartedly trying to turn off the gas with her possessive boyfriend, Brian, and she did feel she'd made some progress. Whenever she opted out of the Gaslight Tango—when she told Brian that she didn't want to continue a discussion or actually left the room to avoid hearing his accusations—he often backed off, and sometimes he even apologized. Katie also felt that she herself was getting better at resisting the Urge to Merge. She was more willing to live with disagreement and was freeing herself from the need to seek Brian's approval. Gradually, she was coming to feel her own sense of being a good person, whether or not Brian validated her.

Nevertheless, Katie told me, Brian didn't seem interested in initiating any changes. If Katie interrupted the gaslighting dynamic, Brian might back off. But he continued to *start* the gaslighting process as often as before, which meant that she always had to be on alert. And when Katie slipped—when she got caught up in defending herself to Brian or in apologizing for things she didn't think she had done—he seemed happy to continue in the old pattern.

"I feel I have to do all the changing myself," she said after about three months of concerted effort. "It's not like Brian won't do *anything* differently, but it's also not like he's giving me much help. It's like he's this big rock, and

I keep trying to push him uphill. I can make some progress if I work really hard. But if I stop, even for a second, he rolls back down. Maybe the rock isn't getting any heavier, but it's not getting any lighter, either!"

So Katie wasn't sure what to do next. She still loved Brian, and she hated the thought of breaking up with him. But she was becoming increasingly frustrated by his constant accusations and his sense that the world was a dangerous, miserable place. How much change could she expect? she wondered. Which expectations were realistic and which were simply wishful thinking? And, most important, how much change did she require to be willing to stay in her relationship?

LIZ HAD BEGUN to realize that things could not continue as they were. She was spending far too much time and emotional energy obsessing about her boss. Sometimes Liz felt as though this boss had become the most important person in her life—more important than her husband, her best friend, or her family. "I'm tired of feeling as though he's eclipsed everything and everyone," she told me. "I want my life back!"

The question for Liz was whether she could get her life back and still remain in the professional position she had worked so hard to achieve. Was there a way to stay in her job and *not* participate in the Gaslight Tango? she wondered. Or was her boss so good at pushing her buttons—and at manipulating the situation—that even minimal contact between them would always produce a gaslighting relationship?

Liz started thinking hard about her options. For the first time, she began to look clearly at her professional choices, thinking about other advertising agencies where she might apply and other contacts who might help her find something. She took a long, hard look at what her current boss's plans might be: How committed was he, really, to getting rid of her or to isolating her in the company? Was there *anything* she could do to alter the situation, or was he really determined to drive her out? She also did quite a bit of soul-searching about her own part in the relationship. Was it realistic to think she could stop responding to her boss's provocations as she had been doing, with panic and a desperate wish to please him? Would the effort to "rewrite" her own responses take so much out of her that she wouldn't be able to enjoy her job anyway? Did it make more sense to try to change the relationship or simply to walk away?

WHEN MITCHELL FINALLY got in touch with how he felt about his mother's gaslighting, he became quite depressed for several weeks. It was as though the sorrow, anger, and helplessness he'd been trying to avoid his entire life had finally caught up with him, and for a while, he felt completely overwhelmed. "I just don't want to have to ever see her again," he kept saying. "I don't need her! Why should I have anything to do with someone who treats me like that?"

Mitchell realized that cutting off all contact with his mother was a major decision, and he kept asking me what I thought about it. I told him that, all things being equal, it's better to stay on speaking terms with family members if we possibly can, simply because those relationships hold so much of our history and often become increasingly important as we grow older, especially if we have children. Still, if a relationship is genuinely abusive beyond the point of repair, and if that abuse is keeping us from moving forward in our lives, or if it causes us so much pain that we can't enjoy the rest of our lives, then we may indeed want to cut the person in question out of our lives.

Mitchell began thinking about all the ways his relationship with his mother affected his life—from his choice in clothes to his ability to make a commitment to his girlfriend. He also thought about all the ways he might relate to his mother. Although part of him wanted simply to cut her out of his life completely, he forced himself to consider other options: seeing her only on holidays, visiting her once a month instead of once a week, spending time with her only in the company of his girlfriend or another friend rather than facing her alone. He also thought about making decisions more slowly, leaving his options open to change his mind in the future, when he might be feeling stronger. Mitchell knew he had to make some kind of change in his relationship to his mother. But for a long time, he couldn't decide what kind of change he wanted.

Taking Time for a Decision

If we're committed to freeing ourselves from gaslighting, there often comes a time when we have to decide whether to stay in a relationship or let it go. As I've said, the only way to really free ourselves from gaslighting is to be *willing* to leave. But then we have to decide whether we *will* leave.

The time may come when you feel that you don't have any choice: that you *must* leave to preserve your sense of self and to be happy. Or you might feel that you have several choices but that leaving is the best one. In other words, you might feel desperate or you might not, but at some point, you come to the realization that the relationship is over.

Alternately, you may come to a decision point and then decide to stay. You may feel that you can make this relationship work or decide that there are good reasons for staying despite the pain and frustration.

Whatever you decide, you may still have many positive feelings about your gaslighter. You may still be madly in love with your husband or deeply fond of your friend. Gaslighters in your family may provoke a complicated mixture of love, anger, sorrow, frustration, affection, and confusion. And if your gaslighter is a boss or colleague, you may still see the benefits of staying in your job; you might even feel appreciation, respect, and affection for your gaslighter.

I want to stress very strongly that the good feelings we have for our gaslighters are not necessarily illusions. Human beings are contradictory and complex, and none of us is perfect. Our gaslighters may indeed have behaved in abusive and problematic ways. But they may also have given us love, affection, attention, advice, adventure, training, or security. They may have been part of important times in our lives, or they may have helped us grow in ways we couldn't have managed alone. They may be people whose other qualities we admire, or people who simply move us for no reason we can name.

Often, when we discover that we've been abused or badly treated, we feel the need for an extreme reaction. We want to make the offender pay. We want justice or retaliation, something to make up for the hurt we have suffered. We can't believe we ever had good feelings for the person whom we now see as dangerous or destructive, and we may even want to cut the offending person entirely out of our lives.

These feelings are natural, and they may indeed be guides to action. But they may not be. Sometimes, our strong reactions against the people who have gaslighted us—especially family members—are at least partly driven by our frustration with ourselves. How could we have been so blind? How could we have let ourselves be treated so badly? Why couldn't we live up to our ideals of being strong, self-sufficient, and impervious to bad treatment? Why couldn't we have been more powerful, more effective? We may feel a complicated mixture of shame, resentment, anger, and sorrow as we start to look more closely at our own part in our gaslighting relationships.

All these reactions are important to notice and to feel. They're all part of helping us know what happened to us and what we want to do about it. Sometimes, too, they're guides to immediate action. "Get out," they tell us. "Don't let this continue one more day." Sometimes, listening to that urgency is the best thing we can do.

Sometimes, though, we need to let the feelings settle and the intensity subside before taking any action. Especially when we're considering a lifelong relationship, a partnership, or children, we may want to give ourselves time to explore all our options. We might want to choose temporary rather than permanent responses: a separation rather than a divorce, a "time-out" rather than a cessation of all contact. We may be able to pull back from a relationship without announcing to the other person that we are doing so, giving ourselves time and space before making a permanent decision about the future.

Mariana, for example, was growing increasingly frustrated by her relationship with Sue. She had come to hate their intense, emotional conversations, which left her feeling judged and controlled. But she'd been friends with Sue since high school, and she also hated the thought of never seeing her again.

She knew she'd have to make some changes, but she wasn't yet sure whether she wanted to end the relationship, pull back from it, or begin the long, hard process of trying—she hoped, with Sue's help—to change it.

Mariana also knew that if she told Sue straight out that she, Mariana, needed a time-out, it would certainly provoke another round of exactly the discussions she was trying to avoid. But she couldn't just stop returning Sue's calls without also provoking her friend's questions and concerns. So she told Sue that she was facing a difficult time at work and explained that she'd be unable to get together for about a month. She found a way to restrict her contact with Sue to brief phone calls and a few e-mails. Mariana hoped that temporarily and "unofficially" limiting her friendship would give her some breathing room to find out more about how she felt and what she wanted to do.

So how do you know what your next step should be? Here are four questions that can help you decide what to do next.

Four Questions to Ask About Staying or Going

1. Can I act differently with this person?
2. Is he capable of acting differently with me?
3. Am I willing to do the work it might take to change our dynamic?
4. Realistically, if I give it my best effort, will I happy with our relationship?

Can I Act Differently with This Person?

As we've seen throughout this book, your gaslighting relationship isn't going to change unless you behave differently within it. Turning off the gas requires that you detach from your gaslighter, opting out of a gaslighting conversation or walking out of the room when the Emotional Apocalypse threatens. It means you have to refuse the Urge to Merge and be willing to allow your gaslighter to have his own views, even if you *know* they're wrong. And it means that when you're feeling anxious, lonely, or insecure, you may not necessarily be able to share those feelings with your gaslighter, since they are often the very feelings that provoke him to gaslight. When you're anxious and he can't fix it, that makes him feel powerless, so he turns to gaslighting to preserve his sense of power and control.

Here are some questions to ask yourself about how much you're willing to change. Then read on to see how Katie, Liz, and Sondra answered these questions.

*When he begins gaslighting me, can I opt out of the conversation or will I often need to prove to him I'm right? Will I keep arguing with him in my head, even if I don't say anything out loud?

KATIE: I don't need to be right so much. I think I could do this with my boyfriend, Brian. Getting out of the arguments isn't the part that's hard for me.

LIZ: It makes me *crazy* to hear my boss distort the truth! Even if I don't say anything to him out loud, I know I'll keep replaying the conversation in my head over and over and over again. I just can't stand to hear him say those things!

SONDRA: The first time I opted out of a gaslighting conversation with my husband, Peter, it really upset me. I got pains in my stomach, and I actually started to shake. I just wanted so much to make things right! But now that I've been doing it for a few months, it's not that hard. So yes, I think I could do this pretty easily now.

*If his gaslighting makes me feel anxious about myself or our relationship, will I need to turn to him for reassurance? Or can I find some way of calming myself down that doesn't depend on him?

KATIE: This is the hard part for me. I want to be able to lean on Brian. So I don't think I can keep myself from asking him to reassure me. In fact,

I'm not sure I *want* to change this part of myself. I *want* to be able to ask my boyfriend for reassurance without upsetting him.

LIZ: Oh, sure, I can do *this*. I don't need *that* man's reassurance that things are okay! I just need him to stop behaving badly.

SONDRA: I think I can do this. It's hard, because Peter will often notice that I seem upset and ask me if I'm all right or if everything is okay with me. Sometimes he really wants an honest answer, and sometimes it's just the beginning of a new round of gaslighting, where he "proves" to me that I have no reason to be upset because he's done everything right. So I'll have to figure out whether he's being sincere or just baiting me. But I think I can do that.

*If I say I'm going to do something—such as leave the room when he yells, or leave the restaurant if he's more than twenty minutes late—will I be able to stick to what I've said?

KATIE: I *hate* this part. I think I can *do* it. But I *hate* doing it.

LIZ: I can do this, no problem. I'm just not sure it applies. It seems to me that no matter what I do, his behavior isn't going to change.

SONDRA: Yes, I can do this. After all, I've had good practice with the kids!

After Katie, Liz, and Sondra had answered these questions, I asked each of them to sum up what they had learned about themselves. Given their previous answers, how would they answer the big question: *Can I act differently with this person?*

KATIE: I probably could, but now I'm not so sure I *want* to! Why be with a boyfriend if you can't go to him with your worries or ask him to reassure you from time to time? Maybe I don't want to do this after all . . .

LIZ: I don't think there's any way I can work with this man and not obsess about what he's doing to me. I just don't think I can.

SONDRA: Yes, I think I can act differently with Peter. It might even be good for me to make these changes in myself.

Is He Capable of Acting Differently with Me?

Let's go back for a moment to consider what drives a person to become a gaslighter. A person turns to gaslighting when he feels threatened or stressed, and he responds to that stress by proving he's right. That's the way he feels powerful and strong in the world, and the way he holds on to his sense of who he is.

Some people are deeply committed to gaslighting because of profound insecurities in their sense of self, which lead them to insist upon gaslighting as their normal mode of interaction. They feel so weak that they'll seek every opportunity to manipulate the minds of others in order to feel powerful and in control.

Some people gaslight in certain relationships but not in others. Maybe they turn to gaslighting with their spouses but not with employees. Or perhaps being boss brings out their gaslighter side, whereas they are kind and loving with their spouses.

Still other people gaslight only occasionally, in response to stresses within or outside the relationship. If you're married to a guy like this, he may go for weeks or even months without an episode. Then all of a sudden you have a big fight about money, or he isn't getting along with one of the kids, or he's having trouble at work, or his mother has to go to the hospital, and suddenly, he's gaslighting you.

So here's first question you need to ask about your gaslighter.

*How committed is he to gaslighting?

KATIE: Honestly, I don't know. Sometimes I think he is *very* committed to it—because he keeps doing it! Other times, I see that he stops doing it when I change. I don't know the answer to this.

LIZ: Oh, he's *totally* committed to it—at least with me. I can see that he's the kind of man who always needs to be right and to get his own way. He really enjoys making me jump through all these hoops. I see the way he smiles as I leave the office. I don't think anything will ever get him to change.

SONDRA: I think Peter will probably always turn to gaslighting when he's stressed. But I've made some efforts to turn off the gas, and they've worked pretty well. It helps that we can talk about this problem, and that we both want to change. I would say that Peter is not *committed* to gaslighting, even though it may always be a tendency of his.

As you can see, Liz and Sondra know how to answer this question, but Katie isn't sure. If you're not sure, either, let me suggest the following exercise. For one whole week, make every possible effort to turn off the gas. Don't accept one single invitation to join in the Gaslight Tango. Don't let one opportunity go by to step away from the dance. Avoid all temptations to control, explain, analyze, fantasize about, or even negotiate with your gaslighter. Almost certainly he will at some point try to draw you in to resume the tango. But see what happens if you continue to refuse.

Katie did this experiment, and here's what she found.

KATIE: When I tried for one whole week to turn off the gas, Brian still kept gaslighting me. I could sometimes interrupt the process. But he still kept starting it. I'm beginning to wonder if it's always going to be like this . . .

If you're still not sure about whether your gaslighter can behave differently with you, there's another question you might ask: *How capable is he of relating to me?* Apart from the gaslighting dynamic, do you feel that he sees you as a separate person whom he respects, loves, and listens to? Or does he always seem more concerned with himself—with proving that he's right, showing you what a good guy he is, or demonstrating how romantic he can be? Do you feel connected to him? Or do you feel that often he's simply putting on a show?

If your gaslighter often relates to you in a way you find satisfying, there may be reason to think the gaslighting could end or at least diminish to a level you can live with. But if you realize that the vast majority of your relationship feels disconnected and unsatisfying, your gaslighter may not be able to relate to you in any other way. Even when he's not actively gaslighting you, he may not connect to you with intimacy and respect. In that case, the gaslighting might diminish as you try to Turn Off the Gas, but you still may not find the relationship very satisfying.

*How capable is he of relating to me?

KATIE: I don't know. When we first got together, I thought Brian was the perfect boyfriend. He was protective and loving, and I felt so safe with him! But now I'm starting to wonder. Maybe he was just trying to prove that he was a strong, protective man. And then when he thinks he's failed, he gaslights me. So I guess he's not very capable of really relating to me.

LIZ: I don't know what this man is like with any other person, but he certainly does *not* relate to me. Every single thing he does is for some end of his own, some power play. I don't think he has any idea of me, Liz. I'm just some pawn in his big chess game.

SONDRA: Peter can get so caught up in his own work and his own problems that he sometimes forgets I'm a person, too. That's when he gaslights me. He needs to prove what a good guy he is, and then I'm not a real person to him, just his audience. But there are other times when he definitely keys in to what's going on with me. He'll notice when I'm upset and ask me to talk about it, and then he gives me really helpful advice. He'll see that I'm tired and say, "I'll put the kids to bed tonight. You put your feet up and take some time out." He'll even make dinner for us when I come home from visiting my family— because he's so relieved that *he* doesn't have to go! So yes, I think he's very capable of relating to me; sometimes he can't, but most of the time he can.

> ## How Capable Is Your Gaslighter of Relating to You?
> ## Does he . . .
>
> - seem capable of understanding and respecting your point of view?
> - at least occasionally key in to your feelings and needs?
> - at least occasionally put your feelings and needs ahead of his own?
> - feel remorse about the times he hurts you—in a way that leads him to change his own behavior?
> - show interest in changing for his own reasons, and not simply to please you or to prove what a good guy he is?

Again, I asked Katie, Liz, and Sondra to sum up what they had learned about their gaslighters. How would they answer the big question: *Is he capable of acting differently with me?*

KATIE: I'm not sure. Right now, I would have to say, I don't think so.
LIZ: Definitely not.
SONDRA: Yes, I think he is. Not all the time, but maybe enough of the time.

Am I Willing to Do the Work It Might Take to Change Our Dynamic?

Because gaslighting is so compelling, it seems especially difficult for couples to break free from this dynamic together. Often, gaslighting relationships create a kind of vicious cycle, in which his aggressive behavior provokes your defensive reaction, which in turn triggers even greater aggression from him.

For example, Katie came to realize that her gaslighting relationship progressed from Stage 1 to Stage 2 and then to Stage 3 in large part because of the dynamic that had been established between her and Brian. When she felt anxious and needy, and he felt powerless to help her, he would engage in gaslighting to make himself feel more powerful. In effect, he would try to convince her that she had no reason to be anxious, or that she didn't really *have* any needs, or that she was wrong to have them. But the more angry he became, the more anxious and defensive and needy she became, which only made everything worse.

Thus, when Brian first started accusing her of flirting, Katie was certain that he was mistaken, and she responded accordingly: "Oh, honey, I was *not* flirting!" "Brian, you're being ridiculous, that man was just being friendly." "You really have nothing to worry about. Why can't you see that?" But as Brian's accusations continued, Katie felt her self-confidence slipping away, and she became increasingly anxious and placating in her responses: "*Please*, Brian, take that back!" "I didn't mean anything. You've got to believe me!" "I can't stand your thinking so badly of me. Now I feel terrible!"

Brian was an anxious, insecure man, but he wasn't a monster. It made him genuinely unhappy to see Katie so upset, and he didn't like feeling that he'd been responsible for it. Moreover, as Katie's self-confidence ebbed, she became ever more dependent and needy, desperate for Brian to reassure her and prove he loved her. As we saw, Brian took Katie's desperation very personally; it made him feel powerless to help her and he hated feeling powerless. So the more desperate Katie got, the more bitter, accusing, and negative Brian became. And so their gaslighting relationship moved into Stage 2.

Brian's Stage 2 insults and accusations made Katie feel even more anxious and desperate, and her pleas for reassurance made him feel even *more* powerless and out of control. Why couldn't he make this woman happy? Why couldn't he force this relationship to work? What was *wrong* with him? No, he couldn't be so weak and helpless, he couldn't be such a bad husband or such a failure as a man. The problem *couldn't* be his lack of power—he *had* to be powerful—so there must be something wrong with *her*. Brian's own desperation and insecurity led him to escalate his accusations and attacks, trying even harder to get Katie to agree that he was right and powerful, and she was wrong and bad. So eventually, the relationship moved into Stage 3.

You Might Trigger an Escalation in Gaslighting by . . .

- **Expecting to be put down.**

    "I know, I'm so stupid."

    "Please forgive me, you know I can be really self-absorbed."

    "I can't believe how selfish I've been."

- **Begging for reassurance.**

    "Even though I'm such a mess, you still love me, don't you?"

    "I just get so lonely, honey. Can't you see how much I need you?"

    "I didn't mean to hurt you. Are you still mad?"

- **Assuming he'll treat you badly.**

    "Now don't fly off the handle again."

    "Please don't get jealous. You know there's no reason for it."

    "I know you'll think I'm stupid, but I can't help it, okay?"

Katie was horrified when she realized that her own responses had helped make Brian feel more anxious and behave even more possessively. Even though she realized she wasn't to blame for his actions, she saw that her responses were part of the dynamic they had created together. "I wanted to think I was good for him," she said one day in my office. "But now I'm starting to think I bring out the worst in him—just like he brings out the worst in me."

As we've seen throughout the book, gaslighting usually involves two people who both have a very low tolerance for disagreement. He needs to be right, and you need his approval. He can't stand it that you don't see the world his way, and you can't bear that he thinks so badly of you. Each of you brings an extra intensity of need to your relationship, and this intensity tends to set off another round of the Gaslight Tango. So here are some questions you might ask yourself as you decide whether the two of you can change your dynamic.

*Do I have a support system? As we've seen, gaslighting challenges your ability to distinguish truth from distortion. It's very difficult to challenge a gaslighter without a support system—friends, loved ones, a therapist—to help you maintain your own sense of what's really going on. Here's a related question: *Can I commit to at least one person—therapist, partner, friend, sister, or brother—with whom I can be completely honest about my communication with my gaslighter, and then get honest feedback about what's going on?*

KATIE: I don't feel comfortable talking to my friends about this. But at least I have a therapist I trust!

LIZ: Oh, sure, I have a support system—husband, friends, therapist. But they're all getting pretty tired of hearing about my work problems.

SONDRA: Yes, I have a good support system. I don't always want to hear what they have to say, but I know they'll always be honest with me.

*Do I have the discipline to insist on my limits? We've already established that you can't control him, but you *can* control your own responses. If you're serious about changing the gaslighting aspects of your relationship, you'll need to stick to whatever limits you set, no matter how bad it sometimes feels.

Suppose you tell him, "Honey, I'm tired of your being late, and I'm tired of arguing about it. The next time you're more than twenty minutes late, I'll just leave."

So far, so good. You've set a limit, made yourself clear, and stood up for yourself. Now comes the hard part: You've made reservations at your favorite restaurant, you've been looking forward to this dinner all week . . . and he's twenty minutes late. Do you have the strength to leave? What about the next time it happens? And the next time? And the next? If you don't have that strength—and nobody could blame you if you didn't—you may not be able to change the relationship from within.

KATIE: I can do this. But I'm not so sure I want to.

LIZ: This doesn't apply to me. If I set those kinds of limits with my boss, he'd just fire me. In fact, sometimes I think he's daring me to do just that—so that he *can* fire me.

SONDRA: I have been doing this, and it's been working. It hasn't been easy, but it's definitely worth it.

*Do I have not only the discipline but the energy to say, "Stop it"?
Let's suppose you've told your gaslighter that you don't like being yelled at. So you tell him the next time he yells at you, you're simply going to hang up the phone or walk out of the room—no matter what the circumstances.

You try this approach a few times when you have a quarrel in private, and it works pretty well. You walk away, he cools off, the yelling stops, and you go on together as though nothing had happened. Sometimes he even apologizes, and you feel terrific—things are finally starting to change!

Then one day he yells at you during a family dinner, when both your relatives and his are present. Do you walk away then? What about late one night, when all you want is to go to sleep in your own bed? Do you get up and go sleep on the couch, or maybe go to a motel? What about early one morning, while you're rushing to get ready for work? Wouldn't you rather just wait out the yelling and not make a fuss about it, just this once?

You see the problem. This kind of change takes deep, concerted effort. And not everyone has the energy to make that kind of effort, particularly if she's got other commitments. Are you willing to put that kind of work into saving your relationship, knowing that it might not even pay off? Or does it seem wiser simply to let this partnership go and move on to someone who isn't interested in gaslighting?

KATIE: I have the discipline, but I'm not sure I do have the energy.

LIZ: Again, it doesn't apply to me. I can't take this kind of stand with my gaslighter, because he's my boss. If I don't do what he wants, he'll fire me.

SONDRA: After dealing with my job and the kids all day, it's *hard* to find the energy. This is my least favorite part of the whole process. Frankly, I hate it! But to save my marriage, I'm willing to do it.

*Am I willing to make sacrifices? Sometimes taking the high road in response to a gaslighter means that *you* miss out—on that romantic dinner, that family party, that quiet evening at home. You may feel that you're giving up much of what made your relationship pleasurable or worthwhile, that your efforts to save your relationship are in fact destroying it.

Sticking to your guns may also make you look like the bad guy—the one with no sense of humor, a short temper, a low tolerance for teasing or mistakes. Are you willing to give up some people's good opinion as they judge you for being uptight or intolerant?

KATIE: I *can* do this, but I'm starting to think I *really* don't want to!

LIZ: Well, here's how this question applies to me: Am I willing to sacrifice this position in my company—the position I've worked so hard for—in order to stop the gaslighting? Will I walk away from this wonderful job simply because this awful boss is making my life miserable? I'm beginning to think I might *have* to do this. But it *will* be a sacrifice.

SONDRA: Okay, maybe *this* is my least favorite part. But I can do it if I have to. And I still think this marriage is worth it.

Once again, I asked Katie, Liz, and Sondra to ask themselves the big question: *Am I willing to do the work it might take to change our dynamic?*

KATIE: Now that I see what's involved, I'm not sure I am willing to do all that work and make all those sacrifices. I thought I would do *anything* for Brian . . . But if this is what it takes, I'm not so sure . . .

LIZ: It doesn't matter what I do. This relationship won't change.

SONDRA: I think we've got a good chance of saving our marriage. And yes, I'm willing to do the work involved.

Realistically, if I Give It My Best Effort, Will I Be Happy with Our Relationship?

This is the question that will really tell you what you want to do. Looking realistically at who you are, who your gaslighter is, and what you'll have to do to change your dynamic, is it worth it to you? Will you be getting enough to make all that effort worthwhile? Or will you be working so hard with so little to show for it that you'd be better off just walking away?

As you look at that question, what's your immediate reaction? Can you already hear yourself saying *Stay* or *Go*? Check in with your Flight Attendants—are they happy with the answer you've come up with? If you picture staying, does your whole stomach clench in protest? Do your friends raise their eyebrows or shake their heads and look away? If you imagine leaving, do you feel an overwhelming dread, or does your anxiety lighten? Are your friends horrified, or relieved? It may take a while to read your Flight Attendants' response, but keep paying attention to them and hearing what they have to tell you. I promise, they won't let you down.

Some Flight Attendants Who Might Signal Danger

- Frequent feelings of being bewildered or confused
- Bad or restless dreams
- A troubling inability to remember details of what happened with your gaslighter
- Physical indicators: sinking stomach, tight chest, sore throat, intestinal difficulties
- A sense of dread or hyperalertness when he calls or comes home
- An extra effort to convince yourself or your friends of how good the relationship with your gaslighter really is
- The feeling you're tolerating treatment that compromises your integrity

(continued)

- Trusted friends or relatives who frequently express concern
- Avoidance of your friends or refusal to talk with them about your relationship
- A loss of joy in your life

If you still don't know the answer, it's fine to take more time. Live with the question for a while. See what emerges. You may wake up one morning knowing what to do, or you may hear yourself talking about your relationship as though you'd already made a choice. Or you may need to give yourself a deadline and allow yourself some quiet, focused time to really think this through.

To help you decide, let me share some of the conclusions my patients have come to about whether to stay or go.

Reasons My Patients Have Given for Staying in Their Gaslighting Relationships

- "I really enjoy the conversations I have with my partner."
- "If there's any way to make this relationship work, I owe it to my kids to try."
- "I hadn't realized how much I was participating in the problem. Let's see what happens when I shift my own behavior."
- "We have a long history together."
- "I admire my friend—she has a unique perspective—and I don't want to give up access to her."
- "I'm willing to see my mother less often, but I would feel deprived not seeing her at all."

(continued)

- "I want my kids to know their relatives, and I'm willing to put up with a lot of unpleasantness to make that happen."
- "This job is probably good for another two years. After that, I'm moving on anyway."
- "I think I can still learn more from this work situation, so I'm going to grit my teeth and find a way to make it work."

Reasons My Patients Have Given for Letting Go of Their Gaslighting Relationships

- "I never want to be in a relationship where I can't be proud and comfortable telling people how my partner talks to me and what he does."
- "Being in a relationship is supposed to make your life bigger and richer, and this one has made my life smaller and poorer. Even if that's my own responsibility, I'm still tired of it."
- "I don't want my children to grow up thinking that *this* is what a marriage is."
- "I don't think my friends would recognize me anymore."
- "When I think about him, I'm always anxious."
- "I don't like to be called names. Period."
- "I'm tired of feeling bad all the time."
- "I just don't want to feel this way anymore."
- "I cried all last night. Enough is enough."
- "I'm sick of thinking about this relationship. It's all I ever think about anymore!"

If you're still undecided about what to do, let me make one final suggestion. Turn to the exercise on page 153, the one entitled "WHOM DO YOU ALLOW INTO YOUR WORLD?" Complete this exercise a second time. Then ask yourself: Would you allow your gaslighter into this world? If your heart brightens at the thought, then perhaps you'll want to stay. If your heart sinks or your stomach clenches or you begin to feel numb or exhausted, you may want to leave. And if you really can't decide, consider a trial separation. Some time apart may really clarify the issue for both of you.

Here's how Katie, Liz, and Sondra went on to answer this question: *Realistically, if I give it my best shot, will I be happy with our relationship?*

KATIE: I'm not sure. But I'm starting to think the answer is no. I know our relationship could get better; it's already gotten better. But maybe Brian and I really do bring out the worst in each other. Maybe I have to let it go. I'm going to live with that thought for a few weeks and see how I feel then.

LIZ: I can't *stand* the thought of leaving this job; it just makes me crazy to give up everything I've worked for. But I can see that it's never going to get any better. And I can't keep living like this. It's taken over my whole life. I wish I could make it work. But I can't.

SONDRA: I think Peter and I have a real chance to improve our marriage. And if there's any way I could keep our family together, I would certainly like to. So I'm going to keep working and trying. It's exhausting, but at least I'm getting rewarded for my efforts! Yes, I think, on balance, I'll be happy with the relationship we're likely to have.

Now that you've decided whether to stay or go, you have a new challenge: keeping your life gaslight-free. Whether you're trying to change a gaslighting relationship from within, to limit one, or to leave one, you've got some work ahead of you. I'll help you with that work in Chapter 8.

Keeping Your Life Gaslight-Free

S o now you've understood your own role in the Gaslight Tango and you've found new ways to step away from it. You've learned how to turn off the gas, and perhaps you've even practiced doing it a bit. And you've decided whether to leave your gaslighting relationship, limit it significantly, or try changing it from within.

What's Next?

Your first step is to decide your objective. Are you trying to change your gaslighting relationship from within in the hope of being able to remain at your current level of intimacy—or perhaps even to get closer? Are you trying to limit the intimacy of your relationship so that you can disengage from the gaslighting? Or are you committed to leaving the relationship altogether? Each choice will require a different mindset and set of actions.

If You're Trying to Change a Gaslighting Relationship from Within

Changing a gaslighting relationship from within may be the most challenging option of all, especially if the gaslighting has been going on for a while.

You and your gaslighter have established a powerful dynamic, and you'll need to be prepared for a lot of work and commitment if you want that dynamic to change. Here's what you'll need to do in order to change a gaslighting relationship from within.

*Be committed. Remember, the only way your gaslighting dynamic will change is if *you* change it. Your own changes are not enough, of course. Your gaslighter also has to be willing to behave differently. But if you don't alter your behavior, it will be virtually impossible for him to alter his.

*Be aware. The only way you can behave differently within a gaslighting relationship is by remaining in touch with your own feelings and responses. I'm not suggesting that you let your emotions run you. We all have times when we know our anxiety, sadness, anger, or loneliness is "just a feeling" that doesn't reflect the reality of our lives, just as we all have moments of hope, excitement, and romantic ecstasy that may not quite fit the truth of our relationships. Still, if an emotion persists, it's important to listen to what it's trying to tell you. This is particularly important when two wildly different emotions coexist—hope and despair, joy and sorrow, anxiety and relief. Our tendency, especially in relationships we don't want to leave, is to pay attention only to the good news and ignore the bad—but to keep your life Gaslight-Free, you need to listen to both.

*Be honest. Sometimes we'll be aware of a problem while we're dealing with it but then conveniently forget it as soon as it goes away. In some cases, this might be a very powerful recipe for serenity and joy, but if you're trying to keep your life Gaslight-Free, you might want to work on holding the long view in mind. I suggest keeping a calendar for one month. Every night, jot down a few words or a sentence that sums up your experience of that day, focusing on your gaslighting relationship. At the end of the month, copy the sentences into a chart with three columns: "Positive," "Negative," and "Neutral." Which column is longest? What does your chart reveal about the overall tenor of your month? What conclusions can you honestly draw about your progress—or lack of progress—in changing your relationship and yourself?

***Be disciplined.** Gaslighting dynamics run very deep, and they exert a powerful pull on both parties. If you've been involved in a gaslighting relationship, particularly one that has lasted more than a few weeks, I promise you that there will be many times each of you will be tempted to fall back into old patterns. You probably won't be able to avoid every temptation; you'd be superhuman if you could. But you do need to take a strong tack with yourself, promising yourself to use every possible opportunity to behave differently. (And, as we saw in Chapter 7, if this sounds too difficult, you always have the option of leaving your gaslighting relationship and starting over in one without such a problematic history.)

***Be responsible.** Let me be very clear: I do *not* mean you should take responsibility for your gaslighter's behavior or even for the outcome of your relationship. In fact, that's one of the problems in a gaslighting relationship: Both parties often agree that the gaslightee is responsible for everything that happens. He's three hours late, and you're responsible for being "uptight" about it. He won't tell you how much money he just spent for a family purchase, and you're responsible for being "demanding" and "suspicious." He showers you with presents you don't particularly want, and you're responsible for being "unspontaneous" and "unwilling to receive." So I'm not suggesting that you continue this pattern of behavior—in fact, just the opposite! Take responsibility for your own part in the relationship, and decide what you want to do if you're not getting what you want. If he's late, consider not waiting for him. If he won't give you financial information, consider withdrawing your money from the joint checking account. If he gives you presents you don't want, return them, either to him or to the store. Don't try to change his behavior, but don't accept it passively, either. And if you find this course of action unsatisfying, then accept that you're in a relationship that isn't working for you, and decide what you want to do about that.

*Be compassionate. That goes for your attitude toward both your gas-lighter and yourself. Both of you are going to make mistakes, and both of you are going to act badly, at least some of the time. You don't have to put up with unlimited bad treatment, but if your gaslighter persists in gaslighting you, you can remind yourself that he is also suffering, perhaps even more than you are. After all, he almost certainly grew up in a home where he was gas-lighted by someone and couldn't make it stop—so now he doesn't under-stand why you have the power to say no. You can also treat yourself with compassion, allowing yourself to be vulnerable, needy, flawed—human. Your compassion may not alter your basic decision to leave or stay, but it can cer-tainly alter the tone you take, with both your gaslighter and yourself.

If You're Trying to Limit a Gaslighting Relationship

Sometimes you feel committed to staying in a relationship even though you realize the gaslighting isn't likely to end. Gaslighting relationships with bosses, colleagues, relatives, old friends, and perhaps a spouse you're unwill-ing to divorce may fall into this category. You may also have decided that cer-tain relationships can remain Gaslight-Free when they're more distant but will inevitably involve gaslighting when they become intimate. If you want to limit a gaslighting relationship while remaining within it, these are the qual-ities you'll need to embrace:

*Be analytic. Make a list of all the situations in which gaslighting in this relationship is most likely to happen: family dinners, private time with the gaslighter, year-end reviews, et cetera. Likewise, make a list of topics, and per-haps also times of the day, week, or year, that set off gaslighting. Identify the aspects of the relationship that are most crucial for you to avoid, or, if you can't avoid them, to defend yourself within.

*Be specific. Use your analysis to decide what aspects of the relationship you need to cut back on and what kinds of contact will work for you. Do you simply want to spend less time with this person? To avoid intimate encounters as opposed to more superficial ones? Are you looking to limit particular types of conversation—to not allow your boss to bring up personal topics, for example, or to avoid long, drawn-out discussions with a friend? Would you prefer seeing this person only in large groups, or only in one-on-one situations? Often, with families, certain patterns get triggered when particular family members are present. Do you want to avoid seeing your gaslighter under those circumstances? Sometimes it's useful to have a support person with you when you're dealing with a difficult person; would that be something you'd find helpful? Think clearly about what might help make your limits work for you.

*Be creative. Often, when my patients and I first discuss setting new limits, they explain to me very insistently why something cannot possibly work. If I suggest an alternate way of doing it—one they haven't thought of before—they look at me in surprise, as though I've just pulled the most amazing rabbit out of a hat. It's remarkable how easy it is for our thinking to get stuck in a rut. If you feel trapped by the way your mother always offers you food you can't eat, maybe it would work to meet her in a museum instead of at her house. If your friend insists on bringing up painful topics and you want to keep things light, perhaps you can make the two of you some "light day" vouchers and playfully hand them to her at your next encounter, suggesting that either of you can use one on days when you feel the need to be cheered instead of challenged. Before proving to yourself that something can't be done, see if you can come up with a creative way to work around the problem rather than confront it head-on.

*Be kind AND firm. I wanted to put these two recommendations together because often, those of us with difficulty setting limits tend to think of these qualities as opposites rather than as two sides of the same coin. When we feel defensive, guilty, or apprehensive about setting limits, we tend to overstate our case, and perhaps, in our desperation to be heard, we forget to be kind. If we're absolutely confident and comfortable about setting limits, it's easier to do so kindly. Even if you don't feel confident, this is one of those times when it's good to "fake it till you make it." Remind yourself that you have the right to set any limit you want, and then, secure in the knowledge that you won't give in, maintain that limit as calmly and kindly as you can.

*Be committed.** Remember, you're the one who wants to make the change; your gaslighter would probably prefer to keep things the way they are, at least at first. That means you need to invest extra energy in making sure you get what you want, knowing that you may face a certain amount of opposition.

*Be disciplined.** It can be hard to stick to your guns, especially if your gaslighter resists. But if you don't give a consistent, steady message about the limits you want to set, you can be sure that, within a matter of weeks, your relationship will be right back where it was before. If you are setting limits in order to preserve a relationship, it's especially important that you maintain your discipline (and commitment); otherwise, you risk the relationship degenerating to the point where you really won't be able to stay in it.

*Be compassionate.** As always, I'm inviting you to show compassion toward both your gaslighter and yourself. Neither of you has chosen to be in a difficult situation, and yet, both of you are. Both of you are suffering, and both of you will make mistakes. Try to view yourselves with compassion, even as you proceed with the tough decisions that you may need to make.

If You're Trying to Leave a Gaslighting Relationship

You may have decided that the only way to avoid the gaslighting in your relationship is to end the relationship entirely. Or you may feel that the gaslighting has so eroded your feelings for the gaslighter that you're no longer interested in remaining connected. If you want to end your gaslighting relationship, these are the qualities you'll need to embrace:

*Be in the present.** It hurts to leave a relationship, even one that's no longer making us happy. There's a strong temptation to project that pain into the future. Our unhappiness feels so real, so present, so overwhelming. We can't imagine that we'll ever feel any other way. If we've had a history of bad relationships, we may be even more certain that nothing good can ever happen to us. And if we've invested a great deal in our gaslighter, we may be able to see only how much we're losing. Alas, you probably need to feel all those painful feelings—but you don't need to project them into the future. Remind yourself that you're unhappy *now*—and that's all you know. The future is as mysterious and full of possibilities as it always was. Stay in the present, live one day at a time, and let the future take care of itself.

*Be receptive to help. Don't try to do this alone. Call on your friends, your loved ones, your family. Find a therapist. Take a yoga class. Start meditating. Do something that offers you some of the comfort, serenity, insight, and connection you need. Our culture tends to place a high value on toughing it out and going it alone. I don't believe in that approach. I think accepting help and reaching out in times of trouble actually make us stronger. If you're in the process of leaving a gaslighting relationship, you're doing something very difficult, and I salute you. Salute yourself yourself—and then reach out for help.

*Be patient. Now that you're making this huge change in your personal, professional, or family life, you may want everything to get better right away. You may be looking for vast improvements in your relationships or your career. You may also be expecting yourself to change a great deal—to become someone who will no longer allow herself to be gaslighted. I promise you that you've taken a huge step toward making the changes you seek. But you can be pretty sure they won't all happen right away, and even if they do, that will bring another kind of challenge. So keep breathing—consider that yoga class!—and be patient. It's taken you your whole life to get to this point; allow yourself a bit more time to complete the process you've begun.

*Be compassionate. I know I've ended every list with this suggestion, but that's because I feel it's crucial, no matter what course of action you choose. It can be very healing to show compassion toward your gaslighter—and even more so to express it toward yourself. Don't allow yourself to say mean things about yourself, or to be cruel, unforgiving, or contemptuous. Accept that you've done the best you can, and offer yourself the compassion you deserve.

Rewriting Your Responses

Now that you've taken action on your most pressing gaslight relationships, how do you make sure that you don't repeat the experience? The key to remaining gaslight-free is not to let your self-worth depend on someone else's approval. If there is even one little part of you that wants the approval of another person to make you feel better about yourself, boost your confidence, or bolter your sense of who you are in the world, then you are a gaslightee waiting for a gaslighter. So developing a strong, clear sense of yourself and your worth is crucial to staying out of gaslighting relationships.

Here are other long-term suggestions for keeping your life gaslight-free:

- Listen to your inner voice (take time to daydream, walk, reflect).
- Write in a journal.
- Keep talking to trusted friends.
- If you're tempted to engage in a gaslighting relationship, think about what a trusted mentor or role model might say to you.
- Ask yourself: Is this guy good enough for my daughter/ sister/ mother?
- Practice positive self-talk. Tell yourself, truthfully, what's good and admirable about yourself.
- Nurture yourself by connecting with your spirit. Make time for prayer, meditation, or simple quiet times to reconnect to your deepest self.
- Recall your values, the ways you believe people ought to treat each other.
- Spend time with people who affirm your spirit.
- Believe that "No" is a whole sentence, and use it more often.
- Take up some form of strengthening physical activity.
- Find an assertiveness class or leadership training workshop where you

can sharpen your skills in effective communication, advocacy for yourself, and negotiation.

- Do only what you want to do. If you're ambivalent, say no; you will feel
  the strength of your convictions.
- Make use of the exercises in this book that strengthen and clarify your
  mind, emotions, and spirit. I particularly invite you to avail yourself of
  that image of the beautiful house surrounded by the gate that only you
  can open (see page 153). Practice letting in the right people and keeping
  out the wrong ones whenever you feel your commitment weakening. Remember that you have *total* control over who comes into your "house," and
  resolve not to let anyone inside who doesn't feel right to you. Promise
  yourself that you won't have even a single conversation in this house that
  feels wrong.

Considering the Future

As you look toward a gaslight-free future, I believe there's one more shift you
can make that will help keep gaslighting out of your life. You might look
more closely at the aspects of gaslighting that make it so attractive and ask
yourself why you find them so compelling.

In my experience, in both my own gaslighting relationships and those I've
observed among patients, friends, and colleagues, gaslighting often holds a
powerful allure beyond the ones we've already discussed. We often feel that
our gaslighting relationships offer us the promise of something more intense, more glamorous, and more special than other connections; the very
difficulty of the relationships is part of their charm.

Think for a moment of the movie *Gaslight*. Paula, the Ingrid Bergman character, falls deeply in love with Gregory because she believes he will offer her
the haven she's been seeking all her life—and she's certainly had a rocky life.
Orphaned young and raised by her beloved aunt, Paula was then traumatized
by her aunt's murder when Paula was still a child. Having lost all the people
who ever took care of her, Paula was sent away from her childhood home to
study in a strange country with another language. She longs for a relation-

ship that will replace the caretakers she has lost, and she brings a special intensity to her need for Gregory, whom she needs not just to love her but to save her.

I believe that many of us come to relationships—in love, friendship, work, and family—with an underlay of that "extra" wish for not just the present connection but also a way to repair the past. It's as though we're starving for a certain type of care, understanding, appreciation, and the gaslighter somehow promises to feed us. No food ever tastes as good as when you're really hungry for it, and the very depth of our hunger for connection can give our gaslighter a kind of savior quality: He's the one who will make us whole, rescue us from loneliness, assure us that someone really does understand. Or perhaps he's the one who will help us prove that we are effective adults in the world, or lovable friends; perhaps he's the one who will assure us that we matter to someone, or that we really are good people after all. Whatever we're longing for, the gaslighter somehow seems to fulfill, and that may make the good times—or even the promise of the good times—more special than anything else in our world. We may also love feeling that we can do the same for him.

Then, as we consider leaving our gaslighting relationships and keeping our lives gaslight-free, we long for that specialness and wonder whether we'll ever have it again. We wonder if our next lover will be as sexually attractive to us, or if he'll seem to be our soul mate, as this one was—or might have been. We wonder if our next good friend will be a "best friend for life" the way our gaslighter was. We wonder if we'll ever have a job that makes us feel as competent, as successful, as glamorous. We wonder if, having given up on a family connection—even if we remain in contact with the person in question—anyone else in our lives will provide us with the security and boundless love that we'd always hoped to get from that person, and maybe sometimes thought we did get.

The answer to all those questions may indeed be no. If we no longer approach relationships out of that great hunger, they may not feel so special, so satisfying. The overpowering relief of ending starvation probably is greater than the simple pleasure of eating something delicious. The thrill of living in combat, of coping with a life-and-death situation, is surely deeper than the ordinary excitement of facing a new day. If we feel compelled to put our emotional lives at risk, if we involve ourselves with unpredictable people, if we view our personal and professional relationships as opportunities to make up for past injuries, then no, simply living in the present with satisfying people and challenging work may not feel as intense, as special, as wonderful.

So as you look toward the future and think about keeping your life gaslight-free, consider whether this extra thrill of emergency, this extra depth of longing, is really something you want to give up. If you don't, you may indeed find yourself attracted to other gaslighting situations, though you may be able to resist them now that you know more about them and about yourself. But if you've had enough of situations in which your entire emotional life is on the line, you may have to accept that you won't feel as intensely about future relationships—though you may very well derive deeper and more lasting satisfactions from them.

This isn't something you have to decide immediately, and it may not be something you decide consciously. But I do believe it's a significant part of keeping your life gaslight-free over the long term, so keep it in mind as you go on to choose new relationships and professional challenges.

Keeping Things in Perspective

Now that you've changed, limited, or left a gaslighting relationship, you may feel another type of trepidation about getting involved with someone else, whether as lover, friend, or employer/colleague. "How do I know," you may be thinking, "when a problem is just 'one of those things,' and when it's a warning sign of gaslighting?"

Indeed, every relationship has its ups and downs, its times when we don't feel heard, its periods when we feel ourselves being dismissed, discounted, ignored. Seeking that perfect union of love and understanding is part of what got us into gaslighting relationships in the first place. So now, how do we distinguish between ordinary imperfections and serious flaws?

I have two suggestions for those of you who are concerned about this question. First, look at your relationship over time. *On balance,* do you feel heard, appreciated, effective within the relationship? *On balance,* do you feel you're getting what you want? Any one incident may not be that important in the grand scheme of things, but is there a pattern of your being discounted and dismissed, or would you say the relationship is characterized by your being heard and respected?

Second, look within, to your Flight Attendants. When you think about your relationship, do you feel joy, pleasure, satisfaction? Or do you feel anxiety, trepidation, uncertainty? Do you feel a wild mix of highs and lows—the glamour of falling in love alongside the agony of being mistreated? Or do you feel a steady glow of appreciation and pleasure, even though there are also some things you don't like about your partner/friend/boss and the way he or she treats you?

Some Flight Attendants Who Might Signal Danger

- Frequent feelings of being bewildered or confused
- Bad or restless dreams
- A troubling inability to remember details of what happened with your gaslighter
- Physical indicators: sinking stomach, tight chest, sore throat, intestinal difficulties
- A sense of dread or hyperalertness when he calls or comes home
- An extra effort to convince yourself or your friends of how good the relationshiop with your gaslighter really is
- The feeling you're tolerating treatment that compromises your integrity

(continued)

- Trusted friends or relatives who frequently express concern
- Avoidance of your friends or refusal to talk with them about your relationship
- A loss of joy in your life

I would say that if you consistently feel your interactions with a particular person discount you and what's important to you, go with that feeling and get out of the relationship. Even if you are just "being neurotic," as so many people worry they are—even if the relationship is theoretically fine and the problem is that you're too anxious, critical, or demanding—your best bet may still be to leave the relationship that is making you feel so crazy and then address whatever was preventing you from enjoying it. Manipulating your own sense of reality—telling yourself that you *should* be feeling something you aren't—is never a good idea. Even if the problem *is* with you, you'll be better off solving the problem than trying to talk yourself out of how you feel.

Living with Integrity

Part of remaining gaslight-free is being vigilant about how, in general, you're living your life. Are you constantly preoccupied by the last fight you had with your boyfriend, your mother, your boss, or are you focusing on the life *you* want to lead, a life of integrity, fulfillment, and joy? Gaslighting takes up a tremendous amount of our mental, emotional, and spiritual energy. Committing to using that energy for the goals and dreams that really matter to us can help keep us gaslight-free.

New Possibilities

Mariana, my patient involved in a gaslighting relationship with her friend Sue, worked very hard at rewriting the rules of that relationship. After her initial month of withdrawal from Sue, she reentered the friendship determined to start responding differently. When Sue would try to initiate a long, painful discussion, Mariana would simply disengage, saying something like "I've heard your concerns, and I don't feel we need to go any further." If she herself felt anxious about disagreeing with Sue or seeming to be misunderstood, she would force herself to detach rather than reach out to Sue for reassurance. And if she did something that Sue objected to, Mariana would look rigorously at her own behavior, decide what she herself thought, apologize if necessary, and move on. She didn't allow Sue to pass judgment on her, and she didn't expect Sue to absolve her of guilt.

To Mariana's surprise, both women began enjoying the friendship more. Although there were times that each of them seemed tempted to return to their old patterns, Mariana stayed committed to avoiding the Gaslight Tango, and for the most part, she succeeded. Her reward was the reworking of a long and durable friendship that meant a great deal to both women, even as the relationship became less intense and all-consuming.

SONDRA, TOO, SUCCEEDED in rewriting her relationship with her husband. She and Peter began spending more time together in ways that they both really enjoyed rather than eating up their time with obligations. Sondra found that a lot of stress was relieved by agreeing that Peter would not be spending much time with her family, which for some reason he found very difficult. As they cut back on their joint trips to her family, Peter also became able to spend less time with his own family—and as a result, he seemed happier and more at peace. Sondra realized that Peter's mother had probably gaslighted him in ways similar to his gaslighting of Sondra, so reducing those family ties was good for both of them.

Sondra also had to learn to change her own behavior. She needed to stop taking out her anxieties about the children on Peter, which gave him the un-intended message that he wasn't a good father. She also needed to take more time for herself, allowing herself to find sources of joy and pleasure besides her family: long walks in the country, with or without Peter; a yoga class she signed up for; more time set aside to have coffee with her friends. Drawing upon a wider support system made it easier for Sondra to opt out of the gaslighting with Peter, which in turn made it easier for him to stop gaslight-ing. Although there's still work ahead of them, Sondra is extremely opti-mistic about her marriage. And she's no longer feeling numb!

KATIE WASN'T SO LUCKY. As she came to look more clearly at her relationship with Brian, she could see that they did, indeed, bring out the worst in each other. Brian's aggressive, negative attitudes tended to make Katie feel defensive, anxious, and needy, while those very qualities provoked Brian's own insecurities and frustrations. Katie came to believe that the two of them would never be able to create a happy, loving relationship together, that they would always be locked in the Gaslight Tango, simply by the way they pushed each other's buttons. She realized that if she stayed with Brian, she would never have lasting joy in her life, whereas if she left, she would at least have the possibility of finding it.

After Katie broke up with Brian, it took her a while to find someone else. In large part that was because she wanted to be sure she really had rewritten her responses to men and romantic relationships. She came to see a pattern in her love life of choosing difficult men who saw her as the only one who un-derstood them. Katie had felt comforted by being special and needed; now she saw that the price she paid for this version of closeness was to be treated possessively and often angrily by men who felt isolated and anxious. If no one else in their world could understand them, that made Katie extremely important, but it also put her under enormous pressure.

"If I succeeded, I was on top of the world," Katie told me one day as she looked back on this pattern. "But when I failed, I felt like the worst person alive. *Why* couldn't I make this man happy? He had depended on me and

I had failed. How could I be such a terrible person? And because they were all such unhappy guys, of course I was going to fail—there was a good reason nobody else had ever made them happy. I guess I liked thinking I could succeed where others had failed. But I didn't like always failing myself."

Eventually, Katie went on to a new relationship that she described as "less intense, less of a soul mate thing," but, in the end, more satisfying. "I don't have to think about Will all the time," she told me, "and in a way I kind of miss that. I still kind of feel like being 'in love'—you know, that kind of 'in love' where all you can think about is *him* and what's going to happen next. With Will, I don't have to think about it—I know he'll just sort of be there. Sometimes I feel like I'm missing something. Most of the time, I'm pretty happy."

LIZ ALSO DECIDED to leave her gaslighting relationship at work. For Liz, the change was extremely painful. Leaving the top position she'd worked so hard for made her question her entire working life. Although she understood rationally that her boss was a manipulative gaslighter who had simply triumphed in a professional contest, she felt overwhelmed by a sense of failure and worthlessness. "What was the point of working that hard?" she kept asking me. And "Why *couldn't* I make it work?"

Eventually, after several months of agonizing, Liz came to see that in many ways her job at the ad agency hadn't been the perfect fit for her after all. She wondered whether she'd pushed so hard for professional achievement because she hadn't found the work itself very satisfying. The more dissatisfied she felt, the harder she worked, almost as though she was trying to force her work life to give her the satisfaction that eluded her. Being pushed aside by her latest boss came to seem like the last straw, the final insult in a long series of frustrations and disappointments.

Liz is still trying to figure out what she wants to do next. Freed from the pressure to make an impossible situation work out, she now has the emotional space to look around and see what kind of work might better fit her true talents, values, and tastes. "I don't know what's coming next," she told me recently. "But whatever it is, I'm excited."

AS FOR MITCHELL, he eventually decided not to cut his mother out of his life but to severely limit contact with her. He resolved to see her only in the company of his girlfriend or another friend, who might at least provide moral support when his mother began to speak to him dismissively. He stopped going to his parents' house for dinner every week, though he still visits at least once a month. And he continues to struggle with the sadness and anger he still feels about his relationship with his parents.

The good news for Mitchell is that, as he made these decisions about his family, the rest of his life took off. As he started to speak up for himself and become more emotionally present, his relationship with his girlfriend deepened, and for the first time, Mitchell felt secure in a relationship outside his family. He also found himself making some new friends with a sense of confidence he'd never felt before. And as he became more assertive, his grad-school situation improved as well. His professors seemed to have more respect for him, and one of them became more of a mentor, offering Mitchell some professional opportunities that had eluded him before. Although Mitchell's relationship with his mother is still fraught and unhappy, turning off the gas brought him another set of satisfactions.

SO NOW YOU have the opportunity to keep your life gaslight-free and go on to a new future. You have the chance to rework or leave unsatisfying relationships and choose new relationships that feed your sense of self, your vitality, and your joy. You have the chance to become a stronger, more solid person who charts her own course and lives by her own values. Most important, you have the chance to discover what you truly want—in your work, your home life, your relationships, and yourself. Freed from the Gaslight Effect, you can make better choices, choices that are right for you. As you begin this exciting new portion of your life's journey, I wish you strength and spirit and all the luck in the world.

Know Your Emotions

Build a "Feelings Vocabulary"

Gaslighting often leads women to repress their feelings or even to become completely out of touch with them. But if you don't know how you feel, you've lost touch with a key source of energy that can help you stand up for yourself and make it clear to both your gaslighter and yourself how you'd like to be treated. Knowing your feelings can help you get in touch with the energy you need either to improve or to leave your gaslighting relationship.

The first step toward knowing what you're feeling is having the words to express it. A feelings vocabulary can help you get in touch with your emotions. Then, when you're ready to tell your gaslighter how you feel and what you want, you'll have the words right there.

Consider the words in the following list. Do any of them apply to you? Can you add more words that describe how you feel?

abandoned	appreciated	creative
adequate	bad	curious
affectionate	bored	defeated
ambivalent	comfortable	dejected
anxious	confident	dependent

depressed

desperate

determined

disappointed

discontented

ecstatic

embarrassed

energetic

excited

exhausted

exhilarated

fearful

frantic

frustrated

glad

good

grateful

guilty

happy

hostile

inadequate

incompetent

independent

infatuated

inferior

insecure

intimidated

isolated

jealous

judgmental

lonely

lovable

loving

miserable

misunderstood

needy

nervous

optimistic

outraged

overwhelmed

paranoid

pleasant

preoccupied

rejected

relieved

satisfied

shocked

shy

silly

sluggish

stunned

threatened

thwarted

tired

touched

troubled

uncertain

uneasy

uptight

violent

vulnerable

wonderful

worried

Regaining Your Voice

Your feelings are a prime source of energy in standing up for yourself and making it clear to your gaslighter how you want to be treated. But it's hard to know your feelings if you can't say how you're feeling, even to yourself. Try the following exercise to help get in touch with your feelings and your ability to express them. Once you've found your voice, you'll be able to speak up to your gaslighter with a new power and clarity that may transform your relationship—or that may, if you choose, give you the power to end it.

Step One

Take a look at the following statements. Do any of them describe the way you're feeling?

- "I don't know how I feel."
- "I feel numb."
- "I don't know what I want."
- "I don't know what would help."
- "I guess I feel kind of weird."
- "I feel flat."
- "I feel pretty down. I don't know why."
- "I'm just not into sex anymore."
- "I don't like being married anymore."
- "My job isn't very satisfying."
- "I feel out of it."
- "I'm angry all the time."
- "Everything seems to get on my nerves."
- "I'm just not having a good time anymore."
- "I'm depressed."

Step Two

Pick the statement with which you most identify. Write it on a separate page. Then pick one of the following phrases:

- I feel this way because —
- This feeling began when —
- This feeling continues because —
- If I *didn't* feel this way, I would —
- What might change or end this feeling is —
- What I want most right now is —

Step Three

Copy the phrase of your choice under the statement. Then set a timer for fifteen minutes and force yourself to write for the whole time without stopping. You can begin by completing the sentence, or you can write anything you like. Just don't stop writing. If you don't know what to say, just keep writing the phrase—or some other phrase—over and over and over again. Sooner or later, something new will emerge.

If you do just keep repeating the same old phrases, try this exercise again the next day and every day, until you find yourself writing something new. (It's fine to pick a different statement and/or a different phrase each time you do the exercise.) Knowing your feelings and expressing them clearly will help move you toward taking healthy, positive actions for yourself.

Draw Your Feelings

Just as being able to speak your feelings helps you connect with them—and with the energy to stand up for yourself—so does expressing your feelings in a different way. If you're more comfortable with drawing than with speaking, try this exercise to help you clarify how you're feeling, which may help you take positive action to turn off the gas.

Step One

Label a blank page "My Point of View." Under that title, draw a picture or design that expresses how you feel about your situation or about a particular problem you've been having with your gaslighter. Label a second blank page "His Point of View," and make a similar drawing showing the situation from his perspective.

Step Two

Sometimes it's important to give yourself time to sit with your feelings and see how they affect you. So put both pages away for twenty-four hours. When you look at them again, have another blank page ready. Write down whatever thoughts and feelings arise from this second viewing. Perhaps this new perspective on your feelings will help you discover an unexpected inner resolve to take action and stand up for yourself.

Visualize Your Relationship

This exercise will help you understand your relationship better so that you have a better sense of what decisions you want to make about it. If you can visualize exactly what is going on with your relationship, you can decide whether to stay, to leave, or to start taking the actions that are part of turning off the gas. But in order to make those decisions, you have to know how your relationship makes you feel. Visualizing your current relationship will help you know that.

If there are problems in your relationship, visualizing your past relationship will make it clear to you how serious the problems are. If your relationship was once good and has since changed, you can decide whether it's realistic to regain the good elements while changing the bad ones. If you discover that your relationship has always upset you or frustrated you or left you feeling lonely, you can decide whether it's realistic to expect it to get better.

Visualizing your future relationship will help you get in touch with how you truly feel and what you genuinely think about the possibilities your relationship holds. Is there a real chance of making it good, or can you not even imagine being happy within it? Asking these questions will bring you closer to a decision about whether to stay or leave, as will visualizing the future without your gaslighting relationship. If you like that future better than the alternative, maybe it's time to leave.

Finally, evaluating your relationship can help you decide what you want to do. Perhaps you need to choose between staying or leaving. Or perhaps you'd like to try turning off the gas. Perhaps you'd like to give your relationship a time limit: If it hasn't improved by a certain point, then you'll reconsider and take new action. Whatever you choose, evaluating your relationship can help you come to a decision that is right for you.

Visualize Your Current Relationship

Close your eyes and allow yourself to think about your current relationship with your gaslighter. What images come to mind? What emotions wash over you? How do you see yourself? How do you see him? Don't censor or judge any of the images, thoughts, or feelings that come to mind. Just allow your mind to drift where it will and then notice where it takes you.

When you've finished, open your eyes and complete each of the following sentences. Write as much or as little as you like. If you prefer, you can draw a picture or create an image that expresses your response.

- The thing I like most about [my gaslighter] is _____.
- The thing I like least about [my gaslighter] is _____.
- Qualities I value in [my gaslighter] are _____.
- Qualities I value in myself when I am with [my gaslighter] are _____
  _____.
- When I'm frustrated with [my gaslighter], I wish I could change _____
  _____.
- When I see us together, I'm most struck by _____.
- My Flight Attendants are telling me _____.
- As I write these answers, I feel _____.
- Right now, my body feels _____.

Visualize Your Past Relationship

Now close your eyes and allow yourself to think about your past relationship with your gaslighter. What images come to mind? What emotions wash over you? How do you see yourself? How do you see him? Again, don't censor or judge any of the images, thoughts, or feelings that come to mind. Just allow your mind to drift where it will as you notice where it takes you.

When you've finished, open your eyes and complete each of the following sentences.

- The thing I like most about our past relationship is _____.
- The thing I like least about our past relationship is _____.
- Something I'd like to recapture from that time is _____.
- Something I never want to repeat again is _____.
- When I look at [my gaslighter] back then, I see a person who _____ _____.
- When I look at myself back then, I see a person who _____.
- When I see us together, I see a couple [pair of friends, set of colleagues, mother and daughter, et cetera] who _____.
- My Flight Attendants are telling me _____.
- As I write these answers, I feel _____.
- Right now, my body feels _____.

Visualize Your Future Relationship

Once again close your eyes and open your mind. Allow yourself to think about a possible future relationship with your gaslighter. Visualize the two of you together next month, next year, five years from now. What images appear? What emotions emerge? Is your gaslighter someone you'd like to be involved with, as partner, friend, employee/colleague, family member? Most important, are you the person you'd most like to be? Are you on the way to reaching your full potential, fulfilling your dreams, savoring the joy in your life? Are you imagining a future full of possibility and excitement, or do you find yourself feeling dread, anxiety, or regret? Again, don't censor or judge anything that comes to your mind. Just keep asking yourself to visualize the future and see what comes up.

When you've finished, open your eyes and complete each of the following sentences.

- The thing I like most about the future I imagine is _____.
- Something that concerns me about the future I imagine is _____.
- The person I want to become is someone who _____.
- My future relationship will help me become that person by _____.
- My future relationship may prevent me from becoming that person by _____.
- My Flight Attendants are telling me _____.
- As I write these answers, I feel _____.
- Right now, my body feels _____.

Visualize Your Future Without Your Gaslighting Relationship

For the last time, close your eyes and allow your mind to wander, this time, toward a possible future relationship without your gaslighter. Visualize yourself without this relationship (or with a far more limited version of it) next month, next year, five years from now. Now what images appear? What emotions emerge? Who are the important people in your life? What activities preoccupy you? How are you feeling? What are you doing? Most important, are you the person you'd most like to be? Without censoring or judging, allow yourself to imagine a possible future without your gaslighting relationship as you know it now.

When you've finished, open your eyes and complete each of the following sentences.

- The thing I like most about the future I imagine is _____.
- Something that concerns me about the future I imagine is _____.
- The person I want to become is someone who _____.
- Not being in my gaslighting relationship (or being in a much more limited version of it) will help me become that person by _____.
- Not being in my gaslighting relationship may prevent me from becoming that person by _____.
- My Flight Attendants are telling me _____.
- As I write these answers, I feel _____.
- Right now, my body feels _____.

Evaluate Your Relationship

Now that you've thought about the past, present, and future of your gaslighting relationship, let's zero in on a possible evaluation of how that relationship is working for you and how you imagine it might work in the future. So grab that pen and paper, and complete the following sentences. Remember, you can write as much or as little as you like.

- When I imagine describing my relationship to my Flight Attendants—my surest guides to what's going on—I hear myself saying _____.
- When I imagine my Flight Attendants witnessing my relationship, what they see is _____.
- I'm picturing a child, younger sibling, or some other child I'm close to, and I'm imagining that child growing up and being in a relationship just like mine. When I imagine this, I feel _____.
- Since I've been in this gaslighting relationship, I feel I've become more _____.
- Since I've been in this gaslighting relationship, I feel I've become less _____.
- When I think about how being in this relationship has affected me, I feel _____.

Now take a new sheet of paper and draw a line down the middle. Over the left-hand column, write, "I might want to keep this relationship because . . ." Over the right-hand column, write, "I might want to let go of this relationship because . . ." Complete both columns. If you like, come back to this part of the exercise over the next several days, as you think of more pros and cons.

Finally, when you've completed all the other steps, take one last sheet of paper. At the top write, "Do I want to stay in this relationship or let it go?" Fill the blank part of the page any way you like—with words, images, sentences, or symbols. Or you can leave the page blank and simply look at the question for a while. Allow yourself to live with the question until an answer emerges that is right for you.

Take Care of Yourself

An Antistress and Antidepression Diet

People struggling with gaslighting relationships also often suffer from stress and/or depression. As you figure out what's going on and what to do about it, it's important to take care of yourself. Consult a nutritionist, or try the following antistress and antidepression diet, which may help you think more clearly and feel more empowered.

- Eat three meals and two snacks a day. Low blood-sugar levels can make you feel confused and hopeless, so keep your spirits up by eating at least every three hours. Make sure each meal and snack contains some high-quality protein: lean meat, fish, eggs, low-fat dairy products, or tofu.
- Eat plenty of whole grains, legumes, low-fat dairy products, fresh fruits, and vegetables. Grains, legumes, and dairy products help your brain manufacture serotonin and other vital hormones that fight depression and boost feelings of self-esteem and empowerment. Fresh fruits and vegetables provide key vitamins and minerals that your brain needs to think clearly.
- Make sure you're getting enough omega-3 fats, found in fish and flax. Studies have shown that omega-3s play a vital role in combating depres-

sion. The hormones they help produce support your self-esteem, feelings of hopefulness, and a sense of empowerment.

For more support on diet, I suggest checking out *The Chemistry of Joy* by Henry Emmons, M.D., with Rachel Kranz, and *Potatoes, Not Prozac* by Kathleen desMaisons.

Supplements for Stress and Depression

The following supplements may help your brain manufacture the chemicals and hormones it needs to respond to stress, withstand depression, and help you think clearly.

- *A daily dose of good vitamin B complex that contains at least*
  - 10 to 15 mg of B_6
  - 400 mcg of folic acid
  - 20 to 100 mcg of B_{12}
- *1000 to 3000 mg of fish oil, taken daily*
- *120 to 250 mg of vitamin C, taken twice daily*
- *400 mg of vitamin E, taken daily, with food*
- *25,000 IU of beta-carotene, taken daily in a supplement of mixed carotenoids*
- *200 mcg selenium, taken daily*

If you're not taking an antidepressant, you can add 50 mg of 5-HTP every night. This supplement will help your brain make serotonin, a hormone that helps you sleep, builds self-esteem, and calms anxiety. If you don't notice any side effects for a few days, increase your dose to 150 mg each night or take 50 to 100 mg three times a day.

WARNING: Do not take 5-HTP if you are taking a prescription antidepressant, and do not stop your prescription antidepressant in order to take 5-HTP. If you are under a physician's care for depression, inform him or her before taking 5-HTP.

For more support on supplements, again, see *The Chemistry of Joy* by Henry Emmons M.D., with Rachel Kranz, and *Potatoes, Not Prozac* by Kathleen desMaisons.

Sleep for Empowerment and Mood Enhancement

Sleep is important, and never more than when you're undergoing a stressful time. You need all your resources to combat gaslighting, so make sure you're getting at least eight hours of sleep each night. If you're having trouble falling or staying asleep, try to develop a calming bedtime routine; avoid caffeine, other stimulants, and alcohol, even early in the day; eat a healthy carbohydrate snack (milk, fruit, nuts, cereal, whole-grain bread, or brown rice) about an hour before bedtime, and consider a natural sleep aid, such as valerian or melatonin.

Most Americans are relatively sleep-deprived and get at least an hour less sleep than they need each night. Just improving your sleep patterns may go a long way toward giving you the strength you need to think clearly and take new actions. However, if you're sleeping more than ten or eleven hours a day, you may want to restrict your sleep to eight or nine hours. In some cases, excess sleep feeds depression and supports a sense of sluggishness and lassitude.

Exercise for Empowerment and Mood Enhancement

The positive benefits of exercise are enormous. Exercise helps you release stress, build brain-healthy hormones, improve sleep, and generally increase your sense of self-empowerment and self-esteem. See if you can give yourself at least fifteen minutes a day of mild aerobic exercise—a brisk walk will do. If you can, work your way up to thirty minutes a day, five days a week, but if this feels like an impossible goal, start small. Even a five-minute daily walk will make you feel better than you do now. And if you're already getting regular exercise? Good for you! That is one positive step you are taking to support your brain chemistry, your emotional balance, and your sense of self.

Hormonal Cycles and Antidepressants

Our bodies and brain chemistry have a great impact on how we feel, which is why I've suggested paying attention to diet, exercise, sleep, and other physical factors in your mood. You may also want to consider how hormonal issues are affecting your mental and emotional condition. Some women have intense responses during the premenstrual portion of their cycles or during ovulation—times when you may feel either more despairing about changing your situation or more desperate about wishing to change. You may find yourself changing your mind about whether you want to make changes—and whether you have the energy to make changes—depending on where you are in your cycle. Many women also experience intense feelings in response to the hormonal fluctuations of perimenopause and menopause.

If you feel that a hormonal imbalance may be making it more difficult for you to see your situation clearly, you might seek the help of a physician and/or an alternative practitioner. A medical doctor can prescribe hormone replacement therapy or other supplementation. A naturopath, nutritionist, or herbal healer (including many acupuncturists and specialists in Chinese and Ayurvedic medicine) can suggest natural products that might help balance your hormones. (The herb pau d'arco, available as a capsule, tablet, or tea, is one of the most potent. I have friends who swear by it.)

If you feel that your brain is foggy and your emotions are out of whack, you may want to see a physician or psychiatrist about prescribing anti-depressants. Antidepressants should always be taken in conjunction with a brain-healthy diet and exercise plan, such as the one I've just outlined. They should always be taken in conjunction with a therapist's care, and they should never be seen as a long-term solution. But they can bring you some short-term breathing room in which you have the opportunity to see life from a more empowered, upbeat place. The most common antidepressants—selective serotonin reuptake inhibitors (SSRIs), including Celexa, Luvox, Paxil, Zoloft, and Prozac—have also been shown in many cases to boost self-esteem, especially among people who have been chronically depressed.

Resources

Domestic and Emotional Abuse Resources

National Domestic Violence Hotline (http://www.ndvh.org/)
1-800-799-SAFE (7233); 1-800-787-3224 (TTY)

The Emotional Abuse Institute (http://www.martiloring.org/)
Dr. Marti Loring LCSW, PhD, Executive Director
Phone: (404) 377-7732; Fax: (404) 377-0590

Safe Horizon (http://www.safehorizon.org/)
1-800-621-HOPE (4673)

State Coalition List—The National Coalition Against Domestic Violence
(http://www.ncadv.org/resources/StateCoalitionList__73.html)

Women's Law Initiative (http://www.womenslaw.org/)
1-800-799-SAFE (7233); 1-800-787-3224 (TTY)

Fostering Leadership from Girlhood to Womanhood

Girls Leadership Institute (http://www.girlsleadershipinstitute.org/)
Phone: (401) 878-2258

The Woodhull Institute for Ethical Leadership (http://www.woodhull.org/)
Phone: (646) 495-6060; Fax: (646) 495-6059

Educate and Empower Yourself
Through Social and Emotional Learning

6 Seconds Emotional Intelligence Network (http://www.6seconds.org/)
Phone: (650) 685-9885; Fax: (650) 685-9880

The Collaborative for Academic, Social, and Emotional Learning (http://www.casel.org/)
Phone: (312) 413-1008; Fax: (312) 355-4480

Daniel Goleman, author of *Emotional Intelligence* (http://www.daniel goleman.info/)

The Consortium for Research on Emotional Intelligence in Organizations (http://eiconsortium.org/)

Mind, Body, and Spirit: Nationwide Resources

Angels Arrien, author of *The Four-Fold Way*—Reflections (http://www.angelsarrien.com/)

The Garrison Institute—Retreats (http://www.garrisoninstitute.org/)
Phone: (845) 424-4800; Fax: (845) 424-4900

International Taoist Tai Chi Society (http://taoist.org/english/directory/)
Phone: (850) 224-5438

National Women's Health Resource Center (http://www.healthywomen .org/)
(877) 986-9472 (toll-free)

Sharon Salzberg, author of *Lovingkindness*—Meditations (http://www.sharonsalzberg.com/)

Yoga Alliance (www.yogaalliance.org)
(877) 964-2255 (toll free); (301) 868-7909 (fax)

Bibliography

Allen, J. G., H. Stein, P. Fonagy, J. Fultz, and M. Target. (Winter 2005). Rethinking Adult Attachment: A Study of Expert Consensus. *Bulletin of the Menninger Clinic* 69 (1): 59–80.

Alter, R. M. (2006). *It's (Mostly) His Fault: For Women Who Are Fed Up and the Men Who Love Them*. New York: Warner Books.

Arrien, A. (1993). *The Four-Fold Way: Walking the Paths of the Warrior, Teacher, Healer and Visionary*. New York: HarperSanFrancisco.

Bacal, H. (1998). *Optimal Responsiveness: How Therapists Heal Their Patients*. Northvale, N.J.: Aronson.

Basch, M. F. (1980). *Doing Psychotherapy*. New York: Basic Books.

Bateson, M. C. (2000). *Full Circles, Overlapping Lives: Culture and Generation in Transition*. 1st ed., New York: Random House.

Baumgardner, J., and A. Richards. (2000). *Manifesta: Young Women, Feminism, and the Future*. 1st ed., New York: Farrar, Straus & Giroux.

Bennett-Goleman, T. (2001). *Emotional Alchemy: How the Mind Can Heal the Heart*. New York: Harmony Books.

Boyatzis, R. E., and A. McKee. (2005). *Resonant Leadership: Renewing Yourself and Connecting with Others Through Mindfulness, Hope, and Compassion*. Boston: Harvard Business School Press.

Bradlow, P. A. (1973). Depersonalization, Ego Splitting, Non-Human Fantasy and Shame. *International Journal of Psycho-Analysis* 54 (4):487–492.

Brandchaft, B., and R. D. Stolorow. (1990). Varieties of Therapeutic Alliance. *Annual of Psychoanalysis* 18:99–114.

Brizendine, L. (2006). *The Female Brain*. New York: Morgan Road Books.

Buirski, P., ed. (1987). *Frontiers of Dynamic Psychotherapy: Essays in Honor of Arlene and Lewis R. Wolberg*. New York: Brunner/Mazel.

Calef, V., and E. M. Weinshel. (1981). Some Clinical Consequences of Introjection: Gaslighting. *The Psychoanalytic Quarterly* 50 (1): 44–66.

Callahan, D. (2004). *The Cheating Culture: Why More Americans Are Doing Wrong to Get Ahead*. Orlando, Fla.: Harcourt.

Carle, G. (2000). *He's Not All That!: How to Attract the Good Guys*. New York: Cliff Street Books.

Carter, S., and J. Sokol. (2005). *Help! I'm in Love with a Narcissist*. New York: M. Evans.

Caruth, E., and M. Eber. (1996). Blurred Boundaries in the Therapeutic Encounter. *Annual of Psychoanalysis*: 24: 175–185.

Casarjian, B. E., and D. H. Dillon. (2006). *Mommy Mantras: Affirmations and Insights to Keep You from Losing Your Mind*. New York: Broadway Books.

Cavell, S. (1996). *Contesting Tears: The Hollywood Melodrama of the Unknown Woman*. Chicago: University of Chicago Press.

Dalai Lama (1999). *Ethics for the New Millennium*. New York: Riverhead Books.

Dalai Lama and H. C. Cutler. (1998). *The Art of Happiness: A Handbook for Living*. New York: Riverhead Books.

Desmaisons, K. (1998). *Potatoes, Not Prozac*. New York: Simon & Schuster.

Dorpat, T. L. (2004). *Gaslighting, the Double Whammy, Interrogation, and Other Methods of Covert Control in Psychotherapy and Analysis*. Lanham, Md.: Rowman & Littlefield.

Duck, S. (1991). *Understanding Relationships*. New York: Guilford Press.

Elgin, S. H. (1995). *You Can't Say That to Me: Stopping the Pain of Verbal Abuse—An 8-Step Program*. New York: John Wiley.

Emmons, Henry, with Rachel Kranz. (2005). *The Chemistry of Joy*. New York: Simon & Schuster.

Engel, B. (2005). *Breaking the Cycle of Abuse: How to Move Beyond Your Past to Create an Abuse-Free Future*. Hoboken, N.J.: John Wiley.

Evans, P. (1996). *The Verbally Abusive Relationship: How to Recognize It and How to Respond*. 2d ed., Avon, Mass.: Adams Media.

Evans, W. N. (1964). The Fear of Being Smothered. *The Psychoanalytic Quarterly* 33:53–70.

Ferenczi, S. (1949). Confusion of the Tongues Between the Adults and the Child. *International Journal of Psycho-Analysis* 30:225–230.

Filippini, S. (2005). Perverse Relationships: The Perspective of the Perpetrator. *International Journal of Psycho-Analysis* 86:755–773.

Forward, S., and D. Frazier. (1999). *When Your Lover Is a Liar: Healing the Wounds of Deception and Betrayal.* New York: HarperCollins.

Forward, S., and D. Frazier. (2001). *Emotional Blackmail: When the People in Your Life Use Fear, Obligation, and Guilt to Manipulate You.* New York: Quill.

Gediman, H. K. (1991). Seduction Trauma: Complemental Intrapsychic and Interpersonal Perspectives on Fantasy and Reality. *Psychoanalytic Psychology* 8 (4):381–401.

Gedo, J. E. (1989). Vicissitudes in the Psychotherapy of Depressive Crises. *Psychoanalytic Psychology* 6 (11):1–13.

Goldsmith, R. E., and J. J. Freyd. (2005). Effects of Emotional Abuse in Family and Work Environments. *Journal of Emotional Abuse* 5 (1): 95–123.

Goleman, D. (1985). *Vital Lies, Simple Truths: The Psychology of Self-Deception.* New York: Simon & Schuster.

Goleman, D. (1997). *Emotional Intelligence.* New York: Bantam Books.

Goleman, D., R. Boyatzis, and A. McKee. (2002). *Primal Leadership: Realizing the Power of Emotional Intelligence.* Boston: Harvard Business School Press.

Greenberg, L. S., and S. C. Paivio. (1997). *Working with Emotions in Psychotherapy.* New York: Guilford Press.

Hirschfield, J., ed. (1995). *Women in Praise of the Sacred: Forty-three Centuries of Spiritual Poetry by Women.* New York: HarperPerennial.

Horney, K. (1942). *Self-analysis.* New York: W. W. Norton.

Jordan, J. V., A. G. Kaplan, J. B. Miller, I. P. Stiver, and J. L. Surrey. (1991). *Women's Growth in Connection: Writings from the Stone Center.* New York: Guilford Press.

Kegan, R. (1982). *The Evolving Self: Problem and Process in Human Development.* Cambridge, Mass.: Harvard University Press.

Kegan, R., and L. L. Lahey. (2001). *How the Way We Talk Can Change the Way We Work: Seven Languages for Transformation.* 1st ed., San Francisco: Jossey-Bass.

Kemp, A. (1998). *Abuse in the Family: An Introduction.* Pacific Grove, Calif.: Brooks/Cole.

Kernberg, O. F. (1991). Transference Regression and Psychoanalytic Technique with Infantile Personalities. *International Journal of Psycho-Analysis* 72: 189–200.

Kohut, H. (1966). Forms and Transformations of Narcissism. *Journal of the American Psychoanalytic Association* 14: 243–272.

Kohut, H. (1984). *How Does Analysis Cure?* Chicago: University of Chicago Press.

Kohut, H., and E. S. Wolf. (1978). The Disorders of the Self and Their Treatment: An Outline. *International Journal of Psycho-Analysis* 59: 413–425.

Komarovsky, M. (1985). *Women in College: Shaping New Feminine Identities*. New York: Basic Books.

Koonin, M., and T. M. Green. (2004). The Emotionally Abusive Workplace. *Journal of Emotional Abuse* 4 (3–4): 71–79.

Lachkar, J. (2000). Emotional Abuse of High-Functioning Professional Women: A Psychodynamic Perspective. *Journal of Emotional Abuse* 2 (1): 73–91.

Lachmann, F. M. (1986). Interpretation of Psychic Conflict and Adversarial Relationships. *Psychoanalytic Psychology* 3:341–355.

Lachmann, F. M. (1988). On Ambition and Hubris. *Progress Self Psychology* 3:195–209.

Lammers, M., J. Ritchie, and N. Robertson. (2005). Women's Experience of Emotional Abuse in Intimate Relationships: A Qualitative Study. *Journal of Emotional Abuse* 5 (1): 29–64.

Landers, E., and V. Mainzer. (2005). *The Script: The 100 % Absolutely Predictable Things Men Do When They Cheat*. New York: Hyperion.

LeDoux, J. E. (1996). *The Emotional Brain: The Mysterious Underpinnings of Emotional Life*. New York: Simon & Schuster.

Lenoff, L. (1998). Phantasy Self-Objects and the Conditions of Therapeutic Change. *Progress in Self Psychology* 14:147–167.

Lenoff, L. (2003). Consequences of Empathy: Rereading Kohut's Examination. *Progress in Self Psychology* 19:21–40.

Lerner, H. G. (1989). *The Dance of Anger: A Woman's Guide to Changing the Patterns of Intimate Relationships*. (Perennial Library/reissued 1989 ed.). New York: Perennial Library.

Lerner, H. G. (1993). *The Dance of Deception: Pretending and Truth-telling in Women's Lives*. 1st ed., New York: HarperCollins.

Lewis, M. J. (1992). *Shame: The Exposed Self*. New York: Free Press.

Lieberman, A. F. (1993). *The Emotional Life of the Toddler.* New York: Free Press, New York: Maxwell Macmillan International.

Loehr, J., and T. Schwartz. (2003). *The Power of Full Engagement: Managing Energy, Not Time, Is the Key to High Performance and Personal Renewal.* New York: Free Press.

Loring, M. T. (1998). *Emotional Abuse: The Trauma and Treatment.* San Francisco: Jossey-Bass.

McKay, M., P. Fanning, C. Honeychurch, and C. Sutker. (2005). *The Self-Esteem Companion.* 1st ed. Oakland, Calif.: New Harbinger.

Mellody, P. (1992). *Facing Love Addiction: Giving Yourself the Power to Change the Way You Love.* New York: HarperSanFrancisco.

Mitchell, S. A. (1988). *Relational Concepts in Psychoanalysis: An Intergration.* Cambridge, Mass.: Harvard University Press.

Modell, A. H. (1991). A Confusion of Tongues or Whose Reality Is It? *The Psychoanalytic Quarterly* 60 (2): 227–244.

Morrison, A. P. (1983). Shame, Ideal Self, and Narcissism. *Contemporary Psychoanalysis* 19:295–318.

Morrison, A. P. (2001). "We'll Be in Touch": Gas-lighting, Transference, Empathy and Forthrightness." (Draft, Revised). For presentation at the SICP retreat, Montauk Point, N.Y., on March 30–April 1, 2001, and the CSPP in New Haven, on January 12, 2002.

Nussbaum, M. C. (2001). *Upheavals of Thought: The Intelligence of Emotions.* Cambridge and New York: Cambridge University Press.

Ogawa, B. (1989). *Walking on Eggshells: Practical Counseling for Women in or Leaving a Violent Relationship.* Volcano, Calif.: Volcano Press.

Reich, A. (1960). Pathologic Forms of Self-Esteem Regulation. *Psychoanalytic Study of the Child* 15: 215–232.

Rosenberg, M. B. (2003). *Nonviolent Communication: A Language of Life.* Encinitas, Calif.: PuddleDance Press.

Salzberg, S. (2002). *Lovingkindness: The Revolutionary Art of Happiness.* Boston: Shambhala.

Santoro, V. (1994). *Gaslighting: How to Drive Your Enemies Crazy.* Port Townsend, Wash.: Loompanics Unlimited.

Sorsoli, L. (2004). Hurt Feelings: Emotional Abuse and the Failure of Empathy. *Journal of Emotional Abuse* 4 (1): 1–26.

Steinem, G. (1992). *Revolution from Within: A Book of Self-esteem.* 1st ed., Boston: Little, Brown.

Taffel, R., and M. Blau. (2001). *The Second Family: How Adolescent Power Is Challenging the American Family.* 1st ed., New York: St. Martin's Press.

Tannen, D. (1998). *The Argument Culture: Moving from Debate to Dialogue.* 1st ed., New York: Random House.

Wallace, B. A. (2006). *The Attention Revolution: Unlocking the Power of the Focused Mind.* 1st ed., Somerville, Mass.: Wisdom Publications.

Weitzman, S. (2000). *Not to People Like Us: Hidden Abuse in Upscale Marriages.* New York: Basic Books.

Wheelis, A. (1975). *How People Change.* New York: Harper & Row.

Whitfield, C. L. (1993). *Boundaries and Relationships: Knowing, Protecting and Enjoying the Self.* Deerfield Beach, Fla.: Health Communications.

Wolf, N. (2005). *The Treehouse: Eccentric Wisdom from My Father on How to Live, Love, and See.* New York: Simon & Schuster.

Yalom, I. D. (1989). *Love's Executioner, and Other Tales of Psychotherapy.* New York: HarperPerennial.

Index